FEMINIST RECONSTRUCTIONS OF CHRISTIAN DOCTRINE

FEMINIST RECONSTRUCTIONS

OF

CHRISTIAN DOCTRINE

Narrative Analysis and Appraisal

KATHRYN GREENE-MCCREIGHT

New York ❂ Oxford

Oxford University Press

2000

Oxford University Press

Oxford   New York
Athens   Auckland   Bangkok   Bogotá   Buenos Aires   Calcutta
Cape Town   Chennai   Dar es Salaam   Delhi   Florence   Hong Kong   Istanbul
Karachi   Kuala Lumpur   Madrid   Melbourne   Mexico City   Mumbai
Nairobi   Paris   São Paulo   Singapore   Taipei   Tokyo   Toronto   Warsaw

and associated companies in
Berlin   Ibadan

Published by Oxford University Press, Inc.
198 Madison Avenue, New York, New York 10016

Library of Congress Cataloging-in-Publication Data
Greene-McCreight, Kathryn, 1961–
Feminist reconstructions of Christian doctrine : narrative analysis
and appraisal / Kathryn Greene-McCreight.
p.   cm.
Includes bibliographical references and index.
ISBN 0-19-512862-1
1. Feminist theology.   I. Title.
BT83.55.G73   2000
230'.082—dc21   99–19374

1 3 5 7 9 8 6 4 2

Printed in the United States of America
on acid-free paper

PREFACE

The main focus of this study is, as the title indicates, feminist reconstructions of Christian doctrine, and that mainly of scholars in the United States and Europe who tend to have the greatest influence on American seminaries and churches. I do not intend to offer here a comprehensive survey of feminist theology. The literature required for such a project would be vast, as feminist theology grows by leaps and bounds seemingly on a daily basis, and not all feminist theological writings are useful for the purposes of this study. Neither is this a historical project: I do not seek to reconstruct attitudes toward women or the voices of women themselves throughout the history of Christianity, nor do I give a typology of those who do. This is important work, but others more competent at this are already doing a fine job here.[1] Also, I do not intend in this project to give justification for women in ministry, even though this, too, is a vitally important project; again, there are plenty of others engaged in this task.[2] This is not an essay on the relationship between feminism and religion, which itself is a compelling topic.[3] And, while I consider the use of the Bible throughout this project, I am not offering a study on the Bible from a feminist perspective per se.[4] Those who expect such will only be disappointed. The task at hand is much smaller: using William Christian's observations, which I outline in the opening chapter, about the relationship between doctrine and truth and the related observations of George Lindbeck and Hans Frei about the biblical narrative and its role in theology, we will examine feminist theologies to see how they fit the patterns outlined in the theory.

Some of the ideas presented here have appeared in previous incarnations in the form of articles, lectures, and seminars. A piece of chapter 1 was presented to the Reformed Theology and History Consultation at the American Academy of Religion in 1994 and was later published in *Modern Theology* 14 (1998): 213–24. A small segment of chapter 2 appeared in my "*Ad Litteram: How Augustine, Calvin and Barth* Read the 'Plain Sense' of Genesis 1–3." New York: Peter Lang Press, 1999. Material from an early version of chapter 3 appeared in an article in *Scottish Journal of Theology* 50 (1997): 415–32. Portions of chapter 4 originated as a lecture to Scholarly Engagement with Anglican Doctrine in January 1997 and appeared in *Rule of Faith*, edited by Ephraim Radner and George Sumner, Harrisburg: Moorehouse 1998 pp 27–35. Bits and pieces of chapters 5 and 6 have appeared in an article in *Pro Ecclesia* 6 (1997): 289–308.

These ideas have been brewing during my years at Yale, even while feminist theology per se was not my central intellectual concern. Important to my understanding of feminist theology was auditing Letty Russell's course at Yale Divinity School on feminist hermeneutics. In addition, my students in my 1995 seminar at Yale Divinity School, "Feminist Theology and the Story of Israel," and in my 1996 course at Yale College, "Feminist Reconstructions of Christian Doctrine," have shared their questions and insights. For these I am thankful. Cynthia Read and Jennifer Rozgonyi of Oxford University Press were supportive at every step. I am above all grateful to the Pew Evangelical Scholars Foundation for their generous grant during the academic year 1996–1997, which enabled the writing of this project, and to Paul Stuehrenberg and Susan Burdick of Yale Divinity School Library for their skill and patience in helping me obtain the material I needed for this project. I am grateful to Fritz Bauerschmidt, Jim Buckley, Garrett Green, George Lindbeck, Joe Mangina, and Claire Mathews, who read and commented on earlier versions of this manuscript. Their advice and comments were helpful, and any flaws which remain are, of course, my own responsibility. Scripture references are taken from the *New Revised Standard Version*.

New Haven, Connecticut   K. G.-M.
June *1999*

CONTENTS

Introduction: Feminist Theology and Biblical Narrative   3

1
Narrative Interpretation and the Bible   8

2
Feminist Hermeneutics, the Bible, and Patriarchy: Governing Doctrines   28

3
Governing Doctrines, Extra-Narratival Claims, and Authentic Doctrine:
Sin and Victimization   55

4
Feminist Christologies   70

5
Feminist Christology and Historical Reconstructions   86

6
Feminist Trinitarian Reconstructions   111

Conclusion: Changing of the Gods?   128

Notes   137

Scripture Index   169

General Index   171

FEMINIST RECONSTRUCTIONS OF CHRISTIAN DOCTRINE

INTRODUCTION

Feminist Theology and Biblical Narrative?

Every woman working to improve her own position in society or that of
women in general is bringing about the end of God. All feminists are making the world less and less like the one described in the Bible and are thus
helping to lessen the influence of Christ and Yahweh on humanity.[1]

What is the relationship between feminist theology and classical Christian theology?[2] Is feminist theology "Christian" and, if so, in what respect and to what
extent? These questions may be approached in many ways. One could ask feminist
theologians if they are Christians. Many would answer positively. For a Roman Catholic
version of the answer, one might inquire of the magisterium, or one could ask feminist
theologians if they honor the church's tradition as a source and norm in theology.
Again, many feminist theologians would answer positively. For a Protestant take on
the answer, one could ask feminist theologians if they affirm the authority of the Bible
for theology. Likewise here, many feminist theologians would answer affirmatively.
However, the answers to these questions will not be helpful in getting us any closer
to a satisfying answer to the first question with which we started: what is the relationship between feminist theology and classical Christian theology? After all, some
feminist theologians admit that they are no longer, or maybe never were, Christian,
and others answer that they are indeed practicing and faithful Christians. The magisterium's hypothetical answer to the question might be extrapolated from the recent
study by Francis Martin, The Feminist Question (1994), which concludes that feminist
theologians pose questions that are not, properly speaking, theological. Most Christian
feminists would answer the question regarding the authority of the Bible in the af-
firmative: yes, the Bible is an important authority in their feminist theology. None of
these answers, however, would give an adequately detailed description of the relationship of feminist theology to classical Christian theology.

The starting point for this study, then, is more specific: how and to what extent
does the biblical narrative identification of God inform and shape Christian feminist
theology? Does the biblical narrative's depiction of God hold authority for feminist

theologians? If so, how and to what extent? These questions give specificity to what would otherwise be an impossibly broad inquiry into how feminist theologians use the Bible and how they come to their conclusions about what counts for truth regarding God and the world. This narrowing of the topic may help to shed more light than heat.

We might take as our point of entry into the discussion Catherine LaCugna's unfavorable review of *Speaking the Christian God: The Holy Trinity and the Challenge of Feminism* and the subsequent response by the editor of the volume, Alvin Kimel.[3] This interchange was an instance in which more heat than light was indeed shed. LaCugna's review opens as follows:

> This book had the potential to make a serious contribution to current discussions of the hotly-debated subject of how to address God. The book is essentially an Evangelical rejection of the feminist plea for inclusive God-language, on the basis that the revealed Word of God (Scripture) is not subject to tampering, adjustment, or even further interpretation.[4]

LaCugna's judgment is that the book did not advance "the conversation in a helpful way, beyond the usual polemics one finds on either side of this topic."[5] She points out that the volume does not distinguish between the different "schools" of feminist theology, instead lumps them all under one category, and yet seems to focus opposition on one feminist theologian—namely, Sallie McFague. Her worry is that the collection of essays represents an "ideological perspective that is quite hostile to feminism, as if the quest for true equality in Christ between women and men, embodied in language, were demonic."[6]

Alvin Kimel, the editor of *Speaking the Christian God*, then wrote a response to LaCugna's review. "It could have been an interesting review," begins Kimel.[7] He complains that, while LaCugna had the opportunity to engage in dialogue with what was the first sustained theological response to feminist God-language, he claims that she "only superficially skimmed" the collection and did not attend to the central issues.[8] These issues, which he understands to be central to the debate between feminist theology and classical Christian theology, are the questions of how we come to know God the Creator and the nature of the language we use to communicate this knowledge of God. As to the first issue, Kimel states:

> If feminists wish to convince the church that their theology faithfully communicates true knowledge of God, then they must demonstrate the unequivocal grounding of their beliefs in the person of Jesus of Nazareth, crucified and risen. . . . Is deity fully and uniquely embodied in Jesus Christ? If yes, then surely we must honor the historical specificities of this revelation. But if the answer is no, then we should honestly admit that the foundational decisions of Nicaea and Chalcedon were wrong.[9]

As to the second issue, Kimel says that contributors to his volume tend to assert a realistic understanding of metaphor, as well as the unsubstitutability of metaphor as language trope, and that the trinitarian names—Father, Son, and Holy Spirit—function as "self-revealed proper names, metaphorical terms that uniquely identify and personally denominate the three persons of the Holy Trinity."[10] Kimel closes his review with a lament that LaCugna did not "engage the book intellectually and decided instead to exploit the occasion for the purpose of disparagement and traducement."[11]

Catherine LaCugna was invited to respond to Kimel's response, but she declined the offer. *Pro Ecclesia* then solicited the publication of comments made by George Lindbeck on the review and its response, in hopes of salvaging the discussion. Lindbeck suggests, "The review of the Kimel volume which is needed, so I proposed, should focus on its failure to communicate. The reply, in turn should explain, among other things, how untraditional is the book's defense of the tradition. Instead, both review and reply end up despite themselves in trading accusations."[12]

LaCugna accuses Kimel's volume of hostility to feminist theology as though it were "demonic," and Kimel accuses LaCugna of an inability to hear and respond to the critique posed by his collection because of "her own prior philosophical and ideological commitments."[13] LaCugna accuses Kimel's volume of "rejecting the feminist plea for inclusive God-language," and Kimel accuses feminist theologians of "rejection of the narrative identification of God."[14] However, according to Lindbeck, Kimel could have helped further the discussion (maybe, indeed, even encouraged the hoped-for reply by LaCugna) by avoiding such accusations and instead modifying and explaining what he had said earlier: "Several of the contributors, including myself, believe that the fundamental weakness of feminist theology (in either its moderate or radical forms) is precisely its rejection of the narrative identification of God."[15] Here, according to Lindbeck, is the understated thesis of the collection. Lindbeck would have preferred, however, that Kimel use the phrase "failure to affirm the narrative identification" rather than "rejection of the narrative identification":

> How can feminists reject a thesis of which they are unaware or, at best, know only through polemical distortions? . . . the primacy of the narrative identification [of God] has been implicit in the church's worship and scriptural interpretation from the beginning, but it is only in the last decades that it has become a topic of explicit, second-order theological reflection.[16]

Lindbeck points out that this second-order reflection of recent years, found particularly in the work of Hans Frei and the so-called Yale School, which is implicit behind the work of many of Kimel's contributors, tends toward the conclusion that the primacy of the narrative identification of God can be a way of ensuring doctrinal fit with orthodox theology.[17] Lindbeck goes on to state that the narrative identification of God may become a crucial safeguard of the gospel in our own day, as was the homoousios in the fourth century. However, he continues, it does not necessarily follow that those who are not "narrativists" are ipso facto heretics. (It is this faulty assumption which, according to Lindbeck, Kimel has made, in addition to the hasty assumption that feminist theologians blanketly "reject" the biblical narrative depiction of God.) Although the homoousios in the fourth century served as an indicator of orthodoxy, failure to uphold the homoousios could not serve as necessary indicator of heterodoxy or heresy. After all, Lindbeck reminds us, Athanasius refused to classify as full-blown Arians those semi-Arians who could not accept the homoousios on the basis of its novelty or nonbiblical origins.[18]

If this is an accurate way of interpreting *Speaking the Christian God*, it becomes clearer why both the essayists and their detractors seem to argue past each other instead of engaging the other's disagreements. One problem Lindbeck has pointed out is that the implicit thesis of the Kimel volume is not self-evident but needs to be explained and demonstrated more thoroughly. In addition, however, there is another difficulty: the very notion of "orthodoxy" is implicitly treated by Kimel and company and by Lindbeck as well as though it were a self-substantiating valuation in theology. That is, even if the biblical narrative identification of God can guide theological hermeneutics in the direction of orthodoxy, so what? Some feminist theologians have posed a prior question: why should orthodoxy be a desirable goal when it is so entangled with patriarchy? The claim that feminist theology is not narratival and therefore not orthodox is with reference to *some* feminist theologians completely obvious. These feminist theologians explicitly avoid following the biblical depiction of God in toto because they claim that the Bible, bearing the stamp of patriarchy, is a potential accomplice in the subjugation of women. There is yet another problem: as LaCugna has pointed out, not all feminists think alike. The claim that feminist theology does not follow the biblical narrative's identification of God is simply not true for some feminist theologians. Others may want to reenvision the biblical depiction of God but nevertheless very much want to remain orthodox, as was the case for Catherine LaCugna.

The task at hand, then, in the present volume is to clarify matters enough so that whichever position we are most drawn to, whether orthodox or feminist of one of the many types or some admixture of the two, we can at the very least agree on our disagreements. At the start, we need to explain and document two opposed modes or patterns by which religions respond to—that is, either accept, reject, or leave undecided—novel claims. Then, we will step back and analyze feminist hermeneutics and its alternatives as discrete ways of construing religious doctrine. Thus, we will not simply hold feminist theology against a putatively orthodox model and point out where feminist theology falls short. Instead, we will attempt to unfold the logic and patterning of doctrine with which each mode of theological inquiry operates. Here, we will rely on concepts drawn from the work of William Christian in particular, as well as from that of Hans Frei and George Lindbeck. We will also introduce the notion of the biblical narrative identification of God. After this, in the main body of the book, we can turn to the writings of feminist theologians to analyze the doctrinal patterns in their reconstructions of primary doctrines and thus attempt to understand how the Bible is used in undergirding their theological reconstructions. This will allow us to engage the task of assessing the extent to which feminist theology adheres to, fails to affirm, or rejects the biblical narrative identification of God.

However, some may ask, why be concerned about feminist theology at all? Indeed, many orthodox women who do not consider themselves feminist theologians have asked and continue to ask this question. Such women might see the present study to be misspent energy. For many who are orthodox, however, the reality of the situation will rarely be so simple as to allow the solution of refusing to consider feminist claims at all. For example, women who consciously reject identifying themselves as feminists for all that the term currently connotes nevertheless may struggle for women's equality and legal rights, and some of them may do so on the basis of the truth claims presented in the gospel.[19] Indeed, for those who are concerned about preserving and passing on classical Christianity, it is clear that feminist theology is crucial to study, in part because it is so terribly influential in our seminaries and churches and in part because some of the claims of feminist can be seen in some respects to be congruent with even a classical reading of Scripture. Where and when feminist claims will and will not be deemed true will be important to consider from this perspective. In addition, feminist theology is important to consider because it can, in some respects, be the worst enemy of improving women's situation in the church. It can and has at times resulted in a backlash that can obscure the discussions about women's rightful place in the church according to Scripture.[20] The very possibility that the advances in women's standing in the Christian community in particular and within Western culture in general could turn into retreats is too daunting to ignore. The task at hand, then, is well worth the trouble.

1

NARRATIVE INTERPRETATION
AND THE BIBLE

Over the past twenty years, a wealth of titles have explored the possibilities in using the concept of narrative as a theological tool.[1] The approach represented in this corpus is usually referred to, not surprisingly, as "narrative theology," and it has yielded inquiry in biblical studies, philosophy, homiletics, and many of the other theological fields.[2] Of the many different ways of using the concept of narrative for theological inquiry, one type has crystallized around the work of Hans Frei and what has come to be known as the "Yale School."[3] While it will not be the goal here to document the theories of the Yale School or to commend the categories of "narrative theology" in general, it will be useful to draw on those insights which can be particularly helpful in analyzing feminist theologies' use of or relation to the biblical depiction of God.

In his watershed book, *The Eclipse of Biblical Narrative*, Hans Frei pointed out what appears so simple once articulated and yet bears unexpected implications: for precritical readers, the Bible was read as one overarching, continuous narrative. This aspect of the biblical text is key in narrative interpretation, and for this reason the term "the Christian story" is used with (what some may consider overdrawn) confidence in narrative theology and interpretation.[4] This "storied" feature of the biblical text, says Frei, is generally no longer accessed in the modern period because of critical approaches that ask different questions of the text of the Bible, questions which implicitly show that the understanding of the location of the subject matter of the Bible has shifted. This shift in the location of the Bible's subject matter has led modern readers to understand themselves and the world in a fundamentally different relationship to the biblical text and the world depicted by that text. Whereas the Reformers and their predecessors understood that they were to read the biblical narrative as depicting the "real world," the larger framework which interpreted their world of sense data, modern readers now tend to interpret the Bible with a reverse logic. That is, the biblically depicted world, rather than absorbing extrabiblical reality, is "inserted" into the world which the interpreter constructs via reason and sense data. This extrabiblical world itself now provides the categories and benchmarks for interpreting the Bible, rather than vice versa.

However, Erich Auerbach observes that the biblical text itself demands the former kind of interpretation rather than the latter, and this observation influences Frei's thought. Auerbach writes that literarily the Bible:

> seeks to overcome our reality: we are to fit our own reality into its world, feel ourselves to be elements in its structure of universal history. . . . But when, through too great a change in environment and through the awakening of a critical consciousness, this becomes impossible, the biblical claim to absolute authority is jeopardized; the method of interpretation scorned and rejected, the biblical stories become ancient legends.[5]

The Bible itself read as a continuous narrative has this power to "overcome our reality." We might say that the Bible "mimics" (after Auerbach's term, mimesis) reality insofar as the biblical characters come to identity gradually but irreversibly throughout the course of the narrative, just as our own personal and communal character is formed and either strengthened or judged through our own interactions with the world around us. In this respect, biblical narrative can be said to be "realistic."

Frei suggests that the hermeneutical option cast aside in the eighteenth and nineteenth centuries was that biblical narrative—in particular, the gospel narratives and much of the Old Testament "historical" material—was formerly understood (at least implicitly) to belong to this category of "realistic narrative." We will not engage the debates over whether Frei was concerned with, or thought that precritical interpretation of the Bible was concerned with, the "facticity" of the narratives. Rather, we will seek to clarify the smaller and, in many ways, more important point for our purposes: the Bible's realistic narrative depiction as significant literary and theological category comes to be overlooked in the modern period.[6] What does Frei mean by "realistic narrative?"

> In that term I include more than the indispensability of the narrative shape, including chronological sequence, to the meaning, theme, or subject matter of the story. The term realistic I take also to imply that the narrative depiction is of that peculiar sort in which characters or individual persons, in their internal depth or subjectivity as well as in their capacity as doers and sufferers of actions or events, are firmly and significantly set in the context of the external environment, natural but more particularly social. Realistic narrative is that kind in which subject and social setting belong together, and characters and external circumstances fitly render each other. Neither character nor circumstance separately, nor yet their interaction, is a shadow of something else more real or more significant.[7]

It is the possibility, according to Frei, of isolating in interpretation this "realistic" quality of the narrative which breaks down in the modern period. It is no longer considered significant for interpretation or inquiry into meaning that characters are rendered within the individual stories and larger narrative movements via interaction with other characters, plot development, and larger canonical developments and crescendos. In the modern period, according to Frei, "the realistic or history-like quality of biblical narratives, acknowledged by all, instead of being examined for the bearing it had in its own right on meaning and interpretation was immediately transposed into the quite different issue of whether or not the realistic narrative was historical."[8] This is not to say that interpreters before the eighteenth century did not ask historical questions, for indeed they have in abundance throughout the history of the Bible's interpretation. However, the historical questions they had previously asked did not blind them, according to Frei, to the history-like or "realistic" quality of the narrative and the bearing this itself had on the very meaning and thematic intent of the narratives.[9] The problem in the modern period is that it is no longer assumed that the biblical narratives' "factuality" or referentiality to the time-space continuum is straightforward enough to be bracketed in hermeneutical inquiry, and now discerning "truth" or facticity becomes integral to interpreting the "meaning" of the narratives.[10]

The Bible "Absorbs the World"

Among readers of the Bible influenced by the Yale School brand of narrative theology, it has become commonplace to speak of Scripture as "absorbing the world" of the reader. Hans Frei and George Lindbeck have both used the metaphor. Lindbeck uses it to describe his cultural-linguistic model of construing doctrine which creates the possibility for a postliberal, intratextual theology: "Intratextual theology redescribes reality within the scriptural framework rather than translating scripture into extra scriptural categories. It is the text, so to speak, which absorbs the world, rather than the world the text."[11] Lindbeck's remarks about intratextual theology are influenced by Frei's observation that the direction of precritical interpretation "was that of incorporating extra-biblical thought, experience, and reality into the one real world detailed and made accessible by the biblical story—not the reverse."

Hans Frei pointed to John Calvin and Karl Barth as examples of those who read the Bible as one continuous narrative, whose reality was overcome by the reality of the biblical world.[12] The description George Lindbeck gives of classical hermeneutics likewise applies to the interpretation of these two figures, for they clearly read the Bible as "a canonically and narrationally unified and internally glossed (that is, self-referential and self-interpreting) whole centered on Jesus Christ, and telling the story of the dealings of the Triune God with his people and his world in ways which are typologically . . . applicable to the present."[13]

While Frei's examples of narrative reading are Calvin and Barth, his examples of non-narrative reading are Paul Ricoeur and David Tracy of the Chicago School, with the larger project of phenomenological hermeneutics embodying modern assumptions about biblical interpretation.[14] Frei points out how, through adherence to the system of assumptions undergirding phenomenological hermeneutics about how texts "disclose" and about the nature of human "understanding," when the likes of Ricoeur and Tracy come to the Gospel texts, one of the results is that Jesus is:

> not in the first place the agent of his actions . . . he is, rather, the verbal expressor of a
> certain preconceptual consciousness which he then, in a logically derivative or secondary

sense, exhibits in action. For example, that Jesus was crucified is not a decisive part of his personal story, only that he was so consistent in his 'mode-of-being-in-the-world' as to take the risk willingly.[15]

Rather than being primarily a character within a plot of a realistic narrative, Jesus becomes for phenomenological hermeneutics a place marker for human consciousness, an icon (in the computerese sense of the term, which, to be sure, correlates with its theological precursor) that points to a reality independent of the narrative. Insofar as this is the case, phenomenological hermeneutics reads the Gospel narratives as though they were allegories rather than "realistic narratives." The word "Jesus" names primarily not a character but rather a meaning, a "generalizable set of attitudes (self-sacrificing righteousness, etc.)," which are in principle independent of their instantiation in the Gospel character named Jesus.[16] Again, the kingdom of God in Jesus' preaching, which traditionally has been understood to refer to Jesus' activity and in turn to the kingdom of God, now becomes "human reality in its wholeness" because "religious language discloses the religious dimension of common human experience."[17] Frei sees the "second naiveté" of Ricoeur to be nothing more than a "verbal pirouette," and not a true option between the first naiveté and suspicion.[18] Frei points to the preference that practitioners of phenomenological hermeneutics hold for parables: the method is more fitting to the parabolic genre than to "realistic narrative."

The type of interpretation Frei suggests is more appropriate to Christian Scripture is therefore "mere description rather than explanation," confining interpretation to "the specific set of texts and the most specific context, rather than to a general class of texts ('realistic narrative') and the most general context ('human experience')."[19] This may come as a surprise to those unfamiliar with Frei, who might have thought that he was attempting to build an interpretive theory around the concept of "realistic narrative," as some instances of "narrative theology" in fact attempt to do. This is not, however, the case for Frei. Indeed, Frei indicates that some versions of "narrative theology" are instances of:

> putting the cart before the horse—but this time the wagon is theological rather than literary—if one constructs a general and inalienable human quality called "narrative" or "narrativity" within which to interpret the Gospels and provide foundational warrant for the possibility of their existential and ontological meaningfulness. The notion that Christian theology is a member of a general class of "narrative theology" is no more than a minor will-o'-the-wisp.[20]

This type of narrative approach would therefore be analogous to New Criticism's literary elevating of the specific case of the Christian doctrine of the incarnation to the level of general theory of meaning, as Frei had pointed out earlier. He had said that New Criticism itself with regard to the doctrine of the Incarnation also put "the cart before the horse and then cut the lines . . . [claiming] that the vehicle is self-propelled."[21] For Frei, any general theory of interpretation is not appropriate for reading the Bible, but rather the Bible demands its own criteria for reading.

Here Frei follows his teacher Karl Barth in claiming a special hermeneutics for the Bible. Of course, the fact that Barth preferred to call this type of special hermeneutics a "general hermeneutics" may confuse readers at this point. Although he proposed a "general hermeneutics," he did not mean by this a general explanatory theory, such as phenomenological hermeneutics applies to the Bible, but rather a reading of the Bible according to which one should then interpret all other "texts" in general. Only in this sense is the Barthian hermeneutic "general," and to a certain extent Frei follows Barth here. Instead of the terms *general* or *special* in describing narrative hermeneutics, we find the terms *extratextual* and *intratextual*. This is a mark in particular of the work of George Lindbeck, who takes the insights of cultural anthropology and applies them to the analysis of religious language. Lindbeck calls this a "cultural-linguistic approach," and he uses the term *intratextual* to describe the kind of theology congruent with such an analysis of religion.[22] Rather than being a general explanatory framework into which Christian doctrine and Scripture are inserted as specific cases, this "intratextual" interpretation allows for "case-specific" readings of the Bible and ultimately, like Barth's own version of general biblical hermeneutics, draws all other "texts" and interpretive data into its orbit.

"The direction in the flow of intratextual interpretation is that of absorbing the extratextual universe into the text, rather than the reverse (extratextual) direction.[23]" This is how Frei described the biblical interpretation of the Reformers and their predecessors in *Eclipse*. With the term *intratextual*, Frei is trying to offer an account of what would be involved in the practice of biblical interpretation if one were to try in a "posthermeneutical" cultural context to retrieve what was lost in the modern period.[24] This is Frei's own analogue to Ricoeur's "second naiveté."[25]

Narrative versus Nonnarrative Interpretation and the Jesus of History versus the Christ of Faith

Frei's analogue to a "second naiveté" is not dependent on a general theory of understanding, as we saw, but on the importance of Christian ruled reading of the scriptures, known as the "literal sense."[26] With the phrase the *literal sense*, he is referring to a specific characteristic of classical Christian interpretation of the Bible:

> The literal sense is the paradigmatic form of such intratextual interpretation in the Christian community's use of its scripture: The literal ascription to Jesus of Nazareth of the stories connected with him is of such far-reaching import that it serves not only as focus for inner-canonical typology but reshapes extratextual language in its manifold descriptive uses into a typological relation to these stories. The reason why the intratextual universe of this Christian symbol system is a narrative one is that a specific set of texts, which happen to be narrative, has become primary, even within scripture, and has been assigned a literal reading as their primary or "plain" sense. They have become the paradigm for the construal not only of what is inside that system but for all that is outside.[27]

That is, the literal sense in Christian interpretation of the Bible favors the narratives about Jesus in such a way that the rest of Scripture is read "through" them, to the effect that the entire canon hums with the playing of texts through and off the Gospel stories about Jesus. When Old Testament texts are played this way off and through the New Testament narratives about Jesus, this is known traditionally as "typological" reading. This privileging of the Gospel stories, because of the nature of the Gospel stories themselves and not because of any general theory, draws the extratextual world itself, as well as the intratextual canonical world, "through" the Gospel narratives. The Gospel narratives about Jesus thus serve as interpretive lens for all of "reality." This version of the understanding of the literal sense of Scripture is not only more in line with precritical Christian interpretation of the Bible but also, unlike the phenomenological hermeneutician's normative way of reading the Bible (which seeks out allegorical rather than literal or its Old Testament correlate to literal, typological readings), is elastic enough to account for the various loci or moments of Christian doctrine, practice, and Scripture: "It will stretch and not break."[28]

It may be helpful here, perhaps, to point out that Frei understood the "realistic" quality not only as an aspect of the text itself but also as an element in or style of reading of the biblical text. "Realistic" refers not only to much of the biblical narratives but also to the reading which takes seriously for the interpretive task this aspect of biblical narrative. And here is the divide between typically modern interpretation of the Bible and Frei's "narrative" interpretation of the Bible:

> Realistic narrative reading is based on one of the characteristics of the Gospel story, especially its later part, viz., that it is history-like in its language as well as its depiction of a common public world (no matter whether it is the one we all think we inhabit), in the close interaction of character and incident, and in the non-symbolic quality of the relation between the story and what the story is about. . . . We cannot have what they are about ("the subject matter") without the stories themselves . . . they literally mean what they say. There is no gap between the representation and what is represented by it.[29]

The assumption that there is, in fact, a gap between the representation and what is represented by it undergirds much of modern biblical criticism and, as a subcategory of this, also the conceptual dichotomy between the Jesus of history and the Christ of faith. This common category in modern theology is used, not surprisingly, with much creative fruit in feminist theologies. However, narrative interpretation of the Gospels cannot embrace such a dichotomy, for since narrative reading understands the subject matter to be borne by the stories, the identity of Jesus present to the believer (Christ of faith) cannot be separated from his narratival depiction in the Gospels (Jesus of history). In discussing modern Christ figures represented in literature, Frei argues:

> A Christ figure must have all three elements—universal redeeming scope, the unsubstitutable personal identity in which the scope is enacted, and the pattern enacted by that person's history. It is therefore important to say that obviously—by definition—the Christ figure's identity is already pre-empted by him who actually is the Christ of Scripture. In short, there can be no Christ figure because Jesus is the Christ, unless an author depicts the figure in terms of a particular identity and pattern wholly different from that of Jesus' story. But in that case it would not make any sense to talk of a Christ figure at all. To speak of Christ involves an enormous claim—a claim so large that it is made exclusively of whomever it is made. The claim is that in one unique case identity and presence are so completely one that to know who he is is to confront his presence.[30]

Thus, for the reader who is able to acknowledge the interpretive import of the realistic depiction of the character Jesus, there can be no Christ figure apart from this narratively depicted man Jesus. This is not yet even a religious claim. At this point, the claim is on a purely literary level but has great theological significance. That is, one could be either a believer or a nonbeliever and acknowledge the interpretive import of realistic depiction, and therefore acknowledge that it is logically nonsensical to speak of a Christ figure as though separable from the representation of Christ in the narratives about Jesus. If one then accepts the narratives' truth claims about the person of Jesus and therefore about the God of Israel, then the literary observation will necessitate a religious decision. Either one will reject the truth claims and therefore reject the God depicted in the biblical narratives, or one will "repent and believe the good news of the gospel." Either response of the narrative reader would fit the logic of the biblical narrative. If Frei is right about the tradition, the case represented by modern theology at large and by feminist theologies as a subcategory, in particular where the believer is not a "narrative" reader, appears to be an odd interim case.

Dogmatics and the Logic of Belief versus Apologetics and the Logic of Coming to Belief

Just as classical theology has historically been characterized by a narrative rather than nonnarrative scriptural reading, it has also practiced a primarily "dogmatic" rather than "apologetic" approach to theology. Dogmatics can be defined for our purposes as theology which unfolds Christian authentic doctrine without particular concern to appeal to such a common ground which would de facto build arguments for Christian truth claims on something other than the biblical narrative. In the modern period, according to Frei, the type of apologetics which comes to win out over dogmatics attempts to translate categories of Christian confession for the "modern mind." Thus, it attempts to win over the cultured despisers of Christianity, whether within the church or without, by offering arguments or warrants for the legitimacy (whether logical, rational, emotional, experiential, or whatever) of Christian claims.[31] Frei defines apologetics as follows: "I have used the term 'apologetics' to cover (among other things) this appeal to a common ground between analysis of human experience by direct natural and by some distinctively Christian thought. This has been the chief characteristic of the mediating theology of modernity."[32] Apologetics of this sort is tied to the loss of narrative reading in modern theology. The only type of "apologetics," if it can even be called that, which is tied to narrative reading is like that of Anselm and Barth: an internal examination of the logic of Christian confession that does not appeal to a common ground between Christian beliefs and experientially derived natural knowledge. This is not deemed to be apologetics in the modern sense at all but rather should be referred to more properly as dogmatics. If, for the sake of ease, we agree with Frei and call this "dogmatics," we can say that this "dogmatics" is "apologetic" in the broad sense that it attempts to make a case for the logic of Christian faith claims and for the integrity and fit of the Christian life against these faith claims. In this sense, indeed, all Christian theology is apologetic.[33] However, when this kind of apologetics turns into apologetics in the modern sense, it finds itself making arguments on behalf of Christian doctrine, language, sacraments, and life, attempting to "translate" the categories and concepts of Christian doctrine into an extra-narratival framework. A patristic analogue to modern apologetics is therefore found, for example, in those elements of Augustine's thought which reflect a Neoplatonic version of the gospel. Frei's observation about the damaging effects of modern apologetics, however, applies to Augustine as well as this point: "I remain convinced that a sound basis for good dogmatic theology demands that a sharp distinction be observed between dogmatic theology and apologetics."[34]

Frei has attempted to point out the danger inherent in apologetics that confuses the logic of belief (e.g., the projects of Barth and Anselm) with the logic of coming to belief (e.g., Bultmann and Tillich):[35]

> [In apologetics as opposed to dogmatics] the rationale of how one comes to believe comes to control, indeed to be virtually identical with the logic of belief, i.e., the meaning and interconnection of dogmatic statements. . . . The order of belief is logically a totally different matter from that of coming to believe or the apologetic justification of Christianity. . . . I am convinced that the passionate and systematic preoccupation with the apologetic task of showing how faith is meaningful and/or possible is largely out of place and self-defeating—except as an *ad hoc* and highly various exercise.[36]

In other words, there is a justification for engaging the apologetic task of unfolding the logic(s) of coming to belief, but when this is confused with the dogmatic task of unfolding the logic of belief, the integrity of the Christian narrative is jeopardized. The logic of belief is expressed in the following statement of Frei:

> [To the believing narrative reader] to think [Jesus] dead is the equivalent of not thinking of him at all. . . . Jesus lives as the one who cannot *not* live, for whom to be what he is is to be . . . there is a kind of logic in a Christian's [narrative reader's] faith that forces him to say that disbelief in the resurrection of Jesus is rationally impossible. But whether one actually believes the resurrection is, of course, a wholly different matter.[37]

The logic of belief (conceptual description) is not systematically correlated with the logic of coming to belief (arguing for conceptual conversion), for there are many logics of coming to belief whereas the logic of belief itself is governed by the Christian story. Frei describes the theology of Karl Barth as an instance of theology which generally focuses its task on explaining and unfolding the logic of belief: "Barth was about the business of conceptual description: He took the classical themes of communal Christian language molded by the Bible, tradition and constant usage in worship, practice, instruction and controversy, and he restated or redescribed them, rather than evolving arguments on their behalf."[38] By contrast, the logic of coming to belief involves constructing arguments on behalf of the classical themes of communal Christian language. These arguments are usually based on the (assumed) common ground between generalizable human experience and the specific language of Christian faith claims. The problem is that one cannot always assume such a common ground between generalizable human experience and the specific language of Christian faith claims. This is what makes focusing on the logic of coming to belief theologically questionable.

The Logic of Doctrines of Religious Communities

The formal distinction between the narrative and non-narrative patterns—and, correspondingly, the logic of belief versus the logic of coming to belief—also has a philosophical correlate in the Yale school. In his study of the logic of the interplay of doctrines of religious communities, William Christian exhibits features also to be found in the work of his younger colleagues Hans Frei and George Lindbeck.[39] Here we have, in effect, the philosophical-theological theory for the observation Frei points to in *Eclipse*. We will see many areas of influence of Christian's work on Frei in particular, such as a formal description of the logic of belief versus the logic of coming to belief, as well as a formal description of Frei's material observation about the specific case of the reversal in the direction of interpretation from the premodern to the modern periods. Even while incorporating concrete examples from the practices and teachings of the world religions' communities (Islam, Hindu, Buddhist, Christian, and Jewish), Christian's study is theoretical insofar as it focuses not on any specific religious community but on the phenomenon of doctrine itself and the logical patterns of its interplay of truth and authenticity. That is, his interest is not so much in exploring the doctrines of any one religious community but rather in examining the function of doctrines as they form, uphold, and promote a discrete constellation of beliefs and practices called religion. His typology for noting the functions and types of doctrine will be useful for our analysis of feminist theology and biblical interpretation.

Primary Doctrines and Governing Doctrines

The first distinction Christian makes which will be useful to us as we turn to feminist theologies is between what he calls primary and governing doctrines of religious communities. Primary doctrines describe the "setting of human life and the conduct of life in this setting."[40] Primary doctrines "propose beliefs about the settings of human activities; they propose courses of inward and outward action to be undertaken in these settings, valuations of human intentions and dispositions, and valuations of the consequences of courses of action."[41] Primary doctrines are usually taken up as the focus of theologians and philosophers of religion alike. However, Christian's interest is not primary doctrines so much as what he calls governing doctrines, which are the principles and rules that govern the formation and development of a community's body of doctrines.[42] Governing doctrines are therefore doctrines about doctrines.[43] Governing doctrines are usually not noticed but operate at an implicit or tacit level. However, at times of upheaval or communal change, a community's governing doctrines may become more important than its primary doctrines in helping to adjudicate and maintain a community's body of doctrines.[44] Christian thus distinguishes primary from governing doctrines as follows:

> The distinction between the primary doctrines of a religious community and its doctrine for identifying its doctrines is comparable with H. L. A. Hart's distinction between the primary rules of obligation in a society (e.g., rules against theft) and the society's "rules of recognition" for identifying its primary rules. . . . Ronald M. Dworkin, in "Is Law a System of Rules?" commenting on Hart's rules of recognition, argued that principles as well as rules are required to determine primary rules of obligation, and that principles, unlike rules, do not dictate results, come what may. They "incline a decision one way, though not conclusively, and they survive intact when they do not prevail."[45]

An example of this which Christian gives is Irenaeus and his consideration of what can be seen as the governing doctrines among the orthodox party and those of the gnostics against whom Irenaeus argues.[46] For Irenaeus, the use of the Rule of Faith functioned as one of his governing doctrines. As Christian notes about governing doctrines, the use of the Rule of Faith does not dictate results. Rather, it inclines a decision in one direction or another, indicating a range of possibilities for primary doctrine, and even when it may not prevail, it survives intact.

Authentic Doctrines and Alien Claims

Christian makes another useful distinction for our purposes, that between authentic doctrines and alien claims. This is not to be equated with the distinction between orthodox doctrine and heresy, to use traditional theological terminology. Instead, it points to a level deeper than these terms indicate—that is, even before the question of truthfulness of a doctrine may be raised. An authentic doctrine of any particular community is one which it is bound to teach. An alien claim can arise from another religious community's authentic doctrines, or it can be a purely secular claim.[47] A secular claim arises in the context of inquiry in which fitness or adequacy is not measured by the distinctive standards of any particular religious community.[48] An alien claim, whether secular or religious, may or may not be true, and it may or may not be consistent with a particular community's authentic doctrine.[49] The community's decision for how to determine the truthfulness of an alien claim depends on that community's "principles or rules for connecting claims to authenticity with claims to truth or rightness."[50] And this is where his work becomes most useful to us.

He sketches two schemas under which religious communities implicitly relate the authenticity of their doctrines and any claims deemed true or right. These are designated in shorthand as T/R-A and A-T/R:

Schema T/R-A

For any sentence (s), if s is true or right, then s is an authentic doctrine of the community. So, if s is not an authentic doctrine of the community, then s is not true or right.

Schema A-T/R

For any sentence, if s is an authentic doctrine of the community, then s is true or right. So, if s is not true or not right, then s is not an authentic doctrine of the community.[51]

These schemas, it must be pointed out, are not to be understood as schemas for determining the truth or falsehood of any claim. Rather, they indicate simply the implicit logic of the relating of truth and authenticity. Determining what counts for truth is another matter entirely and is engaged on the basis of a community's sources and norms. One sees the correspondence here between Christian's schemas T/R-A and A-T/R and Frei's distinction, respectively, between non-narrative and narrative interpretation, between apologetics and dogmatics, and between the logic of coming to belief and the logic of belief. The sets are analogous, although Christian's works on a philosophical and theoretical level and Frei's on hermeneutical and systematic levels.

Christian points out that the second schema, A-T/R, is consistent with the doctrines and teaching practices of the world's major religious communities. That is, whether or not the principle embodied in the second schema is explicitly taught, it is in practice reflected in some of the teaching practices of the Hindu, Buddhist, Jewish, Christian, and Muslim communities. Religious teaching in these communities is conducted in such a way that it is understood that the community is obliged to present teachings (1) which are faithful to its sources and (2) which it claims to be true or right. Such religious communities which operate with the explicit or tacit principle embodied in the A-T/R schema understand the goal of religious formation as resulting in adherents' accepting "the doctrines as true or right, and that they will adopt and live out the pattern of life of which the doctrines are constituents."[52]

In addition, Christian shows how the first schema, T/R-A, is inherently unstable:[53]

> If [the T/R-A] principle is embodied in a doctrine of a religious community, the doctrine would say that if any sentence is true or right, then the sentence expresses an authentic doctrine of that community. . . . It is easy to think of circumstances in which what would be said in utterances of these sentences would be true. Yet it is highly implausible that any of these sentences would count as an authentic doctrine of any religious community. Consider also the following sentences: In an emergency dial 911. Take one tablet four times a day. Put in the stopper before shaking the bottle. Here again it is easy to think of circumstances in which the courses of action proposed in these sentences would be right, prudentially or otherwise. Yet, if we were told that any of these practical sentences is an authentic doctrine of some religious community we would be incredulous.[54]

The first schema, T/R-A, in a sense allows for such a permeable membrane at the juxtaposition between truth and authenticity that true alien claims are de facto authentic doctrines of the religious community to which this schema applies. Such a hypothetical religious community would thus quickly lose any stable identity, if it ever had one. In addition, another conceptual problem arises in this schema insofar as a religious community adopting the principle T/R-A could not with any consistency "grant that there are truths or right actions that it is not bound to teach."[55] That religious community would be bound to teach such a broad range of beliefs and practices that it would seem to lead to irreducible inconsistency and sheer incomprehensibility. However, the appeal of this pattern is its ability to embrace a comprehensive pattern of life, to speak to all circumstances and all understandings of truth, which is part of the appeal of apologetics, of course.[56]

The irony here is that a community which holds and teaches a T/R-A doctrine about its doctrines cannot consistently hold and teach the primary doctrine that there may be alien claims which are true or right. That is, while the community which teaches a T/R-A doctrine about its doctrines may seem, at first glance, to be more "open," "inclusive," and permeable to "outsiders," in fact, it may not be so.[57] It, in effect, leaks its own religious discourse into the larger surrounding communities, either secular or religious, thus "colonizing" other communities, for example, as partial instantiation of its own community.[58]

By contrast, a religious community which holds and teaches an A-T/R doctrine about its doctrines, while initially appearing more "closed" and sure in its own grasp on truth, in fact may be more permeable and open to outside truth than the community adopting the T/R-A principle. For this hypothetical A-T/R community, it would be consistent to hold and teach the primary doctrine that there may, in fact, be alien claims which are true or right.[59] In other words, the community adopting the A-T/R principle may be able to account for the possibility that it does not hold all truths within its own community's constellation of primary doctrines.

Another conceptual problem in the first schema is that, on the one hand, the community which holds and teaches a doctrine about its doctrines that fits the pattern T/R-A would, in effect, be able to say in all consistency that some of its authentic doctrines are not true or right. While this is logically possible, it would seem absurd.[60] On the other hand, a community which holds and teaches a doctrine about its doctrines that fits the A-T/R pattern would have to say that its authentic doctrines are true or right. In addition, it would have to hold and teach that if what is said in a sentence is not true or right, that sentence could not express an authentic doctrine of the community.[61]

Returning now to the notion of alien claims, we find that communities which adopt the T/R-A principle are prone to an inconsistency which the A-T/R community is not prone to, with regard to alien claims. Remember, alien claims usually arise outside a particular community, either in the teachings of another religious community or in secular inquiries. It is possible, however, that claims arising within a community could be deemed to be alien claims to that community. This could be the case if a community decides that a claim which has arisen from within its own rank and file is not required or, more strongly, not consistent with its principles and rules for authenticity.[62]

How would such a decision be made? Never with great dispatch.[63] Along with principles and rules for authenticity, a community would have access to its sources (writings, sages, traditions, ecstatic experience, and so on) and to communal consensus. Christian points out that in the world religions whenever "consensus" is employed as a factor for discerning the authenticity of doctrines of a community, it is never simply a one-person, one-vote poll of the entire community. Rather, consensus is weighted such that some members of the community who are better trained in the community's sources, doctrines, and practices are given greater credence than others less skilled or practiced.[64] What is clear here is that governing doctrines, the principles or rules for adjudicating communal authenticity, are of great importance for the interpretation of the community's sources, doctrines, and practices.[65] Again, we could look to the example within the Christian community of Irenaeus's illustration of the gnostic versus orthodox claims: the gnostics use the same "tiles" as do the orthodox but arrange them according to a different pattern. With these tiles, the orthodox mosaic depicts the King, and the gnostics' mosaic depicts a fox. Irenaeus points out that it is the governing use of the rule of faith which makes the difference in the two mosaics.

"Illustrative" versus "Storied": Relationships between the Christian Story and the Reader or Reading Community

Yet another way of describing the commonalities between the observations of Frei, Lindbeck, and Christian is to point to some helpful comments made by Michael Root.[66] He takes up the concepts of narrative interpretation and applies them to an examination of the doctrine of salvation:

> The soteriological task within Christian theology is then to show how the Christian story is the story of human redemption. What soteriology must make evident is a specific form of what Robert Scholes and Robert Kellogg call the meaning of a narrative, but which I will call the story's significance. Significance is a function of the relation between the story and the world or life of the reader. An insignificant story would be the one that did not illumine or transform the world or life of the reader. A profoundly significant story would be one that in penetrating and thoroughgoing ways illumined and transformed that world and life. Within soteriology, the theologian attempts to show how the Christian story has a particular kind of relation to the reader's life and world. This story is the story of the reader's redemption.[67]

Root suggests two categories of reading the Bible which can result in the relating of the Christian story to the reader. The first he calls "illustrative," the second "storied":

> The story can bear an *illustrative* relation to the reader's life and world. The story illustrates certain redemptive truths about self, world and God. The soteriological task is to bring out the truths the story illustrates and show how they are redemptive. Only when the narrative is transcended does the redemptive relation become clear. The tendency within such an interpretation is to make the story of Jesus only pedagogically necessary and ultimately dispensable to redemption. . . . The Christian narrative can also bear a *storied* relation to the reader. The Christian story and the life and world of the reader do not exist in isolation, but constitute one world and one story. The reader is included in the Christian story. The relation of story to reader becomes internal to the story. As a result, the relations between the story and the reader become storied relations, the sort of relations that are depicted in narratives. The stories of Jesus and of the reader are related by narrative connections that make them two sequences within a single larger story. These storied relations, rather than general truths the story illustrates, mediate between story and reader.[68]

The distinction between *storied* and *illustrative* in relating the Christian story and its reader (or reading community) is the systematic analogue of Frei's hermeneutical observations regarding what I have been calling narrative and non-narrative interpretation. In addition, we could say that both distinctions are examples of the distinction which Christian makes in his schemas of the relating of truth and authenticity. That is, both the "storied" soteriological relation and Frei's narrative interpretation are examples of the relating of truth and authenticity described in Christian's A-T/R schema. Contrariwise, the "illustrative" soteriological relation of story and reader is analogous to Frei's nonnarrative biblical interpretation,[69] and both of these are examples of relating truth and authenticity, as described in Christian's T/R-A schema.

Example of Narrative Interpretation:
John Calvin Reading Genesis

All of this is well and good, but how does it actually function in practice? If it remains on a purely theoretical level, it may not be easy to see the significance of the narrative and nonnarrative patterns for our examination of feminist theologies. Since Frei indicates that an example of narrative interpretation can be found in John Calvin, we may turn to an instance from Calvin's biblical interpretation to illustrate the previous discussion. Here we will find embodied in Calvin's interpretation examples of narrative interpretation, the A-T/R pattern of relating truth to authenticity, a concern for dogmatics rather than apologetics, and a storied rather than illustrative relating of the Christian story of redemption to its readers. The following examines Calvin's commentary on Genesis, which originated as lectures given to his theological students in Geneva. We can see the impact of reading the Bible as one overarching narrative on what Calvin has to say about discrete scenes within the larger narrative. He uses both simple and typological interpretation to render the conclusion that "we are companions of the Patriarchs," that their narrative is also our own.[70]

In the "Argument" which opens Calvin's commentary on Genesis, we find that Calvin reads Genesis itself as both an episode within and a summary or proleptic vision of the "gospel story" as a whole. The story of Genesis is read not only as the "history of the creation of the world" as Calvin calls it, a story about long ago and far away, but also as the sum content of the Christian story itself. Because it is the sum of the Christian story, it thereby automatically is the story of the reader, and it is recapitulated daily in the life of the Christian. Thus Calvin says at the end of his "argument": "We are companions of the patriarchs; for since they possessed Christ as the pledge of their salvation when he had not yet appeared, so we retain the God who formerly manifested himself to them."[71] How does Calvin understand Genesis to tell the Christian story, thereby rendering us companions of the patriarchs? He lays out what he understands to be the "argument" or plot of the book of Genesis: (1) after the world is created, humankind is placed in it, that beholding the works of God, all might reverently adore their Author; (2) all things are ordained for the use of humankind to bind us in obedience and obligation to God; (3) humankind is endowed with reason and thus distinguished from animals that they might meditate on and desire God, in whose image they were made; and (4) next comes the story of fall of Adam, which deprives him of all uprightness, alienates him from God, and leaves him perverse in heart and under the sentence of eternal death. This all seems as would be expected.

However, at this point, Calvin surprises us when he continues: (5) Moses then adds the "history of the restoration of humanity where Christ shines forth with the benefit of redemption." According to Calvin, Genesis relates the providence of God in preserving the church, shows us true worship of God, teaches us of the salvation of humankind, and uses examples of the patriarchs to exhort us to endure the cross. Of course, for Calvin as well as for his contemporary exegetes, whether Roman Catholic or Reformers of different stripes, the word of God to the patriarchs was founded on Christ. Therefore, Calvin says that all the pious who have ever lived have been sustained by the same promise by which Adam was first raised from the Fall. Here we can assume that he refers to Genesis 3:15, the *protoevangelium*, which was considered to be the gospel-before-the-gospel. This verse contains the words of the curse to the serpent: "I will put enmity between you and the woman, and between your seed and her seed; he shall bruise your head, and you shall bruise his heel." Since Moses was ordained to be a teacher of the Israelites, says Calvin, God also intended through Moses to testify to all ages that there is only one true God whom we worship. These, says Calvin, are the main topics of the book of Genesis.

But how does Calvin understand Genesis to speak of Redemption, to tell of the history of the restoration of humanity, and to speak even of the grace of Jesus, and of that as clearly to sixteenth-century Geneva as to Israel of antiquity? Here we see how the whole commentary turns on the assumption of the coherence or wholeness of the book of Genesis and, indeed, the unity of the overall story of Israel, the people of God, the Church. However, this datum has less to do with Calvin's understanding of the nature of the text itself than with his understanding of the nature of the God who addresses the faithful through the text. That is, the fact that the Bible is read as a continuous story is not because of the nature of stories in general or even the compelling nature of this story, although, to be sure, Calvin does find this story to be compelling. The unitary and absorptive character of this narrative issues from the prior claim to the unity and faithfulness of God.

We might illustrate this thesis by outlining two general categories or practices of reading which Calvin uses throughout the Genesis commentary to set forth the character of the One God whom Calvin trusts as both author and subject matter of the biblical text. These two general categories can be seen to fall under the larger rubric of figurative reading.[72] The first is the reading of biblical stories as example, that is, holding up the patriarchs as examples to Calvin's readers such that the struggles of the Christian life are seen to be illustrated or figured in the lives of the patriarchs. In this first category, the patriarchs serve as "types" or figures, which are reiterated daily in the life of the reader. The predicaments and perils, temptations and trials of the patriarchs are gathered up and reappear in the life of the Christian, not merely incidentally but necessarily so, because the God with whom they have to deal is the same God.

This first kind of figural reading is therefore contingent upon a second kind, which entails a specifically christological figurative hermeneutics. This second kind is reading biblical stories as christological prophecy, that is, engaging in figural reading such that Christ and the patterns of his life depicted in the New Testament are understood to be figured proleptically in the story of Israel. Here Calvin sees the story of Christ crucified and risen to be retrojected or folded in backwards into the narratives of Israel. Like the eggwhites folded into a cake batter, it is this forecapitulation of the Christ-event in the stories of the patriarchs that binds the canonical story together for Calvin. It enables and, indeed, requires him to read Genesis as the "Christian story." The "argument" thus opens his commentary by setting the framework within which the figurative rendering of the Christian story takes place: Genesis is both an episode within and a proleptic vision of the gospel story as a whole.

Of the first kind of figural reading, there are two subgroups. One is moral example, and the other is christologically rendered example. Of the first subgroup, instances are many throughout Calvin's commentary on Genesis, in which the patriarchs are examples of both positive and negative responses to the will and grace of God. These examples serve to warn, console, and strengthen Calvin's audience in their daily struggles. The patriarchs can serve as positive examples of behavior which readers are to emulate, as we find in Calvin's comments on Genesis 22. Here, Abraham serves as an example of obedience and subjection to the will of God, even in the thick of severe testing. Indeed, there are also instances of story as negative example, such as Abraham's palming off Sarah as his sister, first on Pharaoh and then on Abimelech, and Sarah's impatience at the delay of the promise, which prompts her to suggest that Hagar bear the son whom they await. In addition to citing stories as positive and negative examples, there are also instances in which Calvin rejects the possibility that a story could serve as example at all, as in his comments on the story of Abraham's servant's offer of gold jewelry to Rebekah in Genesis 24:22:

> But it may be asked whether God approves ornaments of this kind, which pertain not so much to neatness as to pomp? I answer that the things related in Scripture are not always proper to be imitated. Whatever the Lord commands in general terms is to be accounted as an inflexible rule of conduct; but to rely on particular examples is not only dangerous, but even foolish and absurd.[73]

But this more general use of the patriarchs as example is only indirectly linked with Calvin's broader implicit understanding of the absorptive character of the biblical narrative. That is, these instances could conceivably have been part of his comments, even if he did not understand the Christ-story to be typologically rendered in the patriarchs' lives. Thus, this subgroup can be classified simply as moral application. While this in itself would be useful for building the character of Calvin's auditors, moral application is not what makes us companions of the patriarchs, not what draws us into the "strange new world within the Bible." If it were this alone, we would likewise be the companions of the characters of any other narrative.

More interesting for our present purposes is the second subgroup, in which the patriarchs and their struggles are portrayed as directly figurative of the lives of Christians to follow. When commenting on the murder of Abel in Genesis 4:10 at the phrase "the voice of thy brother's blood crieth from the ground," Calvin says:

> This is a wonderfully sweet consolation to good men who are unjustly harassed, when they hear that their own sufferings, which they silently endure, go into the presence of God of their own accord to demand vengeance. . . . Nor does this doctrine apply merely to the state of the present life, to teach us that among the innumerable dangers by which we are surrounded we shall be safe under the guardianship of God; but it elevates us by the hope of a better life, because we must conclude that those for whom God cares shall survive after death.[74]

Thus Abel's own silent death and the crying of his blood to God for vengeance are an example to Calvin's listeners (and, as Calvin would say, to us in our turn) that they submit in their suffering with the knowledge of and trust in God's care, for this is the pattern of the innocent suffering of the vindicated risen Lord. Remarkably, Calvin in effect says that the story of Cain and Abel assures us of the doctrine of the resurrection of the dead. However, instead of spelling this out, he illustrates it by means of comment to the effect that the story of Abel's innocent suffering is to be seen as a type for our own suffering, one we recapitulate whenever we face suffering with the hope of God's vindication.

At the story of God's establishment of the covenant with Noah after the flood in Genesis 9, Calvin argues against what he understands to be the misinterpretation of his theological rivals. At verse 9, which reads "with you and your seed after you," Calvin claims that "the ignorance of the Anabaptists may be refuted who deny that the covenant of God is common to infants, because they are destitute of present faith."[75] Two things in particular are to be noted here. First, the story has direct application to one instance of the present theological polemic Calvin faces, namely, with the Anabaptists who refute infant baptism. According to Calvin, the very words of the text ("with you and your seed after you") indicate a direct engagement in the form of refutation with the Anabaptist position. Second, the obvious implication of this line of argumentation is that the covenant with Noah is the covenant of baptism, namely, the covenant sealed in the death and Resurrection of Christ. Notice how different this is from a strictly "salvation-historical" plan in which God reveals himself in successively clearer covenants until the crowning glory of the covenant mediated by Christ. Here is an instance of our companionship with a patriarch, Noah, based on the understanding that the Christ-story is proleptically present in his story and analeptically present in ours, or at least in Calvin's, and presumably Calvin would say in ours as well. The absorptive capacity of the biblical texts works multidirectionally: the Christ-story is absorbed into Noah's, Noah's into Christ's, and both into ours.

At the story of Abram's offering of the animals and birds in Genesis 15, Calvin claims to avoid the "fabrication of subtleties" and the "wander[ing] in uncertain speculations." Instead, he wants to "cultivate sobriety," saying that the sum of this story is:

> That God, in commanding the animals to be killed, shows what will be the future condition of the Church. Abram certainly wished to be assured of the promised inheritance of the land. Now he is taught that it would take its commencement from death; that is that he and his children must die before they should enjoy the dominion over the land. . . . We see, therefore, that two things were illustrated; namely, the hard servitude, with which the sons of Abram were to be pressed almost to laceration and destruction; and then their redemption, which was to be the signal pledge of divine adoption; and in the same mirror the general condition of the Church is represented to us as it is the peculiar providence of God to create it out of nothing, and to raise it from death.[76]

Thus the "simple sense" of the offering narrated in Genesis 15 tells us of the future condition of the church, of Abram's descendants and the church of Calvin's day, recapitulating the death and Resurrection of the one who calls them into being in their suffering and their hope for the promise.[77] If we wondered how Calvin could see redemption "figuring" into the Genesis story as he claimed in his "Argument," here it is. The attainment of the promised land after the hardships of slavery and the wandering in the desert is a figure of Christ, and, because of this, it is also a figure of the church which shares in the sufferings of Christ. This story of Abram's offering, which Calvin admits is obscure ("I shall not be ashamed to acknowledge my ignorance," he states), figuratively represents the existence of the church and therefore serves as a word of hope. This is because it holds within itself the recollection of creation ex nihilo, narratively fourteen chapters prior to this, and the promise of the Redemption yet to be narrated in the New Covenant.

The second category, christological-prophetic typology, is less prevalent than either subgroup of the first category throughout Calvin's commentary on Genesis. However, this scarcity makes it all the more striking when it does appear, especially in view of Calvin's many comments disparaging allegorical "speculations."[78] Just as it was Ambrose's figurative reading of the Old Testament which "redeemed" the Bible for Augustine and opened his heart to the Catholic Christian faith, so it is such figurative reading which allows Calvin's observations recorded in his "Argument" to come to fruition in the commentary. This claim that "we are companions of the Patriarchs," based as it is on the oneness of God, demands a reading of the Bible which embraces the canon as a whole, even when this may allow for allegorical or typological reading.

For example, in expounding the story of Jacob's dream of the ladder reaching to heaven at Genesis 28:12, Calvin says:

> It is Christ alone therefore, who connects heaven and earth: he is the only mediator who reaches from heaven down to earth. . . . If then, we say that the ladder is a figure of Christ the exposition will not be forced. . . . That the ladder was a symbol of Christ is also confirmed by this consideration, that nothing was more suitable than that God should ratify his covenant of eternal salvation in his Son to his servant Jacob. And hence we feel unspeakable joy when we hear that Christ, who so far excels all creatures, is nevertheless joined with us.[79]

Again, we see the absorptive capacity of the biblical text to be multidirectional: from Jacob to Christ, from Christ to Jacob, from both to us. The multidirectional flow is from the Christ-story outward, both backward and forward. In this way, each Christian whom Calvin addresses shares with Jacob in the joy of being joined with Christ, and, as Calvin says, we have "fraternal society" with Jacob and the patriarchs, because we share a common Head whose "station is on earth." Reading the ladder as a figure of Christ establishes a link not only between Jacob and God but also between Jacob and all those baptized into Christ's death and Resurrection.

Again, Calvin reads the text in christological-typological fashion at the story of Jacob's blessing of Ephraim and Manasseh. Although he regards as absurd the reading which would have the crossing of Jacob's hands to signify the cross of Christ,[80] he does advocate reading the word *angel* at 48:16 christologically:

> Wherefore it is necessary that Christ should be here meant, who does not bear in vain the title of Angel, because he had become the perpetual Mediator. And Paul testifies that he was the Leader and Guide of the journey of his ancient people (1 Cor. 10:4). He had not yet indeed been sent by the Father to approach more nearly to us by taking our flesh, but but because he was always the bond of connection between God and man, and because God formally manifested himself in no other way than through him, he is properly called the Angel. To which may be added that the faith of the Fathers was always fixed on his future mission.[81]

In reading the angel as Christ, Calvin shows that he is assuming that Christ is and always has been the "bond of connection" between God and humanity. Therefore, he also assumes, without sensing that he is "adding" anything to the text or embroidering allegories, that the angel whom Jacob declares to have redeemed him *has to have been* Christ, whose office it is "to defend and to deliver us from all evil." Because of this, argues Calvin, it is indeed proper to say that the faith of the fathers was fixed on the future mission of Christ, the same object of faith shared by Calvin's listeners. Christ is absorbed into the angel of the Genesis blessing, and the angel into Christ. It is this which renders Calvin's listeners as companions of the patriarchs.

Such examples are many within Calvin's commentary on Genesis, as well as in his other commentaries and sermons. What can we learn, then, from these examples of the absorptive power of the biblical text for the narrative reader? First, Calvin's embracing of the unity of the biblical narrative is not pinned to an appreciation of story as theological category or as psychological structure in the human soul. Whether in those examples of Calvin's interpretation in which the Christian struggle is figured in the lives of the patriarchs, or those in which Christ is figured in the stories about the patriarchs, the significant element is this: Calvin does not *establish* a canonical unity via such figural interpretation, but rather such interpretation *assumes* an understanding of canonical unity, which is a derivative corollary of the church's affirmation of the unity of God's will and work.

˙This, then, is a second observation: in beginning with the assumption of canonical unity, Calvin holds a prior assumption of the unity of God. That is, the formal basis of canonical wholeness is the oneness of the divine reality and voice, the God who in Christ appears throughout the Gospel stories, in the stories of Genesis, throughout the entire Bible, and indeed in the lives of Calvin's own parishioners and students. Third, this formal unity is exhibited occasionally via figural interpretation and, at times, even demands it. Thus the Bible is read as a single, cumulative narrative but ultimately not as a direct result of any specific hermeneutical practice at all. Calvin cannot entirely abandon figural reading despite the stock Reformation polemic against allegory, not because of his understanding of what it means to read a text qua text but because of his understanding of the God of Israel and of the nature of this text in particular, the biblical text. That is, Calvin's fugue of figural and literal reading is not an a priori commitment to a specific hermeneutical methodology to unify this random collection of narratives which he knows as the Old Testament. Rather, his interplay of literal and figural interpretation is an ad hoc practice used to interpret the scriptures on which the church's faith stands, the faith that trusts in God's divine caretaking over the storied history which the text is understood to depict.

Thus, we have seen how Calvin reads the Bible as one overarching story with its center point in the narratives about Jesus. Interpretation flows from this center both backward and forward in time, with the result that stories about the patriarchs are echoed in those about Jesus and in our own lives. In Frei's terms, the biblical world absorbs the world of the reader. This, then, is narrative interpretation, which takes for granted the logic of belief rather than the logic of coming to belief and which is dogmatic in approach rather than apologetic. Although this example of narrative interpretation did not contain stories about women, nor was it by a woman, surely we can learn something from Calvin here.

Now, as we turn to feminist theology, we will keep in mind these insights from narrative interpretation to discern more clearly the relationship between feminist interpretation of the Bible and its varied reconstructions of Christian doctrine with that of the narrative pattern. Thus, we might be able to discern among the examples from feminist theologies which direction of interpretive flow obtains, narrative or non-narrative. We will attempt to discern the logic of various feminist theologies' relating truth to authenticity, and which model, either apologetics or dogmatics, best describes the works of feminist theology we will consider. The hope is that, having isolated certain patterns of biblical interpretation, we can, in greater depth and with greater sensitivity and detail, analyze the concrete examples of feminist theology.

In the following chapter, then, we will attempt to discern this specifically with regard to the hermeneutics and biblical interpretation of feminist theologies. This, we will find, will allow us to sketch the governing doctrine(s) of feminist theological interpretation of the Bible. Here we will note the distinction between two broad approaches to feminist theology, one known as "biblical feminism" and one I have termed "mainline feminism," the latter of which will be the focus of our concerns throughout the remainder of this book. The next three chapters will look at the impact of feminist theologies' governing doctrines on their reconstruction of primary doctrines. Chapter 3 will deal with the doctrine of sin, chapters 4 and 5 with key aspects of feminist reconstructions of Christology, and chapter 6 with the doctrine of the Trinity. A final chapter attempts to draw conclusions and make some suggestions for constructive use of feminist theology.

2

>─┼─◆>──0──<◆─┼─<

FEMINIST HERMENEUTICS, THE BIBLE, AND PATRIARCHY

Governing Doctrines

In the previous chapter, we outlined the insights of narrative interpretation and theology. Since Christian and Lindbeck point out that governing doctrines are usually more important than primary doctrines, especially during times of conflict, we should look for the governing doctrines of feminist theologies. We therefore must look to the hermeneutical principles and rules which guide feminist biblical interpretation and theological reflection. This will require, first, looking into the intellectual families of origin from which feminist theology emerges. After this, we can examine the explicit and implicit commitments and principles of interpretation embraced by feminist theologians as they appear in second-order discussion about biblical interpretation. Then we can examine the implicit commitments as they are born out in the practice of biblical interpretation itself.

The two most obvious intellectual forebears of feminist theology are modern theology in general and, more specifically, the feminist movements in America and England. Feminist theology, combining as it does the concerns of modern theology with the sociopolitical concerns of the broader feminist movement, can be analyzed therefore as a subset of either of these two worlds of thought. This is sometimes cause for confusion and debate. The charge is sometimes raised from the side of Christian thinkers that feminist theologians are more committed to feminism than to Christian theology. Conversely, non-Christian feminists sometimes claim that Christian feminist theologians' allegiance to the Christian tradition, with all its patriarchal underpinnings, renders their work untenable. However, both parents of feminist theology, the feminist movement and modern Christian thought, are so thoroughly grounded in the categories and presuppositions of the Enlightenment that these two parents are not in such dire conflict as such charges might lead us to believe. We will examine briefly the phenomenon of feminist theology as a subset of modern theology, and then examine it as a subset of the feminist movement.

Feminist Theology as a Subset of Modern Theology

Without the general acceptance of the hermeneutical presuppositions of modern theology, feminist theology might otherwise have appeared incongruous with Christian theology.[1] In fact, however, it embodies many of the guiding presuppositions—or principles and rules, to use William Christian's terms—of modern theology.[2] These presuppositions include the broad consensus regarding the "turn to the subject" in the study of religion and the necessity to understand the biblical texts as shaped by historical, social, and political factors. This latter element is evident in both the history of religions school and in the broad program of demythologization set forth by Rudolf Bultmann and his successors.

If we were to attempt to pinpoint the most direct intellectual parents of Christian feminist theology, we might credit Friedrich Schleiermacher (1768–1834) with the honor. His focus on the role of experience, in particular, that of God-consciousness, in theology is clearly taken up and metamorphosed in feminist theologies into the concentration on the role of women's experience. We might also look to Immanuel Kant (1724–1804), whose concerns we also see in feminist theologies: the triumph of the ethical over the dogmatic, trust in contemporary experience combined with distrust of tradition, and a vision of theological inquiry as rescuing the tradition from error and irrelevance.[3] To be sure, both Schleiermacher and Kant are important influences in the modern reading of Scripture and theological thinking in general, and not only in feminist theologies, but one clearly sees the influence here. However, it is Ludwig Feuerbach (1804–1872) who is one of the closest intellectual and theological forebears of feminist theology, for his understanding of God and the religious search is most sympathetic to and supportive of the feminist theological project.[4] Indeed, Feuerbach epitomizes and encompasses the weaknesses and strengths of modern theology, following as he does in the steps of both Schleiermacher and his critics.[5] The similarity between feminist theologians and the "antitheologian" Feuerbach is also evident insofar as they, too, have provoked vigorous theological reflection, which has rendered them, like Feuerbach, in some respects potentially "more theological than many of the theologians."[6]

Many of the feminist theologians we will consider are also in general agreement with Feuerbach that religion is "too important a subject to leave to the theologians."[7] For both Feuerbach and feminist theologians, this is because of the notion that religion involves the unconscious projection of individual or communal values or norms onto the grand screen of religious belief. Feminist theologians see a danger in this, however, which Feuerbach did not and could not discern. According to the feminist critique, if it is men to whom theology is left, it is a male projection of God which Christians will worship, and this will serve only to reinscribe patriarchy and strengthen the subjugation of women. Indeed, it is on the basis of Feuerbach's claim that "God is the mirror of man" that Mary Daly can charge that "If God is male, then male is

God."[8] Garrett Green has sketched the logic of what he calls "role model theology" evident in feminist theologies, which he sees to be consistent with Feuerbach's theories of projection.

> Since all religious communities construct their gods as expressions of the social values, a proper theology is one that expresses proper social values. Only such a theology is adequate to a proper religion—namely, one whose god is worthy of emulation by human beings. Since we moderns are committed to the full equality of the sexes, our theology must express that commitment; therefore, we should not speak of God in masculine terms (at least not unless they are balanced by feminine terms).[9]

This "role model theology," on the basis of the theory that our images of God are projections of our desires and values, reconstructs the biblical depiction of God to make it more palatable to our modern egalitarian sensibilities. Here we see but one example of what Frei was speaking when he tried to note the confusion of the dogmatic with the apologetic task.

As Bultmann will do after him, and as many feminist theologians do after Bultmann, Feuerbach understood theology to be, at heart, anthropology: "Theology is anthropology, that is to say in the object of religion, in what we call *Theos* in Greek and *Gott* in German, nothing is specified except the essence of man."[10] Like Bultmann, Feuerbach did not mean this to be derogatory of religion at all, but rather as his "strange *Magnificat* to the beloved God."[11] However, for many feminist theologians, this only increases the stakes involved or ups the ante, so to speak. If theology is anthropology, and theology is left to men, then theology is not anthropology at all but "aner-ology," which excludes "gyn-ecology." Mary Daly thus sees to it that theology as anthropology becomes just this: "gyn/ecology."[12]

Of course, Mary Daly openly states that she has left the Christian community and tradition. Not all feminist theologians admit this so freely; in fact, just the opposite is the case. Many feminist theologians want to remain and, indeed, claim they that they do remain well within the bounds of the Christian tradition. Even Feuerbach claimed to be in good company with respectable Christian theological forebears and traced his theological heritage to Luther, just as Bultmann did in the following century. In the *Essence of Faith According to Luther* (1844), Feuerbach claims that his "feeling of dependence" which marks the religious life is what Luther really meant by his *pro me*.[13] Feuerbach quotes Luther extensively to back up his own view that it is love of self which motivates Protestant piety and which, in turn, creates the God it needs. But the fact remains that Feuerbach adds another block to the foundation on which feminist theologies stand insofar as he, too, seeks in "respectable" theological forebears the justification for his own project.

In turn, Bultmann's program of demythologization is a major influence on feminist interpretation of the Bible, as it is on most modern theology of the twentieth century. Bultmann's demythologizing is driven by an apologetic concern, as is true of feminist theology's depatriarchalizing of the Bible. He attempts to remove the unnecessary stumbling blocks for the modern reader which are present in the ancient writers' mythological worldview, which, according to Bultmann, consisted of "a three-story structure, with earth in the middle, heaven above it, and hell below it."[14] Since this mythological world of Jewish apocalypticism and of the "Gnostic myth of redemption" (itself an uncomplicated term in Bultmann's day) is a thing of the past, the New Testament must be demythologized for modern people to understand the existential decision posed by the gospel. Since "there is nothing specifically Christian about the mythical world picture" of the New Testament, it must be translated, for the "only criticism of the New Testament that can be theologically relevant is that which arises necessarily out of our modern situation."[15] To accept blindly the New Testament mythological world would be to reduce faith to a work and would thus relieve the demand of the existential decision posed by the gospel.

This, of course, is a prime example of the assumption of a gap between the representation and the represented, which Frei pointed out to be a hallmark of modern interpretation of the Bible. Whereas Bultmann understood this gap to be indicated in the mythological worldview, feminist biblical interpretation understands this gap to be located in the patriarchal worldview of the Bible. The feminist alternative to Bultmann's demythologization is "depatriarchalization," or translating the message of the scriptures into nonpatriarchal language and concepts.[16] Like Bultmann's interpretation of the Bible, feminist biblical interpretation demands that criticism of the New Testament be theologically relevant to our modern situation. However, for feminist theologians, the situation which demands the change in interpretation is that of a crumbling patriarchy, not of the modern scientific worldview. The victory over patriarchy for feminists is likened to Paul's eschatological "now and not yet" of the victory of the cross, for the sting of patriarchy is still felt, even though inroads into its destruction are daily being advanced. In addition to the intellectual framework established for feminist theology in Feuerbach's hermeneutics of suspicion, in the concern for the ethical in Kant, and in the focus on experience and feeling in Schleiermacher, we see that Bultmann's plea for demythologization adds another plank to the feminist platform.

Feminist Theologies and the "First" and "Second" Waves of the Feminist Movement

Of course, not only the intellectual parents but also the practical parents of feminist theology have decisively shaped its hermeneutical theory and biblical interpretation. Of the practical parents, the feminist movement of the nineteenth and twentieth centuries is among the more important. The suffragette movement of the nineteenth century, which focused its energies on (white) women's right to the vote, is usually seen to represent the beginning of the "first wave" of the feminist movement. This first wave promoted the rise of "feminist consciousness," the roots of which have been traced deep in the Western intellectual tradition.[17] Arising out of this first wave, the distinctive "consciousness" of feminism affects not only the "second wave" but also the "third wave" of feminist theory. What is feminist consciousness?

> Feminist consciousness consists (1) of the awareness of women that they belong to a subordinate group and that, as members of such a group, they have suffered wrongs; (2) the recognition that their condition of subordination is not natural, but societally determined; (3) the development of a sense of sisterhood; (4) the autonomous definition

by women of their goals and strategies for changing their condition; and (5) the development of an alternate vision of the future.[18]

This consciousness developed in the first wave is then carried through and refined in the second wave, the origins of which are usually traced to Simone de Beauvoir's *The Second Sex* in France and Betty Friedan's *The Feminine Mystique* in North America.[19] While the first wave produced some of the classics of feminist theology and biblical interpretation, such as Elizabeth Cady Stanton's groundbreaking *The Woman's Bible*, it is with the second wave that feminist theology per se properly can be said to begin.[20] Valerie Saiving Goldstein's 1960 essay on women's sin is generally hailed as the pioneering critical work in the task of feminist reconstructions of Christian doctrine.

It is this second wave of the feminist movement that spawns the bulk of both the religious scholarship of feminist theology and the secular scholarship of feminist theory. The two are at times intertwined, but usually it is feminist theory which informs and feeds feminist theology. Rarely is the reverse the case, possibly because of late-twentieth-century Western high-culture's view of the privatized and personalized realm of religion. In any case, because of the influence of theory on theology, to understand some of the debates in feminist theology, we will need to examine some of the questions posed by feminist theory.

Feminist Anthropology and Nature versus Nurture

One of the more unstable areas of feminist theory, which also causes lively debate within feminist theology, is the question of what makes for "woman." For feminist theologians, this topic functions as analogue to theological anthropology which seeks to the answer the question "what is humanity?" For feminist theologians, the question is often posed, "What is woman?" with regard to this debate. Here we find ourselves in the storm of controversy over essentialism and constructionism, or the power of "nature" versus "nurture" to shape identity. Essentialism, in contrast to constructionism, is usually understood to be:

> the invariable and fixed properties which define the "whatness" of a given entity. In feminist theory, the idea that men and women, for example, are identified as such on the basis of transhistorical, eternal, immutable essences has been unequivocally rejected by many anti-essentialist post-structuralist feminists concerned with resisting any attempts to naturalize human nature. And yet one can also hear echoing from the corners of the debates on essentialism renewed interest in its possibilities and potential usages, sounds which articulate themselves most often in the form of calls to "risk" or to "dare" essentialism.[21]

This debate is not merely an intellectual exercise. It has a deep impact on how we engage in feminist analysis in general and therefore feminist theology in particular. As we analyze the power relations between the sexes, can we even say that "woman" is an objective, definable reality? Is her "essence" due to her biological makeup, over against masculine biological form and function? Or is her reality traceable to her socioeconomic placement? If so, can we meaningfully analyze the power relations between the sexes without considering a multiplicity of other factors which play into the creation of the "identity" of "woman"? How we answer these questions significantly affects the question of whether "women" can even be spoken of in a general way. Does the white, wealthy American woman have anything significant in common with the underclass itinerant Gypsy woman in eastern Europe if women are constructed by their environment? Can woman's nature or even women's oppression be analyzed in any meaningful way if we are speaking not of members of underclass but of the wives of the sheiks of the Arab nations or of those few women who themselves are CEOs of major international corporations?

Often, "essentialism" is set off in contrast to "constructionism" as though they were two discrete categories of thought within feminist theory.[22] Constructionist theory wants to examine a multiplicity of factors which play into the establishment of woman's identity. However, others are willing to see through to another possibility, to the effect that:

> there is no essence to essentialism, that (historically, philosophically, and politically) we can only speak of *essentialisms*. Correlatively . . . constructionism (the position that differences are constructed, not innate) really operates as a more sophisticated form of essentialism. The bar between essentialism and constructionism is by no means as solid and unassailable as advocates of both sides assume it to be.[23]

Still other feminist theorists have come to question the distinction between essentialism and constructionism, even to the point where the ability to generalize about women's identity, experience, and oppression becomes problematic. This renders claims about "woman" impossible, for the universalizing assumptions they require import an ethnocentrism which is antithetical to feminist method and analysis.[24] The generalizing necessary in much of feminist discourse, whether essentialist or constructionist, with its more sophisticated parsing of woman's identity and location, can lead to a self-contradictory logic whereby any truths stated are necessarily the victims of their own falsification.[25] Of course, this "inherent shakiness of the designation 'women' " is part and parcel of the flexibility of feminist discourse and can be embraced rather than avoided or shunned.[26]

The inherent instability in feminist theory at this point is best greeted by bracketing the essentialist-constructionist debate. This bracketing ultimately will be useful not only to the present project but also to feminist theology per se.[27] A feminism which attempts to engage Christian Scripture and tradition will need at some point to grapple with the specifically biblical and traditional articulations of what it means to be human, whether or not these articulations will finally be embraced. Deciding in advance for or against one theory over another will get in the way of this. Thus, what is needed is an "agile" (in the words of Denise Riley) or "ad hoc" (in the words of Hans Frei) consideration of the category of gender in general and of the identity of "woman" in particular as we turn to the particulars of feminist theology.[28]

Feminist Theory and Patriarchy

However we decide to deal with the question of nature versus nurture, we do not need to settle the debate to understand feminist theologies. However, understanding what is meant by patriarchy is essential before we can begin to analyze feminist theology, for patriarchy becomes the equivalent to the Fall narrative in Genesis 3, to which the redemption in Christ corresponds. A key understanding of patriarchy within mainline feminist theological scholarship is voiced by Elisabeth Schüssler Fiorenza:

> Just as feminism is not just a worldview or perspective but a women's movement for change, so patriarchy is in my understanding not just ideological dualism or androcentric world construction in language but a *social, economic, and political system of graded subjugations and oppressions.* Therefore I do not speak simply about male oppressors and female oppressed, or see all men over and against all women. Patriarchy as a *male pyramid* specifies women's oppression in terms of the class, race, country, or religion of the men to whom they "belong."[29]

Just how patriarchy "started" is a matter of some debate. For the purposes of this study, we will look to just one of the more influential of the theories, that developed by Gerda Lerner.[30] While her theory regarding the rise of patriarchy is, to be sure, not "provable" in any scientific context, nevertheless, it allows an analysis of patriarchy which can embrace both biological and cultural models of the shaping of woman's identity, which in itself is an advantage for feminist theologies. In her discussion of "patriarchy," Lerner traces the rise of male rule over women throughout the course of civilization. According to Lerner, patriarchy is "a historic creation formed by men and women in a process which took nearly 2500 years to its completion. In its earliest form patriarchy appeared as the archaic state. The basic unit of its organization was the patriarchal family, which both expressed and constantly generated its rules and values."[31] Her theory traces the roots of patriarchy to biological structures inherent in the reproduction and development of the human species. Lerner's analysis of the rise of patriarchy is based on a specific version of evolutionary theory of human development. For example, according to the scientific theory which undergirds her analysis, human bipedalism results in human infants being born at a greater stage of immaturity than other primate species. This, coupled with the human infant's lack of hair covering and the movable toe with which the ape is endowed, means that human infants are entirely dependent on the parent for warmth, physical support, and mobility. This, in turn, leads to the finer development of the human hand, with its opposable thumb and greater reliance on sensory-hand coordination than in the ape. One consequence of this development, according to the theory, is that the human infant's brain develops over the course of many more years than the ape infant's brain. This, combined with the human infant's almost complete dependence for survival on adult humans, results in its being subject to training and shaping of behavior via cultural molding in a way which is distinctly different from the rest of the animal world.[32]

This biological development of the species, combined with the socioeconomic development in agriculture, then leads, according to Lerner, to the gender specifizing of the division of labor. She is swift to point out that, while this was historically a necessity for human survival, no alternative being available than for the females to take on the labor of mothering and raising offspring, this does not indicate an ontological necessity:

The story of civilization is the story of men and women struggling up from necessity, from their helpless dependence on nature, to freedom and their partial mastery over nature. In this struggle women were longer confined to species-essential activities than men and were therefore more vulnerable to being disadvantaged. My argument sharply distinguishes between biological necessity, to which both men and women submitted and adapted, and culturally constructed customs and institutions, which forced women into subordinate roles. I have tried to show how it might come to pass that women agreed to a sexual division of labor, which would eventually disadvantage them, without having been able to foresee the later consequences. Freud's statement . . . that "anatomy is destiny" is wrong because it is ahistorical and reads the distant past into the present without making allowances for changes over time. Worse, this statement has been read as a prescription for present and future: not only is anatomy destiny for women, but it should be. What Freud should have said is that for women anatomy *once was* destiny."[33]

Not only does Lerner's theory therefore allow for the integration of essentialist and constructivist positions but also it lends support for the claim that patriarchy is not necessarily ontologically linked with Western civilization in general, which can be advantageous to Christian feminist theologians whose religion has played such a central role in Western civilization. According to Lerner, patriarchy predated Western civilization without being a prescription for it. We can logically draw the inference that patriarchy is not ontologically linked either with Christianity or Judaism:

The sexuality of women, consisting of their sexual and their reproductive capacities and services, was commodified even prior to the creation of Western civilization. The development of agriculture in the Neolithic period fostered the inter-tribal "exchange of women," not only as a means of avoiding incessant warfare by the cementing of marriage alliances but also because societies with more women could produce more children. In contrast to the economic needs of hunting/gathering societies, agriculturists could use the labor of children to increase production and accumulate surpluses. Men-as-a-group had rights in women which women-as-a-group did not have in men. Women themselves became a resource, acquired by men much as the land was acquired by men.[34]

Indeed, Lerner's theory allows the feminist theorist and theologian to cast the notion of the "reification of women" in a new light. This allows for the possibility of analyzing women as themselves agents, even if only to a small extent but agents nevertheless, in the creation of their own identities. They are not merely victims.

Claude Lévi-Strauss, to whom we owe the concept of 'the exchange of women,' speaks of the reification of women, which occurred as its consequence. But it is not women who are reified and commodified, it is women's sexuality and reproductive capacity which is so treated. The distinction is important. Women never became 'things,' nor were they so perceived. Women, no matter how exploited and abused, retained their power to act and to choose to the same, often very limited extent, as men of their group. But women *always and to this day* lived in a relatively greater state of unfreedom than did men. Since their sexuality, an aspect of their body, was controlled by others, women were not only actually disadvantaged but psychologically restrained in a very special way. For women, as for men of subordinate and oppressed groups, history consisted of their struggle against different forms of oppression and dominance than did men, and their struggle, up to this time, has lagged behind that of men.[35]

According to Lerner, patriarchy then affects Christianity in particular insofar as "male hegemony over the symbol system took two forms: educational deprivation of women and male monopoly on definition."[36] Women are excluded from the process of the production of meaning and from the view of the historian. This adds a cultural seal to the biological constraints.[37]

We begin to see the overlap between Lerner's account and the accounts of feminist theologians as to the exclusion of women's voices from the writing of Scripture and from the shaping of tradition, as we will see. Even while Lerner holds to a purely secular version of the analysis of patriarchy, we see an element which can be taken up as the analogue to "eschatology" within much of Christian mainline feminist theology. In Lerner's words:

> The system of patriarchy is a historic construct; it has a beginning; it will have an end. Its time seems to have nearly run its course—it no longer serves the needs of men or women and in its inextricable linkage to militarism, hierarchy, and racism, it threatens the very existence of life on earth. . . . A feminist world-view will enable women and men to free their minds from patriarchal thought and practice and at last to build a world free of dominance and hierarchy, a world that is truly human.[38]

For Lerner, redemption from patriarchy is on the horizon and will be brought about by cultural and political forces. Feminism itself thus becomes the redeemer of patriarchal culture and, indeed, of the "very existence of life on earth." Among feminist theologians, this often shows up in the presentation of feminist theology as the eschatological redemption of Christianity itself. The Fall was into patriarchy, and Redemption will be into equality, or into separate feminist culture in the thought of some. This, then, is the historical "narrative" of patriarchy with which many feminist theologies implicitly operate. We can now turn to what feminist theologians claim about the scriptures of the church.

Feminist Theologians and the Bible

Feminist theologians hold these questions of the rise and maintenance of patriarchy and the construction of woman's identity before them as they read the Bible. Of course, there are many different ways of approaching the scriptures suggested and used by feminist theologians. These range from that which adopts almost entirely classical attitudes toward the Bible, to that which challenges almost every claim and posture of traditional biblical interpretation. At one end of the spectrum, a perspective infrequently represented by feminist theologians, we find a hermeneutics of trust. For example, Marti Steussy in her essay "My Friend, the Bible" adopts for feminist biblical hermeneutics several classical categories for the task of reading Scripture and proposes her own metaphor of Bible as friend.[39] Friendship takes time and patience, and so does reading the Bible; like a friend, the Bible cares and heals; like a true friend, the Bible is flexible and adaptable. Here, the hermeneutics of suspicion is vastly downplayed, and traditional categories of biblical interpretation are brought to the fore. At the other end of the spectrum, however, the

Bible is viewed as a potential enemy, and feminist consciousness is the "saving grace" which rescues women from the potentially harmful effects of its interpretation:[40]

> Feminist consciousness radically throws into question all traditional religious names, texts, rituals, laws, and interpretive metaphors because they all bear "our Father's names." With Carol Christ I would insist that the central spiritual and religious feminist quest is the quest for women's self-affirmation, survival, power, and self-determination.[41]

However feminists embrace the Bible, the questions of woman's identity and the role of patriarchy in circumscribing that identity are kept always at the fore as feminist theologians approach the Bible.

There are many ways of categorizing the ways in which different feminists use the Bible. On the one hand, feminist approaches to the Bible tend to be classified according to the particular attitudes which feminists hold regarding the Bible. For example, Carolyn Osiek constructs such a typology of different feminist approaches to the Bible: rejectionist (e.g., Mary Daly), loyalist (Susan Foh), revisionist (Phyllis Trible), sublimationist (Joan Engelsman, Leonard Swidler), and liberationist (Elisabeth Schüssler Fiorenza and Rosemary Radford Ruether).[42] On the other hand, they are sometimes analyzed in terms of hermeneutical approaches. For example, Elisabeth Schüssler Fiorenza speaks of her "fourfold" hermeneutical model, which the feminist interpreter can apply to biblical texts: the hermeneutics of suspicion, of remembrance, of proclamation, and of creative actualization.[43] These sorts of typologies, however, often say more about the feminist constructor of the typology than about her understanding of how the Bible actually functions in feminist interpretation. For example, Osiek's loyalist category would presumably also include Mary Stewart van Leeuwen, who is "loyal" but in a completely different way from Susan Foh, Osiek's representative of that category. Apparently, both Foh, who sees a great danger to Christianity in "biblical feminism," and van Leeuwen, who is a biblical feminist, look similar from the remove at which Osiek stands. Again, Osiek's category of liberationist embraces both Ruether and Fiorenza, who would not see themselves as bearing much in common apart from their shared commitment to feminism and to Christianity.

It may prove more helpful instead, therefore, to examine approaches according to the way in which the Bible itself is implicitly construed by feminist theologians. That is, what does a particular feminist theologian understand the Bible to be, and how does she understand it to function? The resulting typology will allow us to see commonalities which otherwise might go unnoticed and, in addition, may tell us more about the actual use of the Bible among the different feminist theologians. We might sketch the categories as follows: understanding the Bible to function primarily as witness to a divine reality, as a vehicle of patriarchy, as a vehicle of patriarchy and racism, and as a cultural artifact.[44]

Feminists of the first group share the understanding that the Bible functions primarily as *inspired witness* to the grace of God in Jesus Christ.[45] This view proceeds on the basis of trust that the scriptures witness to and lead to life and are not fundamentally dangerous but rather life-giving. Understanding the scriptures as inspired witness thus necessitates the strategy of close reading and retrieval of biblical stories of strong women who can serve as role models for contemporary women.[46] This category is occupied by "Biblical feminists" in particular but also by those who oppose biblical feminism as well as by those who are both feminists and orthodox Christians but do not identify themselves as biblical feminists. Biblical feminism, also referred to as "Christian feminism," tends to be an evangelical phenomenon, and is marked by the following traits:

> 1) A commitment to taking the Bible, God's inspired word, seriously as the guide to faith and practice; 2) a biblical understanding of human beings, both male and female, as created in God's image—and marred by sin; 3) an assumption, again based on the Bible, that God intended male and female to live together in this life, caring for the world and each other and practicing love and justice; 4) an appreciation that Christ's redemptive work has changed the possibilities for human beings, that now we can fulfill God's intentions whereas without Christ we could not; 5) a recognition that the imperatives of the Gospel sometimes call us to go against the grain, to oppose received opinion, even when it has been received by the Christian community and thus seems sacrosanct.[47]

That is, as we saw was the case for narrative reading of Scripture outlined earlier, we see here that biblical feminists attempt to read all of reality through the lens of the biblical narrative, and not vice versa. This means that for biblical feminists, the root of the "problem" which feminism must deal with is not patriarchy per se but the larger biblical category into which patriarchy falls, that is, human sin.

> [For biblical feminists,] the root issue is not patriarchy, or even patriarchy-plus-capitalist-exploitation. These themselves are only symptoms of a deeper problem still. The sin that takes its root in the human heart feeds into human and social structures and perverts and distorts relationships. I find it interesting that even though Christians are often accused of having a pessimistic view of human nature with its accent on sin, this view actually emerges as much more optimistic than [non-Christian views]. . . . Christian woman can recognize always the possibility of change and reconciliation. Repentance is a real alternative.[48]

While this is not a logical necessity, biblical feminists tend to rely on essentialist understandings of woman and are sometimes less sensitive than other feminists to the historical and cultural factors which shape the lives of women. Most evangelical or biblical feminists do not seek to reconstruct Christian doctrine but remain concerned with the question of women in ministry and with equality with men.[49] Some are moving into areas of social concern, but even here the focus is not on reconstructing Christian doctrine.[50] However, the importance of their project lies in its use of the Bible as inspired witness to God's grace: for biblical feminists, the Bible can produce and support a feminist vision. The key distinguishing factor between biblical feminists and other feminist theologians is their strong doctrine of Scripture.

Therefore, throughout the remainder of this study we will distinguish between the understanding of the Bible held by biblical feminists and that of other feminist theologians. Those feminist theologians who do not fall into this category, forming as they do the majority of feminist theologians and usually being members either of the "mainline" Protestant denominations or of the Roman Catholic Church, will be referred to as "mainline feminist theologians." While biblical feminists do not use this term to speak of those feminist theologians with whom they differ, they do, indeed, distinguish themselves from mainline feminist theologians. Elaine Storkey, one of the most prominent British biblical feminists, defines biblical feminists over and against what we are calling here mainline feminist theologians:

> [They] do not take their cue from the autonomy of the Enlightenment but from a Christian view of people under God, a view which recognizes the reality of sin and the need of salvation. But it is not an individualist belief, for salvation does not simply affect "personal" or "moral" life, but needs to be worked out in fear and trembling in all areas, including that of sex and gender.[51]

Because it tends to reject a hermeneutics of suspicion in favor of a hermeneutics of trust, biblical feminism tends to be overlooked in the debates of mainline feminist theologians. That is, while the distinction between secular feminism and Christian feminism is at the forefront of the discussion among biblical feminists, among mainline feminists this is not the case. This may be because biblical feminists tend to assume a greater disjuncture between culture and the gospel than do mainline feminist theologians. However, it may more simply be a matter of strategy on the part of mainline feminist theologians: if they do not focus on the distinction and disjuncture between secular feminism and Christian feminism, they can make greater use of secular feminist theory in mainline feminist theology. Whatever the reason, this distinction itself points to the biblical feminist commitment to a traditional hermeneutic, which, according to Frei, is reversed in modern theology.

> Secular feminism centers around gaining equal rights; biblical feminism centers around equal opportunity to serve. The secular feminist says: "I want my rights. I want to be able to compete on an equal basis with men." The biblical feminist says: "I want to be free to be the person God created me to be and to have the privilege of following Christ as He calls me to do." Feminism (or any other "ism") without Christ is just another power struggle. But adding the word biblical to feminism indicates that these feminists want to explore their conviction about equality of women in a biblical way and implement their findings according to biblical guidelines. Therefore, within scriptural parameters, not an "anything goes" approach, biblical feminists will seek to promote a climate in which women are free to act as equal human beings and where Christian women can enter into their full inheritance as equal children of God.[52]

In contrast, most mainline feminist theologians understand the biblical text to be, apart from feminist reinterpretation, a vehicle for the furtherance of patriarchy rather than primarily an inspired witness to the grace of God in Jesus. Of course, these women are Christians as well and so would understand the Bible at some level to serve as witness to divine reality, but primarily the concern is for the extent to which the Bible functions as an instrument of patriarchy. For these feminist theologians, it is only through feminist analysis of the biblical stories and their uses throughout the tradition that the Bible can become one of the means of the overthrow of patriarchy. Without feminist theology, the Bible is understood to be dangerous to women's health. Elisabeth Schüssler Fiorenza exemplifies this understanding of the Bible, for she assumes that the biblical texts are, in the entirety of their scope, story, and interpretation, affected and "infected" by patriarchy and, indeed, that they function to serve the goals and interests of patriarchy.[53] For women not to be harmed or wounded by these texts, the scriptures must therefore be read with a particularly feminist suspicion. This is appropriate because feminist theory and analysis requires the step outside patriarchal thought:

> To step outside of patriarchal thought means: Being skeptical toward every known system of thought; being critical of all assumptions, ordering values and definitions. Testing one's statement by trusting our own, the female experience. Since such experience has usually been trivialized or ignored, it means overcoming the deep-seated resistance within our-selves toward accepting ourselves and our knowledge as valid. It means getting rid of the great men in our heads and substituting for them ourselves, our sisters, our anony-mous foremothers.[54]

Here we see the fundamental gulf dividing biblical feminism and mainline feminism: biblical feminists, because they understand the Bible to be an inspired witness to the grace and life offered by God in Jesus Christ, will not approach Scripture with the degree of skepticism which mainline feminists demand.

Another view of the Bible within mainline feminist theology understands the Bible to be the vehicle of patriarchy and racism. This also requires that the Bible be read through the lens of suspicion. The hermeneutic needed here has thus been termed the "her-meneutics of survival" by Dolores Williams, the well-known womanist theologian.[55] "Survival" is the goal of reconstructive interpretation of the Bible under this view, which underscores the necessity for approaching Scripture with suspicion if (black) women are to survive its slings and arrows. Womanist readings are shaped by the consciousness and struggles of race and class which are particular to African American women. In addition to the obvious differences inherent in racial and class distinctions between womanists and mainline feminist theologians is the distinct struggle in which womanists engage against feminist theorists who have themselves overlooked these very distinctions.[56] Just as mainline feminists critique patriarchal interpretations which posit the normativity of the male subject, womanists observe that feminist discourse about what makes up "woman" is similarly tainted with universalizing, ethnocentric assumptions which fail to include the realities of African American women.

> Feminist and womanist theory assert that the unmarked category "man" is an abstraction masking the contingent and power-steeped positionality of all historical agents. Both call for a suspicion of methods that claim universalism and objectivity as part of their own production, of which the historical-critical paradigm within biblical studies certainly counts as one.[57]

Mainline and womanist theologians share, therefore, a profound reliance on the hermeneutic of suspicion. However, this formal similarity does not entail a uniformity of practice. Viewing the Bible as vehicle of patriarchy and racism can, in fact, embrace three types of practice in biblical interpretation. The first is a genre of Sachkritik insofar as it involves the use of a theme within the biblical material to serve as the criterion for discerning which biblical stories are acceptable to the larger thematic vision, which in this case is, of course, a feminist vision. This first practice is the "prophetic-liberating" approach represented by, among others, Rosemary Radford Ruether in her Sexism and God-Talk.[58] The second is historical reconstruction of women's function and roles in early Christian communities. This, in conjunction with the hermeneutics of suspicion, allows a winnowing and reconfiguring of the historical data presented by biblical texts, either implicitly or explicitly. This second practice is represented by Elisabeth Schüssler Fiorenza in her now-classic work, *In Memory of Her: A Feminist Theological Reconstruction of Christian Origins*, who has been joined in recent years by many others such as Antoinette Clark Wire and Karen Jo Torjesen.[59] The third practice involves a rereading of biblical stories in which women figure as key characters. This practice is somewhat like that of biblical feminism except that the hermeneutic of suspicion is engaged, and either "midrashic" rewritings of the biblical stories or warrants for rejecting the authority of the stories are offered. This practice is represented by the broadest range of feminist scholarship, such as Phyllis Trible's *Texts of Terror* and Elisabeth Schüssler-Fiorenza's later work, *But She Said: Feminist Practices of Biblical Interpretation*.[60]

While most of mainline feminist theological use of the Bible tends either implicitly or explicitly to view the Bible as a vehicle of patriarchy, racism, or both, there is yet another type of feminist reader of the Bible who does not understand the Bible in strictly theological terms at all, not even in the Feuerbachian projectionist view, which fuels the understanding of the Bible as vehicle of patriarchy and/or racism. These feminists of the third group therefore are not concerned to reconstruct the picture of God presented in the biblical narratives, nor do they have much interest in any redemptive or salvific themes in the biblical text or in its interpretation.[61] Instead, the Bible is viewed as *cultural artifact and influence*, and the methods used to interpret the texts tend to reflect the constraints imposed by academic disciplines such as critical theory rather than more strictly theological discourse. An example of this is found in the work of Mieke Bal, who openly states her purposes:

> I do not claim the Bible to be either a feminist resource or a sexist manifesto. That kind of assumption can be an issue only for those who attribute moral, religious, or political authority to these texts, which is precisely the opposite of what I am interested in. It is the cultural function of one of the most influential mythical and literary documents of our culture that I discuss, as a strong representative instance of what language and literature can do to a culture, specifically to its articulation of gender.[62]

This view of the Bible is thus on the border between mainline feminist theology and more secular or nonreligious feminist critical theory. Insofar as mainline feminist theologians are influenced and fed by such work, this approach is important, for it serves as a tributary to more specifically religious feminist readings of the Bible. However, since it is not directly concerned with religious use of texts, it is distinct from mainline feminist theology.

Biblical Authority in Mainline Feminist Theology

Mainline feminist theology tends to understand the nature of biblical authority in a very different way from the understanding adopted by biblical feminists and narrative reading. This is not to say that the Bible holds no authority for mainline feminist theologians, for it certainly does. However, it is a reconstructed notion of authority from that generally held by the narrative hermeneutic. This is not an insignificant addendum but is intentionally incorporated into feminist biblical criticism with profound results. The view that the very notion of biblical authority can strengthen the use of the Bible against women requires for feminist biblical critics a reversal of traditional modes of interpretation: "The authority of the text and canon of the Bible in itself must be thoroughly demystified and deconstructed so that they cannot be used against marginalized women."[63]

Thus, the reversal of the direction of interpretation signaled by Frei as the hallmark of modern biblical interpretation has its own distinct form in feminist interpretation of the Bible. Whereas traditionally the biblical narrative served as the lens through which one interpreted the world, for feminist theological reading of the Bible, the interpretive lens is feminist consciousness itself and, more specifically, women's experience of oppression under the conditions of patriarchy.

> Included in feminist consciousness are some fundamental convictions so basic and so important that contradictory assertions cannot be accepted by feminists without violence being done to their very understandings and valuations. These convictions serve as a kind of negative test for any revelation in knowledge. They can serve, too, as a positive key to the fullness of revelation regarding the reality and destiny of human persons. These convictions must, then, function in a feminist interpretation of scripture—discerning the meaning of the biblical witness as a whole and in its parts and thus (though not only thus) whether it is to be believed.[64]

This means that, negatively, feminist consciousness becomes the test to help the reader of Scripture to determine which texts may not be "revelatory" and positively, it functions to establish or discern that which is "revelatory" ("the fullness of revelation"), apparently both in the Bible and in extrabiblical reality.[65] This is quite similar to the oft-quoted "fundamental principle of judgment" of Rosemary Radford Ruether:

> This critical principle of feminist theology is the affirmation of and promotion of the full humanity of women. Whatever denies, diminishes, or distorts the full humanity of women is, therefore, to be appraised as not redemptive. . . . What does promote the full humanity of women is of the Holy, does reflect true relation to the divine, is the true nature of things, is the authentic message of redemption and the mission of redemptive community.[66]

Certainly, the "full humanity of women" seems to be a worthy principle, a noble goal to attain. Notice, however, that this view sets up a hierarchy of authorities for feminist interpretation of the Bible which allows feminist consciousness pride of place. Ironically, feminist theologians claim to subvert this kind of setting up and maintaining of hierarchies because it is considered anathema. Such hierarchical thinking is understood to be one of the hallmarks of patriarchal thought structures. Now, however, the "full humanity of women" or some analogue to it tops the pyramid instead of a patriarchal equivalent:

> The paradigm that no longer makes sense to feminists is that of authority as domination. . . . Consciously or unconsciously, reality is seen in the form of a hierarchy, or pyramid. . . . In this framework, theological "truth" is sought through ordering the hierarchy of doctrines, orders, and degrees. The difficulty for women and Third World groups is that their perspectives often do not fit in the pyramid structure of such a system of interpre-

tation. . . . The emerging feminist paradigm trying to make sense of biblical and theological truth claims is that of *authority as partnership*. In this view, reality is interpreted in the form of a circle of interdependence. Ordering is explored through inclusion of diversity in a rainbow spectrum that does not require that persons submit to the "top" but, rather, that they participate in the common task of creating an interdependent community of humanity and nature.[67]

In effect, holding as ultimate authority the "full humanity of women" sets up just the sort of hierarchies of truth or doctrine which feminist theologians generally reject. This then places a wedge between explicit theory and implicit practice: in theory, hierarchies are denied, but in practice, setting up feminist consciousness as the hermeneutical guide exchanges one set of hierarchies for another.

To use William Christian's language, we might therefore identify as one of the governing doctrines for feminist theologians this "full humanity of women." This becomes apparent when we turn to examine the rhetorical use of the concept of "experience" in mainline feminist theologies. It is the authority of "experience" in feminist interpretation which subordinates any other authority, whether text, tradition, or reason. This reliance on the category of experience in mainline feminist theology points to the legacy of Schleiermacher, the "father" of modern theology, but the specification of the crucial experience as *women's* experience adds a new twist on an old theme:

> Women's experience and women's praxis are the bases upon which feminist theology endeavors to reconstruct and create new religious forms. The interaction between these categories forms the theoretical basis for feminist theology, resulting in innovation and creativity. Feminist theology has, therefore, been situated in an entirely new context. Women's experience and praxis are the primary resources . . . [and] to include them as starting points and as norms of evaluation is indeed subversive. In according such categories primacy, feminist theologians have effected a methodological revolution.[68]

"Women's experience," which is claimed as ultimate court of appeal in mainline feminist theology, is not, however, defined simply as the experience of women wherever and whenever, as though the mere fact of having been born with a female body gives one special hermeneutical powers. The claim is more sophisticated than this. The "experience" that counts as the basis upon which feminist theology reconstructs religious forms is women's experience of and stance toward *oppression*: "By women's experience as a key to hermeneutics or theory of interpretation, we mean precisely that experience which arises when women become critically aware of these falsifying and alienating experiences imposed upon them as women by a male-dominated culture."[69] The very fact and existence of the womanist critique, however, should be enough to point to the instability of the appeal to experience as norm in interpretation. "Experience," even when it is the "experience" of the feminist consciousness, will never be a monolithic phenomenon. Not only does the feminist appeal to the authority of experience meet with critique within the ranks of feminism itself but also it risks setting itself up as yet another rigid dogmatic theory which feminist theologians had been trying to avoid:

> I suggest that it also makes sense to consider [the myth of women's experience] as a concealed dogma, whose function could be described as the feminist answer to infalli-

bility. By this I mean it has a built-in "not open to challenge" quality about it. This is because as *women's* experience the implication is that it cannot be subject to criticism from men. And because it is women's *individual* experience, the implication is that it is unique and therefore cannot be subject to the criteria of public discourse. Thus, cleverly, it achieves as quasi-dogma status while fiercely denying connection with dogma of any sort. It represents women's claim to authoritative utterance.[70]

In addition, insofar as it can implicitly rely on a denial of human finitude, it indicates another contradictory moment within feminist theology, which in theory had sought to affirm the fragility of human embodiedness.[71] Of course, this is not always the case, but where it is, the notion of women's experience in effect accomplishes exactly that which it sought to overturn. The appeal to experience within feminist theology seems less of an opportunity for women to claim their own voice and rather a foundationalist warrant or grounding for the theological position being recommended.[72]

Since the easiest way to describe feminist theological views of biblical authority is to offer some concrete examples, we will turn first to an example of second-order feminist hermeneutical theory and then to an example of first-order feminist interpretation. The example of feminist hermeneutical theory we will consider is the recent constructive work of Emily Cheney.[73] Here we will see how the governing doctrine of the full humanity of women comes to play out in the reconstruction of biblical interpretive practices.

In an attempt to offer mainline feminist theological readers of the Bible alternative strategies of reading "male-oriented" texts, Cheney proposes three fresh possibilities: gender reversal, the use of analogy, and viewing women as exchange objects.[74] Cheney takes up the Gospel of Matthew (because it has "generally been viewed as unfavorable toward women") to illustrate how her alternative strategies operate.[75] The strategies are designed to help women "examine a text and decide with which texts they want to identify, which ones they want to challenge, and which ones the want to dismiss . . . so that women will affirm themselves and other women as they read. Women must not hurt themselves by identifying against themselves."[76] In gender reversal, by an exercise of the imagination in which the biblical stories are reread with the reversal of gender of the characters, female readers can "recognize more sharply that biblical texts were directed to men":

> The strategy can help female readers assess to what degree biblical writers utilized the conventional gender role behavior of their time to portray the experiences of the protagonists and persuade the audience to share their perspectives. Female readers can decide in what ways their identification with the protagonists, both male and female protagonists, would entail the acceptance of a role that includes self-denigration.[77]

This, as Cheney shows, calls for historical reconstruction itself, and she thus looks to texts from the Bible and the ancient world which can indicate what might have been the constraints on women, for example, if they, too, had been commissioned as disciples in Matthew 10 and 28.

The second strategy, which Cheney calls analogy, is similar to allegorical reading in some respects, insofar as it involves drawing an analogy between the biblical text and contemporary situations: "For example, the struggle to write a poem about a woman who had conceived during a rape is compared to Jacob's wrestling with the angel in Gen. 32. A long and difficult childbirth is compared to Jesus' ordeals in Gethsemane."[78] While the first strategy involved an imaginative leap, allowing the reader to identify with the protagonist, this second strategy involves an opposite imaginative leap. Now the reader requires that the protagonist or the narrative as a whole be made to identify with or conform to her contemporary experience.

The third strategy Cheney suggests draws on Lévi-Strauss's sociological theory of women as exchange objects. This involves a focus on the interaction between male and female characters and on how the female character functions to bond the author and the male reader, to the exclusion of the female reader. The female reader therefore experiences the text differently from the way the male reader would. Attention is focused on the role played by the female characters, and the female reader's identification is with them as opposed to the male characters. This strategy offers yet another version of allegorical interpretation in which the reader deconstructs the narrative identity representation of the characters in the story, in which the text is read "in a direction other than what the text invites its audience to do."[79]

Because feminist theology is still very much in its youth, it is hard to find an example of interpretation which can illustrate Cheney's hermeneutical theory in great detail. However, the following example of feminist interpretation is representative in many ways of the attitudes and goals underlying Cheney's approaches. It also represents those practices held in common by mainline feminist theologians, both Protestant and Roman Catholic, and therefore will prove useful as an illustration of what mainline feminist theologians do with the Bible.

Susan Ackerman's " 'And the Women Knead Dough': The Worship of the Queen of Heaven in Sixth-Century Judah," in *Gender and Difference in Ancient Israel*, is representative of much of mainline feminist reading of an Old Testament text. Ackerman examines passages from Jeremiah in which there are traces of women's cult activity that appear to be subjugated by the editorial hand. Ackerman then attempts to reread these traces. To do so, she posits a distinction between the biblical record and the religion of the masses, so to speak. The biblical texts, according to the historical critic, come from the hands of priests and prophets. Ackerman therefore assumes that they present the priestly and prophetic religion as normative and "orthodox," while any religious activity outside the bounds of priestly and prophetic circles are viewed as heterodox and rejected as deviant.

Ackerman, however, wants to suggest another way of reconstructing the religion of ancient Israel, such that (in spite of the biblical record) neither the priestly nor prophetic cult was normative in the religion of the first millennium BCE. Rather, she claims, "a diversity of beliefs and practices thrived and were accepted by the ancients as legitimate forms of religious expression."[80] To uncover this diversity of forms of religious expression, Ackerman suggests that we need to supplement the biblical picture of Israelite religion with other sources, such as iconographic and epigraphic archaeological evidence from the ancient Near East. This, of course, follows the practice of "historical criticism," and thus she has suggested nothing new that could cause the scholarly guild difficulty. However, she says, since archaeological comparative data are often sparse, we must add another tool to our collection: reading the Bible itself "differently," investigating without prejudice that which is presented in the biblical text as heterodox, such as those cultic practices which the biblical writers condemn either implicitly or explicitly. Ackerman promises that this second venue will allow us to uncover the overlooked aspects of Israelite religion: women's religion.

She examines the two passages in Jeremiah in which the women are depicted as having devoted themselves to the worship of the Queen of Heaven, Jeremiah 7:16–20 and 44:15–19, 25.

> As for you, do not pray for this people, do not raise a cry or prayer on their behalf, and do not intercede with me, for I will not hear you. Do you not see what they are doing in the towns of Judah and in the streets of Jerusalem? The children gather wood, the fathers kindle fire, and the women knead dough, to make cakes for the queen of heaven; and they pour out drink offerings to other gods, to provoke me to anger. Is it I whom they provoke? says the LORD. Is it not themselves, to their own hurt? Therefore thus says the Lord GOD: My anger and my wrath shall be poured out on this place, on human beings and animals, on the trees of the field and the fruit of the ground; it will burn and not be quenched.

> Then all the men who were aware that their wives had been making offerings to other gods, and all the women who stood by, a great assembly, all the people who lived in Pathros in the land of Egypt, answered Jeremiah: "As for the word that you have spoken to us in the name of the LORD, we are not going to listen to you. Instead, we will do everything that we have vowed, make offerings to the queen of heaven and pour out libations to her, just as we and our ancestors, our kings and our officials, used to do in the towns of Judah and in the streets of Jerusalem. We used to have plenty of food, and prospered, and saw no misfortune. But from the time we stopped making offerings to the queen of heaven and pouring out libations to her, we have lacked everything and have perished by the sword and by famine." And the women said, "Indeed we will go on making offerings to the queen of heaven and pouring out libations to her; do you think that we made cakes for her, marked with her image, and poured out libations to her without our husbands' being involved?"
>
> Then Jeremiah said to all the people, men and women, all the people who were giving him this answer: "As for the offerings that you made in the towns of Judah and in the streets of Jerusalem, you and your ancestors, your kings and your officials, and the people of the land, did not the LORD remember them? Did it not come into his mind? The LORD could no longer bear the sight of your evil doings, the abominations that you committed; therefore your land became a desolation and a waste and a curse, without inhabitant, as it is to this day. It is because you burned offerings, and because you sinned against the LORD and did not obey the voice of the LORD or walk in his law and in his statutes and in his decrees, that this disaster has befallen you, as is still evident today."
>
> Jeremiah said to all the people and all the women, "Hear the word of the LORD, all you Judeans who are in the land of Egypt, Thus says the LORD of hosts, the God of Israel: You and your wives have accomplished in deeds what you declared in words, saying, 'We are determined to perform the vows that we have made, to make offerings to the queen of heaven and to pour out libations to her.' By all means, keep your vows and make your libations! Therefore hear the word of the LORD, all you Judeans who live in the land of Egypt: Lo, I swear by my great name, says the LORD, that my name shall no longer be pronounced on the lips of any of the people of Judah in all the land of Egypt, saying, 'As the Lord GOD lives.' I am going to watch over them for harm and not for good; all the people of Judah who are in the land of Egypt shall perish by the sword and by famine, until not one is left. And those who escape the sword shall return from the land of Egypt to the land of Judah, few in number; and all the remnant of Judah,

who have come to the land of Egypt to settle, shall know whose words will stand, mine or theirs! This shall be the sign to you, says the LORD, that I am going to punish you in this place, in order that you may know that my words against you will surely be carried out: Thus says the LORD, I am going to give Pharaoh Hophra, king of Egypt, into the hands of his enemies, those who seek his life, just as I gave King Zedekiah of Judah into the hand of King Nebuchadrezzar of Babylon, his enemy who sought his life."[81]

Here the women are said to bake cakes in the image of the Queen of Heaven as offerings and to burn incense and pour out libations in her honor. Ackerman understands the mere presence of these details in the narrative, which itself condemns such practices, to be evidence of the women's intensity of devotion despite the high degree of risk. Seeking to identify the Queen of Heaven, Ackerman suggests that she is "a syncretistic deity whose character incorporates aspects of west Semitic Astarte and east Semitic Ishtar."[82]

Ackerman notes that, while the cult of Ishtar and Astarte attracted women in particular, the text indicates that the entire people are won over to her devotion. Ackerman points out that the women are depicted as the chief agents in the cultic activity surrounding the Queen of Heaven but that the texts also indicate that the women enlist the aid of the men and children: "The children gather wood, the fathers kindle fire, and the women knead dough, to make cakes for the queen of heaven" (7:18.) Ackerman points also to 44:17 and, 21 to strengthen her argument that this cultic activity involved not a marginal or fringe group, but that it was well integrated among all the people. Thus, instead of crediting Hebrew narrative style with the wording here, she suggests that the phrase "kings and princes of Judah" is to be taken as indicating that "the Queen of Heaven was a part of the religion of the monarchy, [and] the Queen's cult may also have been at home in what was essentially the monarch's private chapel, the temple."[83] Thus, implies Ackerman, the Queen of Heaven was indeed a viable option for worshipers of Yahweh in the temple cult.

After excavating this obscured tradition of what she calls women's religion, Ackerman then incorporates an aggregate version of the theses of Bauer and Marx for her concluding remarks:

> Since it is winners who write history, the importance of this women's cult in the history of the religion of Israel has been obscured by our sources. The ultimate "winners" in the religion of early sixth-century Judah, the Deuteronomistic historians, the priest-prophet Ezekiel, and the prophet Jeremiah, were men. The biblical texts these men wrote malign non-Deuteronomistic, non-priestly, and non-prophetic religion, and in the case of the cult of the Queen of Heaven they malign the religion of women. But fortunately for us, the sources have not completely ignored some women's cults. The losers have not been totally lost. If historians of Israelite religion continue to push beyond biblical polemic, we should hear more and more the voices of the women of Israel witnessing to their religious convictions.[84]

Aspects typical to feminist biblical interpretation illustrated in Ackerman's article are the use of commonly accepted historical-critical tools, a sharpened hermeneutic of suspicion, the conviction that the use of such will "redeem" an otherwise oppressive text, an essentializing of women's activity and identity (such that the activity of some renders an identifiable "women's religion"), and a reading of the text which disregards the narrative context of the passage at hand. Of course, this is both well intentioned and intentional. If we were to respect the narrative context in which the passage is embedded, we would risk having the patriarchal wool pulled over our eyes, so to speak, as to the integrity of this women's goddess cult, for the redactors who covered her tracks were presumably all male. This line of argument is water-tight: there is no disputing the thesis, because once we attempt to do so, we betray our own "false consciousness," which prohibits us from seeing the veiled monster of patriarchy, understood to be stifling the religious experience of women.

These examples of feminist hermeneutics and interpretation emphasize the different understandings of Scripture's authority among mainline feminist theologians over against those among biblical feminists and narrative biblical interpretation. The Bible is held at arm's length because it is potentially dangerous, and when it is brought close, it is reconstructed to illumine women's experience. The Bible is authoritative but carries no ultimate or overriding authority: "Female readers resist the text or give partial consent to the authority of the biblical text because total acceptance of the values in the text and identification with the protagonists would perpetuate oppressive situations in their communities."[85] However, for most of the tradition, at least in the West, of the history of biblical interpretation up to the Enlightenment, the functions of biblical interpretation were usually held to be the upbuilding of faith in and love of God and love of neighbor. Representative of this traditional hermeneutic is the exegetical program set forth in Augustine's *De Doctrina christiana*. A brief detour into this text can provide an illustration of the kind of narrative reading against which much of mainline feminist theology works.

In Augustine's pre-Christian stage, he had rejected Christianity partly because of what he deemed to be the obscurity of Scripture, particularly the Old Testament. Augustine found the Bible distasteful because of the immoral acts of the people of Israel and because he felt that the Bible was literature of an inferior class when compared with the classics which had formed the foundation of his own education. The experience of listening to Ambrose's allegorical sermons on the Old Testament, however, allowed Augustine to make the breakthrough beyond his Manichean rejection of the Bible, and it is in this sense that allegory is the key which opens the scriptures to Augustine.[86] The Pauline statement that God chooses the simple to confound the wise (1 Corinthians 1:27) becomes for him programmatic for his understanding of the Old Testament, and he comes to believe that what he had previously considered obscurity and barbarity in the Bible is more profound than even the wisdom of the classical authors whom he had previously held in such high esteem.

Begun in 396 and completed in 427, *De Doctrina Christiana* represents Augustine's mature view on the interpretation of Scripture.[87] This treatise is extremely influential on subsequent biblical interpretation throughout the centuries at least up until the Enlightenment. Because Augustine understands the biblical text to be inspired and therefore divinely arranged and ordered, he expects it to bear a thematically unified story or message from the Divine to humanity. Thus, the text is to be read with respect to the hermeneutical guidance of the rule of faith, which sets the parameters for the outer limits to this "message."[88] To this, Augustine adds the rule of charity, for he understands the goal of this divine message to be the upbuilding in love of God and neighbor. The rules of faith and charity thus function as "controls" on interpretation, excluding as improper those interpretations which either contradict the inseparability of the doctrines of creation and redemption (the rule of faith) or which do not inculcate love of God and neighbor in the reader (the rule of charity). Notice here the functional similarity between the rules of faith and charity and the rule of the "full humanity of women." Both serve as outer limits of interpretation. Most often the rules of faith and charity do not prescribe a "correct" interpretation but rather serve to draw a circle around an array of allowable interpretations from which the interpreter may choose. Here we are reminded of William Christian's description of governing doctrines' ability to indicate but not to determine what counts for authentic doctrine. In fact, Augustine states that any interpretation which does not lead to the building up of faith and love of God and of neighbor is simply a misunderstanding or underinterpretation of the text: the interpreter "does not yet understand as he ought."[89] For Augustine, there should be no anxiety on the part of the exegete or doubts of one's abilities in interpreting the text if one "is bent on making all understanding of scripture to bear upon these three graces,"[90] for that is the sole purpose of interpretation, and one need not feel constrained to find a single meaning in the text.

Indeed, the variety of interpretations a single text may have (provided these criteria of faith and love are met) emphasizes Augustine's understanding of the Bible's richness and its divinely inspired quality instead of detracting from it.[91] Interpretations which might be seen as "mistakes" or "eisogesis" by a modern critic (e.g., reading the story of the Good Samaritan as an allegory of the Christian life) are allowable in Augustine's plan insofar as the goals of building love of God and neighbor are met. The obscurities and difficulties in Scripture are part of the divine plan and serve to spur the reader on to greater understanding.[92] The "plainer passages satisfy our hunger, the more obscure ones stimulate our appetite," according to Augustine.[93] Therefore, the very act of reading the Bible, with the proper goal set ahead of one, can be part of the redemptive process. In approaching Scripture, therefore, one must adopt an attitude of teachableness and receptivity to the divine nurture of faith, hope, and love. Exegesis is, to be sure, an exercise of the mind, but it also edifies the soul; in Augustinian terms, it is a matter of both loving and knowing.

Whereas for Augustine the function of biblical interpretation is the building up of the reader(s) in faith and love, for mainline feminist readers of the Bible, the intended function of biblical interpretation is, first, protecting women and, second, seeking their betterment. This necessitates a different understanding of the authority of Scripture from that which was operative among the wider tradition. Indeed, this is considered a positive aspect: Cheney openly acknowledges that these strategies "could be viewed as ones that uproot women from tradition and orthodoxy."[94] This is not to be considered a fault among mainline feminist theologians, for discontinuity with the tradition, which itself is understood to be tainted with patriarchy, is indeed valued and sought. This is true not only in Christian mainline feminist theology but also among Jewish feminist theologians.[95]

This willingness to leave behind a traditional understanding of the authority of Scripture dovetails with a general theory of religious language held by most feminist theologians which is required for the feminist theological project. This understanding operates under the assumption that religious language, the larger umbrella category under which the specific case of biblical language is subsumed, is a result of the human search for the divine. The claim to "revelation," that God seeks to be known by humanity, is viewed as an outdated tool used to shore up the power base of the theological or religious elite.

> Everything we say about God represents our human efforts to create, recapture, and evoke experiences of God sustained within linguistic and cultural frameworks that already color our experience and interpretation. All our images have an "as if" or "as it were" in front of them that reminds us they are to be taken neither literally nor as final, but as part of an ongoing quest for language that can provide a framework for meaningful living and give expression to our experience. . . . [Religious symbols] emerge out of the Godwrestling of our ancestors and represent their efforts to name and comprehend the God they knew as with them on a long and various journey. These traditional symbols are privileged insofar as they are a formative part of [our tradition]. . . . They are not privileged, however, in giving us access to the "true" reality of God or a knowledge of God of which we ourselves are incapable. They are arrived at through the same methods of listening, struggling, and constructing meaning in historical context that we go through in trying to make sense of our religious experiences.[96]

This clearly assumes Feuerbach's projectionist model of religious language and concepts, which, in turn, allows for and even necessitates a hermeneutics of suspicion, provided we also hold some version of the doctrine of sin. That is, if there is the influence of sin in the projector, there will be influence of sin in the projected, and this would require a hermeneutics of suspicion. We also see here once again the importance of the "ethical" in the feminist project. The mainline feminist theologians who operate with this understanding of religious language claim that, while traditional symbols may be privileged insofar as they are a part of our religious heritage, whenever they contradict what we understand to be ethical, we are not bound by them either normatively or authoritatively. The question, of course, is what exactly we consider ethical and how we come to that decision. "Once images become socially, politically or morally inadequate, however, they are also religiously inadequate. Instead of pointing to and evoking the reality of God, they block the possibility of religious experience."[97] It is therefore the moral or ethical implications and effects of biblical interpretation which govern mainline feminist theological hermeneutics. Here we note the inheritance from Kant as well as from Feuerbach.[98] We arrive at a judgment about what is "ethical" apart from a holistic understanding of the biblical narrative. This is usually done through the acceptance of what Christian calls alien claims, and what we might less pejoratively call extra-narratival claims, as true and fitting expressions of Christian doctrine. The extra-narratival claims often implicitly appealed to in mainline feminist theologies seem to be those linked with notions of democracy, the protection of individual rights, and utilitarianism. The claim is implicitly made that such presuppositions for how Scripture is to be read are superior to traditional presuppositions insofar as they allow for a range of interpretations which are possible and do not attempt to find the one proper interpretation of any specific biblical text which is true. However, as we saw with Augustine, traditional hermeneutics rarely holds one single interpretation to be the only "true" one.

First of all, we are interested in decentering, by example, the notion of a singular interpretation by presenting several simultaneously compelling readings of the same text. That one can identify several viable womanist and feminist readings of the same text is not symptomatic of a problem requiring a solution (i.e., women can't make up their minds), but rather enacts what this entire volume seeks to explore and enable: a foundational shift in biblical criticism *away* from a hermeneutical project whose goal it is to find the correct key to unlock the unitary truth of the text and *toward* projects focused on multiplicities of meanings, interpretations examining layers of ideology and shifting meanings—in short, toward cultural critique.[99]

This claim to hermeneutical superiority is itself part of the ethical appeal of feminist theology. The feminist claim to reject rigid theoretical positions in favor of dynamic, flexible categories and practices is touted as morally or ethically superior to any traditional hermeneutics. That is, it is not merely the potentially damaging content of patriarchal constructs and theories which is objectionable to mainline feminist theologians but rather the very structure of them which is dangerous. Mutuality is thus to be sought over against hierarchy, and flexibility over against rigidity.

Feminist theological readings of the Bible claim to offer a variety of interpretations over against the supposed unity enforced by patriarchal interpretations.[100] Alicia Ostriker, for example, calls for a "hermeneutics of indeterminacy," which exults in the multivalent quality of the text over against any claims to its unitary voice.[101] However, the claim that traditional reading of the Bible leads to a "single interpretation" or the development of rigid theoretical positions is simply an unsubstantiated caricature of most of the history of Christian biblical interpretation, as we illustrated in our brief summary of Augustine. In fact, the tradition of biblical interpretation up to the Enlightenment was highly flexible and allowed for a broad range of possible interpretations to any specific text.[102] The objection seems to be to Enlightenment-based understandings of how to read the Bible.

This, then, poses a question regarding the interpretation of the Bible by mainline feminist theologians: have they truly overcome the patterns which they intend, and indeed have claimed, to subvert, or have they come to mirror what they most want to avoid? A possible way to address this question will be, again, to consider some actual examples of such patterns deemed destructive which feminist biblical interpretation seeks to overcome. One such example we have already considered: the use of a hierarchy of truths or values. Another such aspect which has become the topic of much discussion within the ranks of feminist theology is anti-Judaism. Feminist theology explicitly rejects in theory any tendency to anti-Judaism but implicitly often embraces it in practice despite the best of intentions.

For example, we can turn again to Susan Ackerman's interpretation of the Queen of Heaven passages in Jeremiah, which we considered previously. A Christian who adopted such a reading of this Old Testament text would be put into the position of engaging in anti-Jewish revisionism. Instead of allowing the sacred text of a religious community its own integrity, Ackerman's reading undermines the story's own self-presentation, such that Jeremiah's prophetic condemnation of the cultic activity is no longer understood to be a word from Yahweh but rather from the male hierarchy of religious power. No longer is the text allowed to speak of the One God of Israel who demands faithfulness to the covenant (as religious Jews and Christians have tradition-ally read the text); it speaks instead of the male struggle to silence the female. This disrespect of the sacred text is also, in turn, a disrespect of the religious community which passed it on through the generations.

Indeed, anti-Jewish strains within feminist theology have been explored at some length, with the result that some scholars claim that Christian feminist theology has tended to support implicitly an attitude of "anti-Judaism."[103] How can this be? In theory, after all, feminist theologians reject out of hand any attitude of intolerance toward the "other." How then can intolerance of the Jewish "other" be held and taught by feminist theologians, even if only implicitly? We could easily argue that this has relatively little to do with feminist theology itself and is simply part of the baggage of modern theology. This is not to say categorically that premodern theology was not anti-Jewish, because certainly there are times and places where it was. However, the attitude and stance toward the Old Testament is one of the loci of the shifts in modern interpretation. When the Old Testament is relegated to a "thing of the past," a new and virulent form of anti-Judaism is admitted as though through the back door.

The now-classic definition of anti-Judaism which is operative in the most recent exploration of religious feminist anti-Judaism is as follows: "If the three pillars on which Judaism stands are God, Torah, and Israel, then a fundamental attack on any of the three would be anti-Jewish."[104] According to Judith Plaskow, one of the first to point out the anti-Jewish sentiments inherent in some Christian feminist theologies, there are three areas in which this anti-Judaism tends to display itself:[105] "the contrast between the supposedly wrathful God of the "Old Testament" and the New Testament God of love, blaming Jews for the death of the Goddess, and the "Jesus was a feminist" theme."[106] She points out that the impulse to rid Christianity of patriarchy often lays blame for the patriarchal elements of Christianity on its Jewish roots.[107] While she points out that feminist theology by no means holds the monopoly on Christian anti-Judaism, this is an element in feminist theology from Elizabeth Cady Stanton in the nineteenth century through to the present. She points out that Judaism is presented either implicitly or explicitly in Christian feminist theologies as the antithesis which Christianity redeems or overcomes; for example, "Jesus-was-a-feminist" who liberated women from the patriarchal shackles of Judaism. Again, Judaism can be seen as a scapegoat, insofar as this patriarchal religion is claimed to have "killed the Goddess" who was worshiped before the arrival of Hebrew worship. Likewise, Judaism can be presented as mere prologue to Christianity, which can turn the Old Testament into a relic of the past.[108]

However, all of these three stances toward Judaism represent non-narrative readings of Christian Scripture. That is, if we read narratively, it is arguably impossible to read the Old Covenant as mere antithesis or prologue to Christianity which can, after the arrival of Christianity, be cast aside. Neither can narrative readers consistently claim that Jews are "Jesus-killers" (the feminist twist on this is that Jews are "Goddess-killers"). This is not to say that narrative readers are automatically free from anti-Judaism, or to deny the anti-Judaism of prominent Christian theologians such as Martin Luther and others, but simply to say that narrative reading logically (if not practically in all cases) applies a constant pressure against anti-Judaism. Narrative read-ers know that, while it is clear from the Gospels that the Jews demanded Jesus' death, his executioners were Romans, and his death is seen theologically as necessary and willingly taken on; reading narratively would put the lie to blaming Jews for Jesus' death. We cannot be consistent narrative readers and determine that the Old Testament no longer bears any of the divine voice and will for Christians, for one of the marks of narrative reading is the yoking of the two testaments in dialectical relation.

However, it is often the case in modern readings, even among sophisticated scholars, that the Old Testament is understood such that it does not bear the divine voice for Christians, or that the voice there is at best muffled. We find this in Rudolf Bultmann's "Prophecy and Fulfillment," in which he claims that the Old Testament is a "miscarriage," and in his "The Significance of the Old Testament for the Christian Faith," in which he states that "to the Christian faith, the Old Testament is no longer revelation as it has been, and still is, for the Jews."[109] While we could make the argument that Bultmann is here simply conveying his Lutheranism, this is not an adequate explanation. The difference between Bultmann's appraisal of the Old Testament as "miscarriage" and Luther's statement in his sermon "How Christians Should Regard Moses" that "not one little period in Moses pertains to us" is clear.[110] The background for Luther's reaction in his sermon is in part his opposition to the radical Reformation's literal appropriation of Moses in their iconoclasm and their tendency to push for replacing the *Sachsenspiegel* with the Law of Moses (or the Sermon on the Mount!).[111] For Bultmann, in part the problem is simply modernity.[112] While we cannot deny the devastation wrought by Christian persecution of Jews throughout the centuries before the Enlightenment, it must be remembered that the most systematic evil perpetrated against the Jews occurred in "Enlightened" Germany, the cradle of modernity.[111] The very program of "demythologization" itself implies a sense of futility in the reading of Scripture in any narratively meaningful sense.

We have seen how some mainline feminist theologies, despite the proclaimed concerns for avoiding hierarchies and intolerance in favor of inclusivity and mutuality, have admitted the influence of modern theology's own particular brand of imperialism, which results in a relegation of the Old Testament to "a thing of the past."[113] My point here is neither to fault feminism with anti-Judaism nor to suggest that before the modern period Christians were free of anti-Judaism. Neither would I agree with those who suggest that the remedy to such anti-Judaism is simply the "teaching of respect," which in itself is important but not sufficient. The point here is simply that where and when Christian feminist theology exhibits anti-Judaism, it can be seen to be a result of non-narrative reading, which runs throughout modern theology in general. The remedy here thus will not be a simple relearning of civility and respect, although that could not do us harm, to be sure. The narratively read Fall story underscores the impossibility of our relearning adequately how to love without the intervention of God's grace. The remedy here suggested for feminist theology in particular and for modern theology in general is a reappropriation of narratival reading, which is linked to key assumptions about God's relationship to the world, which, in turn, form the cluster of governing doctrines on which the classic hermeneutic depends. This would, at the very least, allow for the possibility for feminist theology to extricate itself from the anti-Jewish sentiments catalogued here, even though this would not necessarily rule out anti-Judaism on other unforeseen fronts. In addition, this would also enable some feminist theologies to embrace the Old Testament as a witness to the healing presence of Jesus Christ instead of dismissing it as patriarchal prologue to Jesus' liberation.

We have thus positioned some mainline feminist theologies within the tradition of modern theology descending from Kant, Schleiermacher, and Feuerbach and have seen how they fit within the secular movements of the first and second waves of the feminist movement. We have seen how mainline feminist theology makes use of feminist theory regarding the origins of patriarchy and the nature of woman in constructing modes of feminist interpretation of the Bible. Feminist consciousness is now held to be the epistemological sine qua non and, as such, takes on the status of governing doctrine. Thus it maintains the pinnacle position on the pyramid of authorities which govern the mainline feminist's use of the Bible. In the following chapter, we will turn to the primary doctrine of sin, where we will see how accepting the claims of feminist critique as governing doctrines affects the understanding of the doctrine of sin.

3

GOVERNING DOCTRINES, EXTRA-NARRATIVAL CLAIMS, AND AUTHENTIC DOCTRINE

Sin and Victimization

In the previous chapter, we saw how feminist theologies embrace what Christian called alien claims and what we might less pejoratively call extra-narratival claims. These extra-narratival claims in the case of feminist theologies arise within the discourse of the feminist movement. They are embraced as what Christian calls authentic doctrines and then elevated to the status of, in Christian's terms, governing doctrines. It is the process of discernment regarding the status of the extra-narratival claims of feminism, among others, with which we are struggling in the mainline denominations and seminaries. Are all of the claims of feminism indeed authentic doctrines, or do they cohere with authentic doctrine of the Christian community? Clearly, Christian feminist theologians answer this question, in general, affirmatively, depending, of course, on the specific claims entailed.

Proclaiming extra-narratival claims to be authentic doctrine in and of itself would have had little impact, if any, on a classically conceived web of belief. However, we saw how mainline feminist theologians take this one step further, by absorbing such extra-narratival claims at the level of governing doctrine. An example of this is Rosemary Radford Ruether's "critical principle of feminist theology" which we explored in chapter 2. When these newly acclaimed governing doctrines displace classical governing doctrines, a reshaping of the web of belief begins. Turning now to primary doctrine, we can examine how this affects the web of belief, in this chapter with particular reference to the doctrine of sin.

I was once questioned after a lecture as to whether feminist theologians were really interested in sin at all. My questioner wanted to know if there is even a place for a discussion of sin in feminist theology, for he was under the impression that there is not. His impression is caused, in part, by the relocation of the doctrine of sin among mainline feminist theologians: yes, indeed, there is a "place" for the discussion of sin, a very significant place in fact, but it is different from the classical "place." While the fact that the doctrine of sin is reconstructed is sometimes taken as evidence for its absence, this is far from the case.

There have been two patterns identified in feminist reconstructions of the doctrine of sin, called the "aesthetic" and the "ethical."[1] Since the aesthetic tends to be post-Christian and our present concern is with mainline Christian feminist theology, we will be concerned with the ethical considerations of the doctrine of sin. How, then, does sin affect the human individual and her social context?

Our examination of feminist hermeneutics in the previous chapter would suggest that feminist reconstructions of the doctrine of sin are tied directly to the very practice of biblical interpretation. That is, since feminist analysis of sin examines not so much sin and the individual but sin as it distorts the structures and institutions which organize our communal life, we can find even within discussions of feminist hermeneutics itself the implicit reconstruction of the doctrine of sin. Sin as an alien force which inflicts harm on humanity through patriarchal structures is claimed to be inherent in the canon of Christian Scripture itself, not only in the process by which the canon was formed but also in the use of the canon in the contemporary moment. Scripture both then and now is implicated in patriarchy. Elisabeth Schüssler Fiorenza claims in her feminist commentary project *Searching the Scriptures* that the purpose of the commentary's casting its net beyond the traditional bounds of the Christian canon is expressly *not* intended to develop a "new" feminist canon, which might, in turn, become only yet another vehicle of cultural hegemonic oppression:

> Yet it cannot be overemphasized that this transgressive approach of proliferation and analysis, which has been adopted by this commentary, does *not* seek to establish a new *feminist* canon. Its aim is not constructive but deconstructive insofar as it seeks to unsettle and destabilize the fixation of feminist debates on the canon and its claims to authority. By destabilizing canonical authority, this commentary seeks to deconstruct oppressive cultural and religious identity formations engendered by the ruling Christian canon. Its goal is not a rehabilitation of the canon but an increase in historical-religious knowledge and imagination.[2]

Here, the Christian canon of Holy Scripture itself is understood to be the locus and perpetuation of sin. The remedy for this is not the construction of an alternate canon, but the destabilization of the accepted canon via both historical criticism and imaginative reconstruals. Here again, the "savior" which relieves humanity of sin is the feminist and her (or possibly his) colleagues and the tools of the history of religions. Again, we have stepped completely outside the narrative, purposefully so, to escape the poison within.

To be sure, one of the fishbones of classical Christianity on which feminist theologies often choke is the doctrine of sin, especially in its Augustinian form of "original sin."[3] This, of course, is not surprising. Insofar as both mainline feminist theology and modern theology embrace the Enlightenment notion of the perfectibility of humanity, this reaction to the doctrine of original sin is another example of feminist theologies' fitting into the larger pattern of modern theology. As it becomes inconceivable in the modern period that, as St. Paul explains in his letter to the Romans, one man's sin would affect all of creation without regard to any subsequent personal agency in the matter, so it is equally inconceivable to many feminist theologians. For feminist theologians, however, it is not simply the perfectibility of humanity which makes the doctrine of original sin hard to swallow, but it is this viewed with a distinctly feminist consciousness. That is, as was shown in the previous chapter, any doctrine which places undeserved blame or unmerited responsibility on anyone, particularly on women, is, according to feminist theological governing doctrine, not to be embraced; if it is oppressive to women, it cannot be of God. The rhetoric of "blaming the victim" has been too often used against women, such as is apparent every time a rape victim is accused of provoking the rapist. To the extent that the Adam-Christ typology can even remotely appear to be an instance of blaming the victim, it is to be rejected, according to the standards of feminist theologies. A "narrative reading" of Scripture at this point, as at others, becomes impossible for the feminist theologian—indeed, undesirable—and thus to be avoided.

Not surprisingly, the doctrine of sin is the locus which sparked the first major piece of feminist theological scholarship. The pioneer essay in feminist theological scholarship, Valerie Saiving Goldstein's "The Human Situation: A Feminine View," was first published in 1960. It implicitly asked the question about the nature of woman from the explicit standpoint of contemporary theological framings of the doctrine of sin. Saiving objected to what she saw to be an overwhelming identification of sin with "pride," for she understood this to be an example of "blaming the victim." For Saiving, women are not the agents of prideful sin but rather the objects of men's prideful acts which wound women.

Saiving began by examining the interpretations of sin and love in the work of Reinhold Niebuhr and Anders Nygren, contending that:

> there are significant differences between masculine and feminine experience and that feminine experience reveals in a more emphatic fashion certain aspects of the human situation which are present but less obvious in the experience of men. Contemporary theological doctrines of love have, I believe, been constructed primarily upon the basis of masculine experience and thus view the human situation from the male standpoint. Consequently, these doctrines do not provide an adequate interpretation of the situation of women—nor, for that matter, of men.[4]

Here we see, even at the dawn of feminist theological inquiry, the reliance on the objectification of experience as theological norm. The assumption even at this early stage is that men's experience is categorically different from women's experience, and the claim that men's experience should not be writ large in theological definitions and applied to women simply follows from this. Saiving then attempted to reexamine how sin would manifest itself in the lives and experience of women:

> The temptations of woman as woman are not the same as the temptations of man as man, and the specifically feminine forms of sin . . . have a quality which can never be encompassed by such terms as "pride" and "will to power." They are better suggested by such terms as triviality, distractibility, and diffuseness; lack of an organizing center or focus, dependence on others for one's self-definition; tolerance at the expense of standards of excellence. . . . In short, underdevelopment or negation of the self.[5]

The influence of Betty Friedan's "the problem with no name" is clear here. The stereotypical postwar American housewife who is defined by her responsibilities to her home and husband and who is stifled by the trivialities of the *Ladies' Home Journal* depiction of her reality is not one who readily typifies "will to power" and "pride." In this respect, Saiving's article was a quintessentially American piece of feminist writing.

This question about the nature of women's sin was addressed again fifteen years later in the now-classic 1975 Yale dissertation of Judith Plaskow, published as *Sex, Sin and Grace: Women's Experience and the Theologies of Reinhold Niebuhr and Paul Tillich*. In Plaskow's words, her attempt was to "take up Valerie Saiving's cudgel" in hopes of furthering the work of feminist systematic theology.[6] Until that point, Plaskow notes, most feminist scholarship had been devoted to questions of women's ordination, liturgical reform, and the reinterpretation of specific biblical texts. These are the issues which most biblical feminism is still engaging, and in many ways it is with Plaskow's dissertation that "mainline feminist theology" began to crystallize and precipitate out from the larger fluid of Christian feminism. Here we begin to see feminist reconstructions of primary Christian doctrines.

According to Plaskow, with Reinhold Niebuhr and Paul Tillich, two of the most influential theologians of the twentieth century in American mainline Protestant Christianity, it is the case that "certain aspects of human experience are highlighted and developed while others are regarded as secondary or ignored . . . the effect of this tendency, which is not incidental but springs from the very definitions of sin and grace, is to identify human with male experience."[7] Plaskow also uses, much as did Saiving, the category of "experience" as foundational for analyzing Niebuhr and Tillich's account of sin. She also accepts Saiving's definition of women's sin as "the failure to take responsibility for self-actualization."[8] Therefore, according to Plaskow, women do not necessarily need to be humbled or to deny the self, because more often than not they have little of their own "self" to be humbled or to deny. They need, rather, to come to know themselves, to acknowledge that they are a "self," to define and assert that self over and against the often enslaving cultural definitions and gender stereotypes applied to them. Women's problem is not pride, but, according to Plaskow, it is sloth.

While Saiving's claim seemed to be without reference or regard to cultural conditioning, Plaskow refines the argument such that women's experience is identified as "the interrelation between cultural expectations and their internalization."[9] For Plaskow, "Women's experience means simply this: the experiences of women in the course of a history never free from cultural role definitions."[10] Saiving is silent on the matter, but Plaskow openly acknowledges that her argument does not necessarily apply across cultures and socioeconomic conditions. Yet, even while feminist theology has thus expanded its vision in the work of Plaskow, these factors are not yet brought in for any systematic analysis. That task will await another decade.

This task of examining the role played by the factors of race and class within the understanding of women's sin is then taken up in Susan Thistlethwaite's *Sex, Race, and God: Christian Feminism in Black and White*. She recounts the episode which opened her eyes and brought her to such analysis:

> In my Introduction to Theology course last year, I had occasion to teach the by-now famous article by Valerie Saiving, "The Human Situation: A Feminine View." . . . I had

not gotten too far into the presentation of Saiving's views—in fact I had merely to utter the word "sloth" as representative of "women's sin" (sic)—when a black woman student jumped to her feet and explained to me in no uncertain terms that "sloth" could never be construed as the besetting sin of black women. . . . The protest of the female black student is totally valid: without a historically accurate definition of what it means to be female in different racial, class and sexual role definitions, Saiving's contribution to understanding "sin for women" is misleading.[11]

In an attempt to redirect the discussion, Thistlethwaite then examines African American women writers' understanding of women's experience. Not only is the effect of sin understood differently from the vantage point of women's experience than it is from that of men's experience but also she finds that it will differ as to the "woman" who experiences, in all her socioeconomic and racial specificity. Thistlethwaite thus pushes feminist theological analysis further by examining the effect of sin on women while factoring in the variables of race and class. She looks to the writings of Zora Neale Hurston, Katie Geneva Cannon, Carter Heyward, and Alice Walker, among others, to add depth to the understanding of women's sin informed by the categories of race and class.[12]

What we see, then, over the generation of feminist scholarship on the primary Christian doctrine of sin, is a parsing and refining of the particularities of women's sin.[13] The extra-narratival claim that women's experience and therefore women's sin are distinct from men's experience and men's sin becomes a governing doctrine which then determines the understanding of sin. The unintended net effect is a virtual cataloguing of the difficulties, both personal and social, faced by women of different races and classes. Indeed, such cataloguing was too strong a temptation to be avoided even before the additional refining according to race and class. For example, Mary Daly lists some of the characteristics of "women's sin": psychological paralysis, feminine antifeminism, false humility, emotional dependence, lack of creativity.[14] This becomes a logical move, of course, at the point where evil is defined as the systemic structures or patterns of oppression in economic, political, and social life, and where sin is defined as "those free, discrete acts of responsible individuals that create or reinforce these structures of oppression."[15] This is the case not just because of the general appeal of the idea that women's sin would manifest itself differently from men's sin, but it is tied directly to the very definition of the root of sin for many feminist theologies.[16] Where the root of sin is understood to be sexism itself, it is an easy and logical step to understanding the fruit of sin for women to be self-denial and submissiveness, with the concomitant tailorings according to race and class.[17]

However, this only reinscribes totalizing assumptions about "women" and reinforces stereotypes about women's submissiveness rather than overcoming and subverting them. In addition, this cataloguing only adds to the burdens of guilt imposed on women for not fulfilling their potential.[18] Therefore, despite the layered analysis of the factors of culture, race, and class on the effects of sin on women, which we might have hoped to nuance and qualify the discussion, a surprisingly objectifying and unqualified understanding of women's sin ultimately has held sway in the field of feminist theology: women's sin is women's response to the oppressions of patriarchy, racism, and classism. Women's sin, in other words, becomes a passive reality.[19]

A more recent and theologically fuller attempt to reconstruct the doctrine of sin in a feminist vision is that of Serene Jones in her forthcoming *Cartographies of Grace*. Jones suggests the notion of "imputed sin" as a way to speak of women's sin that would fit the needs and goals of a feminist Christianity:[20]

> In my initial feminist reinterpretation of this metaphor, I suggested that we think of imputed righteousness as a kind of Divinely scripted performance we are called to undertake in the life of faith. . . . Taking this image of imputed justification as "faithful performance," let us now ask in the context of this chapter what it would mean to imagine "imputed, original sin" in a similar manner but in reverse—as the "false performative scripts" into which women are born?[21]

Jones clearly wants to fulfill the requirements of the doctrine of "original sin" with her notion of "imputed sin." This is evident in particular in a footnote which states that "sin is 'imputed' from one generation to the next by virtue of the false identities which we wear that are passed on to us via the institutions and cultural forms we inhabit."[22] However, this is an explanation of how "sin" is transmitted, a matter which is only peripheral to the doctrinal function of original sin. The function of the doctrine of original sin within the greater web of Christian doctrines is to strengthen and balance the doctrine of grace: the saving grace of Christ covers and atones for the sins which are, to use the words of the old confession, our "own grave fault." In this respect, grace is hailed as "amazing." From this perspective, the notion of "imputed sin" can be seen to muffle the word of grace.

Of course, the benefit of this use of the concept of "imputed sin" is that it makes the doctrine of sin more palatable to feminist sensibilities, for it takes out the sting of women's responsibility for sin. This is to be valued insofar as feminist theologies seek to deflect women's responsibility for their own oppression and victimization in an attempt to undermine the rhetoric of "blaming the victim," all too pervasive in instances of abuse of women. Certainly one can be sympathetic with this goal of a feminist reconstruction of the doctrine of sin: "Seeing the self as a site 'attacked' by sin also has the salutary effect of allowing women to be more direct about naming as 'sin' the personal harms which are perpetrated against us, a naming that is particularly important in situations of domestic violence and abuse."[23] However, saying that women are victims of sin which attacks from the exterior, even though it is consistent with Paul's own exposition in Romans 7 and with apocalyptic literature, comes close to saying women are not responsible for their own sin. This in and of itself runs the risk of reinscribing sexist assumptions which put women in the passive role. This might lead one to believe that women are not agents of sin, but merely its victims, innocent of all participation in evil, oppression, injustice, and hatred. However, Jones wants to allow space for women's agency in sin as a possibility, for she realizes that to state otherwise would again cast women in the role of the passive female upon whom identity is conferred rather than casting them in the role of agents and enactors of their own identity:

> It is important for feminists to affirm that women are not only the *victims* of harms perpetrated against them; they are also potentially active *agents* of injustice, capable of personally doing harm to others as well as, more indirectly, participating in and supporting institutions that perpetrate oppression against persons at [a] more systematic level. Again, keeping this emphasis on women's agency is critical to the feminist project because part

of women's oppression over the centuries has been a denial of their role as leading actors on the stage of history. Given this, to assert women's responsibility for sin is, paradoxically, crucial to women's empowerment. Correspondingly, women's agency needs to [be] affirmed in contexts where they occupy the role of the abused rather than the abuser. In such situations, I suggested, women need to take responsibility not for the harm done to them but for their response to that harm. Taking responsibility for how we deal with the injustices done to us is a crucial part of breaking the cycles of oppression that are often repeated if harms go unaddressed.[24]

Thus Jones wants to include a role for women's agency in sin but stresses the possibility that sin can "attack" as though a power from without. This is especially important for those women who have been victims of abuse that they can be free from blaming themselves or being burdened with low self-esteem.

Despite the difficulties in the feminist debate over the doctrine of sin, the question of how sin actually "cashes out" in the life of the believer is indeed a fascinating question. Since one of the key theological descriptions since Luther of the human creature in Christ has been that we are simul justus et peccator, we can assume that this also involves a simul justa et peccatrix. The problem with the debate is not, therefore, the asking of questions about the impact of sin on women of certain socioeconomic locations and conditioning. The problems with the debate, even as it is refined in the work of Plaskow, Thistlethwaite, Jones, and others, stem from two moves, one philosophical and the other more properly theological, both of which are results of a non-narrative reading of Scripture.

The philosophical difficulty is the unexamined totalizing assumptions which run throughout the debate and which even the qualifications of race and class cannot fully negotiate. Most American mainline feminist theological scholarship has explicitly repudiated essentialist definitions of "woman."[25] However, most feminist theologies nevertheless implicitly tend to operate with some analogous form of essentialism or totalizing thought, even if it is refined in terms of cultural construction, economic factors, or racial shaping.[26] To claim that "women's experience" is in any way a clearly discernible phenomenon, even over against "men's experience," is to create a foundation on shifting sands.[27] Claiming that "women's experience" is an identifiable, discrete category rests on the assumption of a totalizing anthropology of the feminine, even granted that we allow for the shaping of race and class.[28] The logic of this totalizing is similar to the logic of colonialist discourse: just as "structures of colonialist discourse . . . set conditions for respect that revolve around a requirement of identity or sameness,"[29] so feminist constructions of the doctrine of sin tend to require, despite their best intentions, a universalizing of anthropology of the feminine. This tends to be the case even when qualifiers of race and class are added. The implicit norms undergirding recent feminist discussions of sin, in effect, can undermine a true respect for the differences which pertain between individuals, insofar as generalizing (whether about a class, a race, a proneness to one kind of sin over another, or something else) is integral to the rhetoric. Thus, while feminist work of all types has sought to liberate women from the constraints placed on them by the interplay of biology and culture, this particular element of feminist theological debate tends merely to "redraw" the boundaries rather than engage in true gender reconciliation within the Body of Christ.

The more properly theological difficulty in following the claim to a discretely identifiable category of "women's sin" is the extent to which it is another example of non-narrative reading of Scripture. At first glance, this might appear to be an unjustifiable way of describing the theological problem, for, to be sure, there is no "text" in the Bible, whether narrative or non-narrative, which explains or defines sin per se. It is because of this very fact, however, that the feminist approach to the doctrine of sin becomes an extremely interesting instance of non-narrative reading. For narrative reading such as we have described, sheer familiarity with the contents of the Bible becomes particularly crucial, for one must rely on the picture of sin painted by the canon as a whole.

Narrative reading of the type required at this level disallows focusing on any one portion of Scripture and requires a more holistic view. This is analogous to what we saw illustrated in Calvin (and in Augustine, on whom he draws) in the concern for Scripture's commentary on itself. The phrase "Scripture is its own interpreter" was never intended to indicate an "objectified" text which required no interpreting subject but rather to insist on interpretation at the level of metanarrative. At this point, feminist theologians' consideration of the doctrine of sin shows itself to be non-narrative, insofar as it defines women according to an anthropology constructed almost entirely independently of the biblical drama.

If we were to follow Saiving, we would have to look far beyond the scope of the biblical narrative to define humanity. This is indeed a live option for the non-Christian and the post-Christian alike, from Starhawk to Daphne Hampson. But for those feminist theologians who are self-consciously Christian, this seems an odd move to make. This is specifically not to say that the insights available from the world of experience or from fields of humanist or scientific study cannot be useful in theology, because, of course, they can be and, indeed, are useful. However, Christian theological investigation usually presumes a significant degree of reliance on some combination of the biblical narrative and Christian tradition. This is not the case in the feminist reconstructions of sin we have examined. The only possible exception to this is Serene Jones's notion of "imputed sin."

Another problematic move in the feminist doctrines of sin examined is that after defining "woman" extra-narrativally, they tend to jump back into the biblical drama. That is, after considering woman as defined according to the extra-narratival claims of a particularly late-twentieth-century North American framework, the feminist theologies then want to make use of this picture as a governing doctrine through which to reinterpret the biblical concepts of sin, grace, and divine agency. This move is not logically required and may only serve to build constraints that would not be ultimately fruitful to the theological task conceived extra-narratively. This is, of course, part of the critique implied in Daphne Hampson's *Theology and Feminism*. Indeed, such use of biblical and traditional categories at this point comes across as somewhat opportunistic, in the words of Angela West, coming close to making of the scriptures and tradition "a great rummage sale in which [theologians] hope to pick up a valuable antique with which to furnish their own apartment."[30] This is the biblical-hermeneutical analogue of the blunder in the field of anthropology known as ethnocentrism; it involves stretching the biblical narrative beyond its own (already) highly elastic capabilities. Once this process has begun, further reshaping of the doctrinal web and of the narrative structure of the biblical drama is required to accommodate the extra-narratival or alien depiction of women earlier introduced. A cycle of reshaping, tearing, and repairing the web of belief sets in, the end of which we have yet to see.

Of course, not all feminist theologians engage in complete reshaping of the web of belief. One example of a feminist consideration of the doctrine of sin which adheres more closely to the metanarrative of the canon is the definition offered by Mary Grey:

> sin is a deliberate blocking of the relational grain of existence . . . it can also be seen as a ghastly mimicry of the energies of creation, a mockery of the story of Genesis. *Sin is structural de-creation—the structural un-making of the world*—and can be seen as such in the many forms in which it is manifest, in interpersonal as well as political contexts.[31]

This is not simply because she mentions the creation stories in Genesis but because the canon itself depicts sin as the chaos which works against the creative activity of God. Grey then takes this narrative depiction of sin and unfolds it, making the connections with feminist concerns in such a way that the biblical narrative "absorbs" them rather than the reverse.

There is also an occasional modern analogue to Julian of Norwich, who understood her life's work as fitting into the narrative framework of the scriptures rather than vice versa. One such example is Sarah Coakley, who in a recent essay attempts to demonstrate how the narratively rendered tradition can "absorb" the norms and goals of feminism:

> the rhetoric of kenosis has not simply constituted the all-too-familiar exhortation to women to submit to lives of self-destructive subordination; nor (as Hampson believes) can it be discarded solely as a compensatory reaction to the 'male problem.' The evocations of the term have been much more complex and confusing even than that; just as the Christian tradition is in so many respects complex, confusing and (as I believe), continually creative. . . . My aim here is to show how wordless prayer can enable one, paradoxically, to hold vulnerability and personal empowerment *together*, precisely by creating the "space" in which non-coercive divine power manifests itself, and I take this to be crucial for my understanding of a specifically Christian form of feminism.[32]

Coakley's claim is that vulnerability and empowerment are held together within the meta-narrative of the biblical canon and within the discourse of classical Christian theology. The task then becomes, instead of non- or extra-narratival reconstructions of Christian doctrine, rather, the rereading and redescription of doctrines which show the ability of the biblical narrative to "absorb" extrabiblical questions and modes of discourse. Coakley's work in this essay is thus implicitly close to Frei's understanding of theology as internal redescription. This is simply to point out that feminist theology does not necessarily negate narrative hermeneutics and that a feminist theology which seeks to reclaim a narrative hermeneutic is possible. It is, however, in the minority and only at a beginning stage.

Narrative Reading and Sin: Karl Barth

One example of how a feminist reconsideration of sin might proceed from these small steps that would engage narrative reading is to consider building on the work of Karl

Barth on sin in his *Church Dogmatics*. While we certainly cannot claim that Barth was a feminist, he is, according to Frei, a modern example of narrative reading. Barth probably would not completely understand what "feminism" is or be very sympathetic with its analyses of the human condition, insofar as they depart from the biblically depicted reality. However, we can take the complaints which Valerie Saiving and others have made about contemporary Protestant discussions of sin and address them with Barth's discussion of sin, for it evidences significant congruences with—yet also divergences from—the concerns of the feminist discussion of women's sin. Therefore, it may help us draw on the strong points of the feminist discussion without tripping up on its difficulties.

Sin in Barth's *Dogmatics* is understood in much broader terms than merely pride alone, which is itself, according to Barth, only one form of human rejection of Jesus Christ. In paragraphs 65 and 66 of the *Church Dogmatics*, Barth examines sin as sloth or, to be precise, sin as our slothful response to the lordship of the Son of Man. Even sloth, however, in Barth's terms is not merely lack of self-assertion or submissiveness but a far-reaching inverse and mirror image of pride. Because Barth's discussion of sin and sanctification is thoroughly guided by and centered on the biblical narrative, the only way we know what sin is, in and of itself, is by knowing first who Jesus is: "Where there is genuine knowledge of sin, it is a matter of the Christian knowledge of God, of revelation and of faith, and therefore of the knowledge of Jesus Christ."[33]

The only way to view sin and sanctification, in fact, is from the standpoint of the Resurrection: "For who and what is overcome in the death of the Son of Man is revealed in His resurrection."[34] Here, of course, Barth is merely following the witness of the New Testament, which moves logically from solution to plight.[35] For Barth, therefore, the nature and extent of the disturbance between humanity and God created by sin "can be measured only by the fact that it is met and overcome by God Himself."[36] This, in and of itself, necessitates a lengthy and layered description of sin. For Barth, especially in paragraph 65 of the *Church Dogmatics*, sin is defined as that which God does not will, in which he has no part, which he did not create, which has no possibility before him, which is absurd before him, and therefore which he has rejected and forbidden.[37] As sloth, it manifests itself in disobedience, unbelief, stupidity, inhumanity, dissipation, care or anxiety, even panic, and is described as misery or bondage of the will.[38]

With particular reference to the feminist concerns about the doctrine of sin, we pick up Barth in paragraph 66, *The Sanctification of Man*, part three, "The Call to Discipleship." Can Barth be used to advantage by feminists in establishing the claim that women need primarily not to deny themselves but rather to assert themselves? His treatment here can cut both ways. Following Jesus in fact means denying the self, the very act which, according to the feminist discussion, women must not and cannot do. As Barth says, "To follow Jesus means to go beyond oneself in a specific action and attitude, and therefore to turn one's back upon oneself, to leave oneself behind. . . . Inevitably the individual who is called by Jesus renounces and turns away from himself as he was yesterday. To use the important New Testament expression, he denies himself"[39] Referring later to Matthew 26:72, Barth points out that true discipleship is the opposite of Peter's denial of Jesus: we must be able to say of ourselves instead of about Jesus, "I do not know the man." Yet Barth claims that even such self-denial involves a degree of what some feminists may be referring to when they speak of "self-assertion," for "self-denial in the context of following Jesus involves a step into the open, into the freedom of a definite decision and act."[40] Self-denial thus is not simply the opposite of self-assertion and cannot be corrected by it.

Indeed, in Barth's discussion of sin as sloth, we can see an overlap or congruence with the feminist concerns about sin first raised by Saiving. This comes, in part, as a result of Barth's weaving together three streams of traditional christological categories via which he creates a masterful structure for setting forth the doctrine of reconciliation.[41] In making use of the traditional "offices" of Christ as prophet, priest, and king (for Barth, priest, king, and prophet), as well as the traditional "states" of Christ's humiliation, exaltation, and manifestation, and the Chalcedonian formulation of the God-human unity, Barth brings the doctrine of sin under the wing of reconciliation, which, in turn, he organizes via christological categories. This means that the doctrines of reconciliation and sin are linked in such a way that "sin" cannot be divided up and parceled out, this sort to these individuals and that to those. Indeed, the doctrine of reconciliation precedes and controls the doctrine of sin such that each of Barth's christological considerations corresponds to the ways in which humanity rebels against Jesus Christ. Sloth is the form our rebellion takes which rejects the exaltation of the Son of Man and is countered by sanctification. Pride is the form our rebellion takes which rejects the humble obedience of the Son of God and is countered by justification. Barth insists, of course, that there is no consequential ordering to this, but that justification is the ground of sanctification and sanctification the purpose of justification. The implicit effect is the joining of the otherwise apparently incongruous "sins" of pride and sloth such that they are an inseparable unity. And here, of course, comes the rub for feminist doctrines of sin:

> But as reconciling grace is not merely justifying, but also wholly and utterly sanctifying and awakening and establishing grace, so sin has not merely the heroic form of pride but also, in complete antithesis yet profound correspondence, the quite unheroic and trivial form of sloth. In other words, it has the form, not only of evil action, but also of evil inaction.[42]

Here the classic confession comes to mind, "we have sinned against thee . . . by what we have done and by what we have left undone."[43] Barth begins to pit sloth against pride in setting them in "complete antithesis," yet immediately he claims that there is also a "profound correspondence" between the two. In a most significant statement, Barth says:

> The sin of man is not merely heroic in its perversion. It is also—to use again the terms already introduced in the first sub-section—ordinary, trivial and mediocre. The sinner is not merely Prometheus or Lucifer. He is also—and for the sake of clarity, and to match the grossness of the matter, we will use rather popular expressions—a lazybones, a sluggard, a good-for-nothing, a slow-coach, and a loafer. He does not exist only in an exalted world of evil; he exists also in a very mean and petty world of evil (and there is a remarkable unity and reciprocity between the two in spite of their apparent antithesis). In the one case, he stands bitterly in need of humiliation; in the other he stands no less bitterly in need of exaltation. And in both cases the need is in relation to the totality of his life and action.[44]

What is this remarkable unity and reciprocity between the two? The correspondence between pride and sloth is that both reside in the larger field of hatred of God:

> In its form as man's tardiness and failure, sloth expresses much more clearly than pride the positive and aggressive ingratitude which repays good with evil. . . . He turns his back on God, rolling himself into a hedgehog with prickly spikes. . . . It may be that this action often assumes the disguise of a tolerant indifference in relation to God. But in fact it is the action of the hate which wants to be free of God, which would prefer that there were no God. . . . This hatred of God is the culminating point of human pride, too.[45]

In our sloth, according to Barth, we reject the man Jesus Christ, wanting to be free of him and of his command. We reject him because we want to be the ones to elect and to will, and we "do not want to be disturbed in this choice."[46] Barth's notion of sin as sloth thus appears to be very different from the feminist understanding of women's sin as lack of self-definition and assertion. Indeed, for Barth, self-definition is itself integrally a part of sloth: "A life which moves and circles around itself, which is self-oriented but also self-directed, seems to hold out far greater promise than one which is lived in this fellowship [with Jesus Christ]." [47] This may indeed be a useful notion for feminist theologians to take up in the attempt to nuance the notion of woman's sin: even attempts at self-definition are fundamentally slothful insofar as they allow the Christian to move and circle around herself rather than engage in fellowship with the crucified and risen Christ and his church.

Another area in which Barth's discussion of sin may help nuance the feminist discussion comes from Barth's explicit statement that the effects of the Fall are entirely equalizing for all of humanity.[48] CD 4.2 390–1 We are all "unequivocally opposed to Him," and we are all like Peter, sinking into the sea because we doubt and reject him. Measured against him, we all exist on a different level from him but indeed precisely on the same level as one another. Humanity is "united in the fact that it doubts Him, that it does not understand Him, that it forsakes Him, that it rejects and denies and betrays or at the very least impotently bewails Him, that it judges Him either on spiritual or secular grounds, that it brings Him to the cross and that it finally abandons Him on the cross."[49] This equalizing of all humanity in contrast to Jesus, and in the reparation of the breach between humanity and God wrought by him, itself logically bridges the gulf between the two halves of humanity, male and female. Barth cannot see the ultimate struggle to be that between the sexes or the races, but the struggle between humanity and its Creator. This he sees to be a direct conclusion to a holistic reading of Scripture. Indeed, sin, even in its manifestation as sloth, is absolutely equalizing:

> We are in the process of denying and destroying and dissipating ourselves as individuals. We are busily engaged in setting up our own caricature. We are sawing off the branch on which we sit. Yet it is true that we cannot reproach one another in this respect. The one can take comfort in the fact that the other is at least not much better and probably much worse. We are all alike at this point.[50]

Not only are we all alike in our sloth, which in itself recapitulates and mirrors and mimics pride while existing as its inverse and counterpart, but also we are all equally under the shadow of the cross. Insofar as we may be said to bear our own cross, which we should not and will not seek, but which, by definition, we will end up bearing if we follow Jesus, our cross resembles that of our neighbor more than it resembles that of Jesus. There is only an indirect connection between our suffering and his, and therefore the gulf lies not between male and female, European and Asian, or gay and straight. The gulf lies not between our respective crosses, but between our cross and his. His cross entailed being rejected by God, and ours does not. This, again, is not simply an instance of Barth unreflectively reinscribing the universalizing claims of patriarchy but rather of his commitment to the thorough prioritizing of the witness of the biblical narrative. Thus he says that our cross will bring on us equally humility, vulnerability, throwing us back on the strength of God, resulting in our being persecuted and treated with scorn and suspicion, but ultimately bringing us a foretaste of joy.[51]

It would seem, then, that Barth's discussion of sin would push the feminist discussion in a direction which would break down some of the distinctions made between women's sin of self-denial and submissiveness versus men's sin of pride. But, a feminist might object, what of the example of Barth's reading of 1 Samuel 25 and the story of David, Nabal, and Abigail? Doesn't his reading of this specific text present a positive understanding of women vis-à-vis human sin, which the feminist can refine and use to her profit? Cannot his reading of this story further establish rather than break down the categories of men's sin and women's sin as have developed over the previous generation of feminist theological discussion of sin?

In Barth's reading, Nabal, whose name Barth notes means "fool," portrays human stupidity while Abigail manifests the wisdom of God. It is Abigail who comes out the heroine, indeed the heroine in a positive sense, not in a "Promethean" or negative sense. According to Barth, the reason Abigail is wise is that she hears the name of David and knows with whom she has to deal. She knows immediately what her husband does not, that it is Yahweh's chosen who is requesting their hospitality. She knows this in spite of her husband. And, Barth points out, without consulting her husband, she repairs the near-fatal blunder he had previously committed. Abigail, in effect, prevents David from exacting vengeance on Nabal's stupidity and inhumanity, which, in turn, would have made David, God's chosen, the fool. Abigail in effect "saves" David and thus the promise from self-destruction. According to Barth, Abigail "towers above David" for she knows Yahweh, and therefore she knows David, in a sense better than he knew himself, for he was about to act the fool instead of fulfilling his own role and identity in the wisdom of God.[52]

A feminist reading of this story could take these observations and conclude that Abigail is a biblical example of the assertive (in a positive, not "Promethean" sense) wise woman, the woman who does not fall prey to stereotypical women's tendency toward self-denial and silence. Barth indeed does this, but only as an aside. His main commitments are not toward promoting healthy role models for women for the sake of the well-being of humanity, despite all he says about Abigail.[53] After all, when he comes to the story of David and Bathsheba, he does not care to comment much on Bathsheba at all, not even on the injustice done to her by David.[54] Barth's main point in his consideration of Abigail is that Abigail's wisdom comes from her recognition of David as God's chosen, "and therefore of the will and promise, the secret and covenant, of the God of Israel." To stop at the conclusion that the story represents a role model for women's assertiveness and intuition would be to trump the story's inner witness to God, according to Barth. The reason that Barth cannot be constrained by the reading of Abigail as a female role model is not merely that he is reinscribing patriarchy but that he is constrained by his prior commitment to the biblical narrative's depiction of sin as the shadows cast behind us from the "backward-shining rays of the Risen One."

Of course, one of the key points of divergence between Barth and many feminists—indeed, the point which may broker all other points of divergence—is their fundamental hermeneutical posture, their very understanding of Scripture and of the nature of theology. For Barth, the claim that Scripture witnesses to God's grace and that theology is the explication of the witness of Scripture means that we must trust Scripture. Within paragraph 66, Barth says that the only reason he can claim the real possibility that the works of the Christian would both praise God and receive praise from God is because the witness of Scripture attests to it. He does not base his argument for the dual nature of the praise of works on the psychological and social benefits which would accrue from it but solely from the presence of such a possibility within the witness of Scripture: "If we are to accept the witness of Scripture, we cannot ignore this, let alone deny it. Scripture not only trusts the God of the covenant, Jesus Christ and the Holy Spirit, that this will be the case. It attests it as a reality within its witness to God the Father, Son and Holy Spirit and His works."[55] For mainline feminist theology (again, evangelical "biblical feminism" is not being considered here within the range of mainline feminist theology proper), we have seen that the very notion of trusting Scripture in any fundamental or overriding way is usually denied explicitly and openly. Since Scripture is so tinged and tainted by the patriarchy of the cultures which produced it, so the argument goes, it cannot and must not be immediately trusted. It must be approached with a hermeneutics of suspicion. Here is the fundamental divide between Barth and much of mainline feminist theology. How one constructs a doctrine of sin, Christology, soteriology, or anything else is fundamentally (although by no means finally) determined by the side of the divide on which one stands. In any case, for Barth, it is not ultimately the text of Scripture which one must trust, but the God who uses Scripture to attest to his will and his work. Here we see the instability of the mainline feminist hermeneutical position: the governing doctrines of feminist theology ("Warning: the Bible may be hazardous to your health," for example) pull the rug out from under the classical hermeneutic.[56] It seems inherently contradictory for feminist theologians to claim to be able to read Scripture as witness to the divine reality *and* to claim that it needs a warning label indicating its toxicity, if the God we are talking about is that of the biblical narrative.

Barth's discussion of sin has helpfully addressed some of the inadequacies of the feminist discussion. His work has shown that self-denial for the Christian is not simply the opposite of self-assertion and cannot be corrected by it. His insistence that pride is not the only manifestation of our rebellion against God has taken much of the force out of the feminist claim that defining sin as pride is reflective of "male" experience, and his insistence on the inner unity between sloth and pride could help refine future feminist reconstructions of the doctrine of sin. Indeed, Barth's discussion has pointed out that sin is not a character flaw in need of amelioration, but a radical rebellion against God that can be overcome alone from the side of the divine rather than by any human efforts, no matter how noble, at dismantling social evils such as patriarchy.

We have also seen that, far from the intentions of the authors involved in the feminist debate on women's sin, the generation of discussion over feminist reconstructions of the doctrine of sin has produced potentially harmful results. The well-intended concern with the effects of sin on women and the refining of this according to race and class implicitly permit an overbearing focus on women's weaknesses and difficulties in the face of social evil. This can, of course, in fact, be, counterproductive to any sense of well-being for women. Thus, what was intended to be helpful can, with an ironic twist, end up enslaving further rather than liberating. In addition, making self-assertion into the goal of sanctification for women threatens to generate chronic guilt and constant self-assessment that can lead to disappointment and a sense of failure.[57] Not only is this potentially damaging both psychologically and spiritually but also, even more profoundly, it ultimately contradicts a central primary doctrine of the Reformed tradition at least, namely, justification by grace through faith alone.

4

FEMINIST CHRISTOLOGIES

Turning now to the primary doctrine of Christology, we will see how feminist theological governing doctrines affect the reconstruction of the consideration of the person of Jesus. Remember that it was the stories about Jesus with which Frei's narrative project was most concerned. Is Jesus to be regarded as a character within a series of stories about him, his life, his followers, his teachings, or is he to be understood as a representative for some greater idea or reality? How will feminist theological reconfiguring of governing doctrine affect the answers to these questions?[1]

Feminist Christologies and the Gender of Jesus

For feminist theology, Christology is inherently problematic because Jesus was male. The complaints against Jesus' masculinity go back to Mary Daly, who viewed the "myth of sin" and the "myth of redemption" as symptoms of the disease of male arrogance and who understood the doctrine of sacrificial atonement to create a "scapegoat syndrome" which encourages women to imitate Jesus' model of self-sacrificial love.[2] Of course, such charges against classical Christianity cannot go unaddressed.[3]

The Christian doctrine of the incarnation, the claim that God became incarnate in a specific male, is problematic on more than one level for feminist theologies. First, Jesus' maleness, claim feminists, is interpreted throughout Christian history as deifying the male and making his rule over woman his divine right. Thus, to claim with Chalcedon that Jesus is fully human and fully divine is to risk playing into the hands of the oppressors. This was Mary Daly's charge; "If God is male, then male is God."[4]

This charge is widely accepted as though it were self-evidently true, despite some valiant attempts to address the misinformation on which the charge is based.[5]

Second, it is claimed that women are not empowered to claim their own identity if Jesus is held up as the role model, the "pioneer and perfecter of our faith" as he is described in Hebrews 12:2.[6] It is claimed that a Christology which concerns itself with the maleness of the incarnate savior therefore can impede women's own self-definition and ability to find their own voice. In fact, some mainline feminists claim that the "Christ serves as a religious tool for marginalizing and excluding women" when his maleness is interpreted as "essential to his redeeming christic function and identity."[7]

Third, since the records about Jesus gathered in the New Testament were written and collected by men for men (so it is claimed), and the canon ratified by hierarchical androcentric political maneuvering, women's voices were excluded from the canon. This makes the Bible, according to a feminist theological approach, potentially "dangerous to our health," as we have already seen, and this, in turn, renders the picture of Jesus in the Bible potentially harmful as well.

Imago Christi and the Priesthood

Part of the problem with the masculinity of Jesus, of course, touches on the relation of Christology to the doctrine of creation, specifically the creation of male and female in the image of God. The Roman Catholic understanding of the role of the priest as representing or imaging Jesus in the eucharistic feast makes this problem especially acute. The Catholic feminist Elizabeth Johnson puts the problem this way:

> As stated in an official argument against women's ordination, for example, men, thanks to their "natural resemblance" enjoy a capacity for closer identification with Christ than do women. While women may be recipients of divine grace, they are unsuited to carry out christic and especially eucharistic actions publicly due to their sexual difference from his maleness. Thus men alone among human beings are able to represent Christ fully. Women's physical embodiment becomes a prison that shuts them off from God, except as mediated through the christic male. For this mentality, the idea that the Word might have become female flesh is not even seriously imaginable, so thoroughly has androcentric Christology done its work of erasing the full dignity of women as christomorphic in the community of disciples. . . . As a logical outcome. . . . women's salvation is implicitly put in jeopardy, at least theoretically.[8]

Working backward from this argument to the question of what exactly it means to image Christ, Elizabeth Johnson then finds herself asking whether women, who cannot "image" Christ in the eucharist because they are not male, are indeed saved by this male.[9] This is, in a sense, a logical extension of the maxim of Athanasius that what is not assumed is not redeemed: if Jesus did not assume a female body, are female bodies redeemed? If they are redeemed in him, what then does it mean to "image" Christ? If he redeemed females even while not assuming a female body, is there not something in his gender and ours that is adiaphoron when it comes to being saved by and in the image of Christ?

The guiding model for the *imago Christi* is not replication of sexual features but participation in the life of Christ, which is founded on communion in the Spirit: those who
live the life of Christ are icons of Christ. Furthermore, the whole Christ is a corporate
personality, a relational reality, redeemed humanity that finds its way by the light of the
historical narrative of Jesus' compassionate, liberating love: Christ exists only pneuma-
tologically. Finally, what is essential to the saving good news about Jesus is not his bodily
sex but the solidarity of the Wisdom of God in and through this genuine human being
with all those who suffer and are lost. To make of the maleness of Jesus Christ a christological principle is to deny the universality of salvation.[10]

However, it is then a long jump from there to the statement that Jesus' maleness itself
is adiaphoron. But why is this? Because as a human, he was constrained within the
bounds of human categories of time, race, and gender. Jesus' very masculinity is one
of the non-negotiables over which we stumble as narrative readers: we cannot turn
his gender into a symbol of something other than what it is, an aspect of his human
life. This imputes a fixity which prohibits the gender bending required by some of
the moves made in inclusivizing Scripture and liturgies. The very fixity itself of Jesus'
gender, however, insofar as he saves all, allows for more fluidity than the Roman
Catholic magisterium's understanding of "imaging" Christ would imply: "No distinction on the basis of sex is made, or needed; being christomorphic is not a sex-
distinctive gift. . . . The image of Christ does not lie in sexual similarity to the human
man Jesus, but in the coherence with the narrative shape of his compassionate, liberating life in the world, through the power of the Spirit."[11] Johnson's remark here
is well stated in its reference to the potential christomorphicity of both male and
female but reflects a non-narrative Christology. In fact, it presupposes a Christology
which casts Jesus as a "role model" of compassion and liberation, which is specifically
not congruent with the "narrative shape" of his identity as it is depicted in the storied
world of Scripture. It is this non-narrative Christology which then allows the more
egregious distortion to be made, whereby the interpretive flow is reversed. This is
evident in the assumption that since male and female are made in the image of God,
they should be able to "return the favor" and name God according to both male and
female categories:

> Insofar as God creates both male and female in the divine image and is the source of the
> perfections of both, either can equally well be used as metaphor to point to divine
> mystery. Both in fact are needed for less inadequate speech about God, in whose image
> the human race is created. The "clue" for speaking of God in the image of male and
> female has the advantage of making clear at the outset that women enjoy the dignity of
> being made in God's image and are therefore capable as women of representing God.[12]

It is, in fact, the Roman Catholic presupposition that a male represents Christ more
adequately than a female which feeds the reversal of narrative logic, thus nourishing
the reconstructive theological work of Elizabeth Johnson here. It allows Johnson to
assume, by using the same logic, that women can "fully represent Christ, being themselves, in the Spirit, other Christs."[13] That is, if a male priest is able to image Christ,
then Christ must, indeed, have left women out of the loop, so to speak, of salvation
because they are less in the image of Christ than males. The need then arises to
"supplement" God language with a feminine dimension to fill in the missing (fem-

inine) piece, for humanity is created in the image of God, male and female. If the debate over ordination had not been resolved by saying that the role of the priest is to represent Christ, this whole chain of assumptions could have been short-circuited. If it were to be accepted that, according to a narrative reading, Jesus is the unsubstitutable messiah who cannot be"imaged" by anyone, whether male or female, just as there is no real "Christ figure" in literary terms, this whole path of arguing might be avoided.

The Scandal of Particularity

Christology also poses difficulties for feminist theology insofar as feminist theology shares in modern theology's difficulty with the "scandal of particularity." The notion that the one eternal God, creator of heaven and earth, could come to dwell with humanity in the person of a Jewish carpenter is often offensive to modern sensibilities, which are drawn instead to the universal and the general.

At the heart of these attempts at reconstructing Christology, we find the problem which has throughout history caused difficulties for Christian confession: the claim that a first-century carpenter named Jesus from the backwater village of Nazareth was the Son of God, the Messiah of Israel, the fulfillment of the promises to Abraham. This marks the "scandal of particularity," the stone of stumbling, over which many have fallen, from the first century to our day.

Feminist theologians are by no means the first to have difficulty with this aspect of Christian confession, for, indeed, modern theology in general tends to view Jesus as the container of a mysterious divine gift rather than the Son of God, the exterior packaging rather than the inextricable union of the container and the gift within the very life of God. However, feminist theology has found new fault in the Nicene creed's confession of Jesus as "God's only son, our lord." The problem now is deemed to be not the divinity of Jesus, not his relation to the Father, not even Jesus' humanity, but his very maleness. Here is the problem: the maleness of Jesus"leaks" into the Godhead like an infectious disease, rendering unclean our understanding of God and therefore also our understanding of our own maleness and femaleness. Now, decades after Mary Daly's charge that "if God is male, then male is God," as the result of its tacit acceptance across the denominational spectrum of American Christianity, we have seen numerous revisions of prayerbooks and hymnals, new "translations" and paraphrases of the scriptures, not to mention the reworkings of Christology such as we have seen here. This is done with the intent of plugging up and blocking the leaking masculinity of Jesus from infecting the Godhead, thus preventing the perception of the masculinity of God from deifying the human male.

Lift High the Cross

While a significant problem for feminist christologies is the maleness of Jesus, the very image of his cross also poses a problem for some feminist theologians. The charge is occasionally raised that insisting on the centrality of the cross in Christian theology is detrimental particularly to women insofar as it (so the charge goes) promotes and glorifies violence and abuse.[14] This, as we have seen, bears the legacy of Mary Daly. The following quote from Rita Nakashima Brock is indicative of this critique:

> Paternalistic grace functions by allowing a select group to be in a favored relationship with the powerful father, but the overall destructiveness of the oppressive systems of the patriarchal family is not challenged by such benevolence. . . . Such doctrines of salvation reflect, by analogy, I believe, images of the neglect of children or, even worse, child abuse, making it acceptable as divine behavior—cosmic child abuse, as it were. The father allows, or even inflicts, the death of his only perfect son.[15]

Not all feminist theologians agree with this charge, but often even those who do not agree nevertheless attempt to disprove it on the basis of the logic of the charge itself. For example, Mary Grey claims that it is not the cross itself as narrative moment but our inadequate interpretations of it which form the basis of the problem. Her suggestion, however, for avoiding the misinterpretation is not to increase attention to the cross through offering a more careful reading of its place in the canonical narrative but to detract attention from the cross.[16] In other words, the "remedy" is not to attempt to give a closer reading of the biblical narratives of the crucifixion, for example, but to examine the inner "meaning" of the narratives. Feminist spirituality here, according to Grey, begins with the assumption that the narratives about the cross are really "about" something else other than the mode of execution of a convicted criminal in the ancient Roman world, something other than the specific cross of a certain rabbi from Galilee who was given the death penalty on account of treason. Since they are "about" something else, feminist "spirituality" can plug its metaphors and symbols into the same slot occupied by the cross and still point to "values" it represents.

The unlikelihood of mainline feminist theologies giving greater attention to or more careful consideration of the place of the cross in Scripture and Christian theology is apparent when one understands that the cross is not interpreted in most feminist circles from within the narrative framework of the Gospel stories. Instead, the larger framework within which the cross is interpreted is "women's experience (of oppression)." When the cross is understood as, from the very outset, an example of abuse which can only wound further, redemption cannot come in the form of the cross and, indeed, may come only by removing the offense of the cross.[17]

Dolores Williams is one of the most vocal proponents of this view. For Williams, the word of the cross legitimates what she calls the "surrogacy experience" of black women, the bearing of others' unbearable burdens, and therefore must be reconstructed if it is not to be completely rejected by black women:

> The image of Jesus on the cross is the image of human sin in its most desecrated form. . . . The cross thus becomes an image of defilement, a gross manifestation of collective human sin. Jesus, then, does not conquer sin through death on the cross. Rather, Jesus conquers the sin of temptation in the wilderness (Mt 4:1–11) by resistance—by resisting the temptation to value the material over the spiritual ("Man shall not eat by bread alone"); by resisting death (not attempting suicide; "if you are the son of God, throw yourself down"); by resisting the greedy urge of monopolistic ownership ("He showed him all the kingdoms of the world and the glory of them; and he said to him, 'All these

I will give you, it you will fall down and worship me' "). Jesus therefore conquered sin in life, not in death. . . . What this allows the black female theologian to show black women is that God did not intend the surrogacy roles they have been forced to perform. God did not intend the defilement of their bodies as white patriarchal power put them in the place of white women to provide sexual pleasure for white men during the slav-ocracy [sic]. This was rape. . . . The cross is a reminder of how humans have tried throughout history to destroy visions of righting relationships that involve transformation of tradition and transformation of social relations and arrangements sanctioned by the status quo.[18]

The death of Jesus is not salvific, according to Williams, but it is his life which is redemptive. Again, the Gospels are read as though their narrative focus and apex were the stories of Jesus' ministry, miracles, and teachings, and if one could bypass the death of Christ and still have the Resurrection, that would be far preferable. Indeed, while the Resurrection may be a helpful piece of the narrative of Jesus to proclaim to black women, his death on the cross bears "nothing of God":

> The resurrection of Jesus and the kingdom of God theme in Jesus' ministerial vision provide black women with the knowledge that God has, through Jesus, shown human-kind how to live peacefully, productively, and abundantly in relationship. Humankind is therefore redeemed through Jesus' life and not through Jesus' death. There is nothing of God in the blood of the cross. God does not intend black women's surrogacy experience. . . . However, as Christians, black women cannot forget the cross. But neither can they glorify it. To do so is to make their exploitation sacred. To do so is to glorify sin.[19]

This critique presents itself as posing a theological question, that is, whether the image of the cross and the atoning sacrifice of Jesus contribute to violence, surrogacy experience, and abuse. However, the "question" in fact functions as an accusation, deemed true until proven false, and is in fact not a question at all. The critique assumes a priori that the images of the cross as atoning, the blood of Jesus as cleansing, the sacrifice of the Son of God as satisfying the wrath of God toward us, and the agony of Christ on the cross as substitution for the agony rightfully due us at the very least do not disallow and at worst contribute to the mounting violence and abuse in our society, in particular, violence against women and children at the hands of men. To assume this to be true without considering the story itself is to have already stepped outside the narrative scope of the canon.

Responding to such a charge, especially when the legitimacy of the charge is not a matter for reasoned debate and dialogue, is extremely difficult and for the most part has not been attempted within circles of feminist theological scholarship. However, such a response might be possible if first we were to admit that caricatures of atone-ment theories, or what we might call "heresies," may indeed possibly contribute to abuse and violence. How we would document such influence is another matter en-tirely. When and where such abuse and violence are perpetrated, the offenders must repent. While admitting the possibility of misuse, we must nevertheless point out the doctrinal safeguard against this misuse inherent in a narratival approach. That is, read-ing the Gospel stories in their canonical context as one great overarching narrative allows the New Testament emphasis on the once-for all character of the atoning work of Christ its power to prohibit, in effect, the transference of the task of redeeming sacrifice to anyone else.[20] This does not mean, of course, that abuse and violence will necessarily stop but that they will appear so terribly incongruent and obvious in their injustice and hypocrisy. Even in Roman Catholicism, where the claim can be made that the sacrifice of Jesus becomes ever contemporary in the celebration of the mass, the sacrifice is nevertheless not claimed to be "transferred" (except in instances deemed to be in error) to someone or something apart from Jesus of the Gospels and the bread and wine of his body and blood.

Another helpful element in the narratival reading of the cross in countering the charge is the extent to which the cross is often "narrated" in postbiblical tradition in terms of the doctrine of the Trinity. That is, the charge of "abusive Christology" can be also be countered by the claim, derived from a narratival reading, that theologically the cross cannot be separated from the incarnation. It follows from this that the cross cannot be adequately interpreted apart from the doctrine of the Trinity. At this point, we see the convergence of biblical interpretation and doctrinal formulation, for the cross in a narratival reading spills into discussion of the inner life of the Trinity. That is, the cross may indeed be incomprehensible apart from its "exegesis" within the context of a Trinitarian understanding of God's self-giving love. The cross can be "exegeted" via the doctrine of the Trinity as an agreement between God the Son and God the Father for the sake of the world, "an event for which the Father expressly sent him, and which he himself deliberately embraced."[21] The atoning work of Jesus on the cross is not to be interpreted as the hostility of God the Father vented on the Son, but as the self-giving of the Father in the Son through the love and power of the Holy Spirit. Such a self-giving draws an alienated and hostile humanity into the divine life, which could be done only by God's entering into that human alienation and hostility and overcoming it.

The charge of "abusive Christology," however, upon which the critique of Williams and others depends, is in part a result of and in part contributes to a materialist utilitarianism which judges doctrine on the basis of what it does for us rather than on the basis of what is says about God. This is not to say that the Christian community should not be concerned about the ethical and moral payout of its doctrinal commitments. Certainly, no one wants Christian doctrine to reap violence, but it is part of the logic of narrative interpretation that readers may trust that it will not do so. To question this is already to have stepped outside the logic of narrative interpretation and to have undercut the power of the doctrinal safeguard tied to narrative interpretation.

"Not All Who Say to Me, 'Lord, Lord' "

In addition to the problems presented by the incarnation, cross, and Resurrection, feminist theologians also face the difficulties posed by the claim to the lordship of Jesus. Feminist theologies seek to target and correct any instances of the reinscription of patriarchal hierarchies of domination and oppression and find in the claim that Jesus is the "Lord" of all to be yet another instantiation of this series of hierarchies inherent in patriarchy. Christianity, it is claimed, is:

afflicted with a hierarchical view of power that undercuts its understanding of love in its fullest incarnation—that we are all part of one another and cocreate each other at the depths of our being. In recognizing how we have been afflicted with the broken heart of patriarchy, we can begin to see the territories of connection beyond patriarchal powers. Heart is the guide into those new territories; erotic power is the energy of incarnate love.[22]

One might then wonder why feminists would not ultimately "give up" on this Jesus and let go of him and the community that worships him as "irredeemably patriarchal," as did Daphne Hampson, for example.[23] For many feminists such as Carter Heyward, Christianity is simply part of the fabric of their lives. They also may not be able to "let go" of Jesus, like Heyward, because they feel that Christology is so potentially damaging that one cannot leave it to anyone else's concern. Women must deal with Jesus, lest Jesus be used as a weapon against women:

> Am I then suggesting that Christians should have no Christ? . . . I believe not. The primary danger of faith in nonspecific revelation of what is beautiful, true, and just is that any of us can locate, name, and attach ourselves to whatever we want, or believe, to be most ultimate, best, highest, "divine." To each his/her own: Aryan supremacy, male headship, white superiority, private property, and national security can float with equal ease under the banner of Christian commitment or the logos of any symbol we may choose to employ: symbols of light, cleanliness, racial or moral purity; symbols of being "God's chosen people," of possessing a "promised land" or "kingdom" as ours and ours alone.[24]

Since there cannot be a Christianity without a Christ, feminists such as Heyward deem their task to be a reconstruction of "the Christ."

The Solution: Reconstruction

These factors render the very figure of Jesus problematic for most mainline feminist theologians. The fear of patriarchy bleeding through Jesus onto the church is the catalyst for creative reconstructions of Christology. Several different implicit models can be found within feminist theology for constructing Christologies.[25] The first, what I will call "internal apology," tends to offer rereadings of either biblical or traditional texts. In this way, Jesus can be redescribed as liberator, prophet, and overturner of patriarchy, who "has renounced this system of domination and seeks to embody in his person the new humanity of service and mutual empowerment."[26] In internal apology, Jesus is implicitly understood primarily as a character enacting his identity within the narrative of the Gospel stories. The narrative "center" of these stories is implicitly taken to be the healings and teachings, thus marking a shift in focus from the Gospel's own apex in the Passion accounts.[27] Jesus is an agent but an agent of a story that, while many of the details of that story may remain the same, has nevertheless in effect a different beginning, middle, and end. The second model engages in doctrinal relocation, such that Christology plays the part which is played by another doctrine within the web of belief. In this model, Jesus functions as a theological place holder. Here, the story in which he is an agent is implicitly perceived to be somewhat like an algebraic equation in which the properties of x could be satisfied with either one of two numbers or, in this case, one of two doctrinal loci: Christology or the doctrine of creation. To be sure, there are strong traditional warrants for proposing the link between Christology and creation. But Jesus in this model has little narrative importance, even if profound theological significance. The third model is closest to ancient allegorical reading, insofar as it is an exercise in independent imagination. In this third model, the focus is on the power of the incarnation found in relationship, love, and interdependence, which are deemed to be feminist values. Attention can thus be shifted away from Jesus himself either to the community gathered around him, the "Christa community," or to the mythic figure of Christa.[28] In the third model, Jesus is at best minimally understood as a character whose identity is shaped by the interplay of his actions and plot development, but he is the stand-in within the narrative framework of the Gospels for us and our community, such that the Gospels are really "about" us. Alternatively, he functions as a stand-in for an equally plausible (according to feminist methodology) hypothesized female character. In both the second and third models, the Gospels are not "about" Jesus at all; rather, he serves as an allegorical pointer to another dimension of reality, either a theological or ideal reality. The fourth, historical reconstruction, uses the methods and categories of modern biblical scholarship to reduce the offensiveness of the masculinity of Jesus. This is done either by use of the Jesus-of-History–Christ-of-Faith dichotomy, thus reducing the theological focus on the maleness of the incarnation, or by portraying Jesus in light of the Sophia-Wisdom tradition, thus bringing a feminine aspect into the category of the incarnation itself.[29] In the fourth model, Jesus is to some extent implicitly understood as a character within a set of narratives, but as a character he serves either as the stand-in for Sophia, whose identity he enacts after her suppression by patriarchal oppression, or for the Christ of Faith, who is deemed more interesting anyway. The Jesus of the Gospel narrative thus points away from himself either to Sophia or to the Christ of Faith, much the way John the Baptist points to Jesus in the famous Grünewald altarpiece depicting the scene in John 3. The lens through which the Gospel narratives are read here is a hyperobjectified historical-critical reconstruction. The first three models are discussed in the rest of this chapter, and the fourth is given a chapter of its own.

Internal Apology and Rereading Texts

In this first model, feminists seek to make an internal apology for Christian doctrine.[30] They do this by offering rereadings of biblical and/or traditional texts which would either help feminists see that some of the complaints they raise against these texts are not well founded and must be reexamined before the charges can be fully addressed, or by offering rereadings of the biblical model of Jesus such that he is less offensive to feminist sensibilities. Anne Carr and Rosemary Radford Ruether, respectively, are examples of practitioners of such an approach.

In her *Transforming Grace*, Anne Carr points out that Christian feminists can demonstrate that classical Christology is not, in truth, a threat to women, but that it can be shown through careful interpretation to be "supportive of the full humanity of women." However, she says, this does not eradicate the problem of the misuse of Christology, which can itself be harmful to women. She takes on the work of Rosemary Radford Ruether, who charges Aquinas with the fault of such misuse. According to Carr, Ruether's version of Aquinas's Christology maintains that only the male represents full human potential and that woman is originally, and not only after the Fall, a defective human being physically, morally, and mentally. Ruether's Aquinas holds that the incarnation of the Word of God in the male Jesus is not simply a historical, contingent fact but indicates that the male is, in himself and as "head" of woman, the fullness of the image of God. Ruether's Aquinas, says Carr, holds that because women cannot represent headship or leadership in society or in the church, it is ontologically required that the incarnation occur in a male body.[31] Carr then seeks to correct Reuther's reading:

> Little of this argument occurs in Aquinas' treatise on Christology but is derived from his discussions of human nature and sacramental priesthood. Like the rest of the tradition, his Christological statements are general, and emphasize the fullness of the divine and human natures in Christ. Yet when Aquinas' anthropology is incorporated with his Christology, the distortion is clear: the Christological emphasis on the truly human is skewed by androcentric bias. The logic of Aquinas' Christological pattern rests on the notion of "headship," which in one sense is an organic model in which Christ is the head of the body of the faithful; when considered in another way it is a hierarchical and dominating model that is used to justify the subordination of women.[32]

In other words, Carr does not necessarily disagree with Ruether but wants her reading of Aquinas to be more accurate and nuanced. The problem, then, according to Carr, is not with Aquinas's Christology but with his anthropology, and when the two are combined, the problems which Ruether points to arise. While this may sound like nit-picking to the feminist who has little stake in theology, if the church, especially the Roman Catholic Church, is ever to consider revising its position on women's ordination, at the very least, fair and accurate reading of the traditional texts would be necessary. Carr takes on this task and offers an internal apology of the pertinent traditional texts.

Rosemary Radford Ruether, in a different sample from her work, offers an internal apology for the scriptural texts, in particular, of their presentation of the person of Jesus. For Ruether, Jesus' identity is to be considered through the distinctive lens of his office as liberating prophet. According to Ruether, the Christology of Chalcedon is not a "faithful rendering of the messianic announcement of Jesus of Nazareth and his views of the coming Reign of God."[33] Classical Christology is thus a deformation of Jesus, and feminist Christology must reach back and strip off the layers of accreted dogma to uncover the liberating Jesus. According to Ruether, Jesus does not "evoke hope for the Davidic Messiah" but refuses the crowds' efforts to crown him king.[34] Instead of the religious authorities, he favors the lowly, the poor, and the oppressed. Jesus proclaims the nearness of the kingdom of God, which is neither nationalistic nor other-worldly. However, "Over the five centuries during which the Christian Church itself is transformed from a marginal sect within the messianic renewal movements of first-century Judaism into the new imperial religion of a Christian Roman Empire," Christology itself becomes deformed, beginning with the crucifixion.[35] The disciples' experience of the resurrected Lord allows them to reject the possibility that the crucifixion indicated a failure of Jesus' mission. Instead, his mission is rescued by God and lives in the present in the prophetic Spirit. The early Christian community experienced the power of this prophetic Spirit in their "ecstatic utterances and gifts of forgiveness and healing" and understood this prophetic Spirit to be the "Risen Lord alive in their midst." This stage of the prophetic community, according to Ruether, was superseded by the developing institutional hierarchy, which "cut off this ongoing speaking in the name of Christ."[36] It is now the task of feminist theology to recover this prophetic Jesus and to reclaim the vocation of the Christian community's prophetic speech and action in his name. In this community, women were equal participants. A "reencounter with the Jesus of the synoptic gospels" will prove that "Jesus renews the prophetic vision whereby the Word of God does not validate the existing social and religious hierarchy but speaks on behalf of the marginalized and despised groups of society."[37] Jesus thus liberates us from dualisms and hierarchies and calls us to renounce the claims of status and privilege. Ruether's vision of Jesus through the lens of liberating prophet intends thus to redeem him from the clutches of patriarchal hierarchies and schemes of domination.

Doctrinal Relocation: Christology to the Doctrine of Creation

Because of the scandal caused by the particularity of the doctrine of the incarnation, we find that the doctrine of incarnation itself is relocated in some feminist theologies and positioned in the place of the doctrine of creation. This is done to relieve stress on the masculinity of Jesus and to maximize his relation to all creation: "In a post-patriarchal context, I suggest, incarnation refers to an immanent, ongoing divine creation, preservation and regeneration of life. Where there is healing and affirmation of life, there is the redeeming body of God."[38] This offers a more universalistic, less narratively tied version of the understanding of incarnation. Here, the claim is not being made that God becomes incarnate in the man of Nazareth in any specifically irreplaceable or unique way, but that the character in the Gospel stories functions as type for the antitypes of incarnation available around us and within us as they manifest themselves in the "healing and affirmation of life." Cooey claims, and rightly so, that this retains a version of traditional Christian theology's insistence on Jesus' soteriological centrality, but for her this is so because it is Jesus who is the type against whose pattern we hold up for confirmation the antitypes of "incarnations" around us:

> An alternative view of the incarnation, one perhaps more attuned to both biblical and twentieth-century sensibilities, claims that Jesus saves us by directing our attention through the events of his life, death and resurrection, as narrated in scripture, to God at work throughout creation, upholding nature and acting through human activity in history, to restore and reconcile all life, including especially life usually considered the least noteworthy. Interpreted in this manner incarnation is always going on, but Jesus in relation to others remains pivotal as the specific revelatory source by which those who call their faith Christian come to recognize, and by grace, quite literally to remember

divine activity at work throughout nature and history. Jesus thus retains epistemological and soteriological centrality for Christian faith without reference to his ontological status, in this respect relieving him of the burden of idolatry.[39]

Jesus is central for soteriology and "remains pivotal" but in such a way that the logic or direction of the interpretation of the reality around us has been reversed. Cooey thus reconstructs an approach to the incarnation which opens the claims about God's presence in Jesus and makes them available to all instances in which we can recognize or "re-member" divine activity. This bears a vague resemblance to some views of Eastern Christianity. However, those views of Eastern Christianity which may be congruent with this generally do not encompass the concern for what Cooey and many feminist theologians see to be the need to "relieve" Jesus of the "burden of idolatry." This marks the feminist hesitation in front of the face of Jesus and returns us to Mary Daly's charge, "If God is man, then man is God." The risk that males in a patriarchal culture will abuse the doctrine of the incarnation, making idols of themselves, is too great to take, and so Cooey offers a "post-patriarchal" telling of this aspect of the Christian story.[40]

> I have maintained that [the doctrine of the Incarnation] is best understood as a claim stated in metaphorical language about a process, namely divine creativity, rather than a human person somehow infused with divine plasma. Taken at face value, I suggested, the doctrine represents a failed attempt to reject as heresy the denial of the human nature of Jesus. This failure leaves the doctrine open to charges of idolatry and nonsense. Nevertheless, the teaching reflects metaphorical imagination at work making up, making real, attempting to make sense, and further making value that remains central to Christian faith to this day. In short, the doctrine of the incarnation plays a major role in the making of Christian faith and therefore the making of Christians. It is appropriately re-envisioned, not discarded, in a post-patriarchal context.[41]

In addition to reconsidering the incarnation, for many of the same reasons, Cooey also takes on the task of tailoring Jesus' Resurrection for a post-patriarchal Christianity.[42] She seeks to reconstruct the understanding of the Resurrection, which she takes to be normative in contemporary and biblical texts in which it signifies "the survival of an individual ego." Cooey finds inadequate both fundamentalist and modern views of the Resurrection, which logically threaten the claim, she feels, that it is God who redeems:

> Just as the doctrine of the incarnation can be interpreted to support docetism in ways that lead to idolatry, so the creedal claim to resurrection, taken literally or as a metaphor for the survival of individual human personality in some form, likewise disguises yet another attempt to circumvent the full implications of human embodiment, in this instance in ways that reveal a tendency to spiritual narcissism. In either case death becomes a necessary but merely temporary inconvenience on the way to eternal self-perpetuation. Furthermore, both fundamentalist and modern views run the risk of denying that God who redeems is also the God who creates; they do so by denying the full material reality of creation, as this creation involves coming to be and passing away in continual change. Whatever the resurrection may have meant or continues to mean to Christians, the survival of an individual ego for all time, especially when made the driving force of human agency, reflects a response to death by way of its denial. Concern for

survival beyond our own death means ironically that we continue to live in bondage to death.[43]

While it is clear that Cooey has correctly observed some of the weaknesses of fundamentalist and modern views, it is curious that she does not seek a view which is closer to the biblical narrative's portrayal (or alternatively that of the classical tradition) of what "resurrection" signifies in the context of the canonical scriptures. Of course, the "scandal of particularity" has historically spun, as if with centrifugal force, its sufferers further and further from the texture of the biblical narrative.

Like Cooey, other feminist theologians, when faced with the difficulties posed by traditional Christologies, attempt to shift the locus of incarnation from narrative specificities of the Gospel stories about Jesus to the more general categories of human existence. This, so feminist theologies promise, allows for an uplifting of divine immanence in creation. The work of Sallie McFague, in particular, has been noted for this turn. The story of Jesus for McFague becomes "paradigmatic" for the immanence of the divine life in all of creation:

> From the story of Jesus of Nazareth and his followers we can gain some sense of the forms or patterns with which Christians might understand divine immanence. That story, both in its beginnings and its history, suggests a shape to the body; needless to say, other religious traditions would propose very different shapes, and even within Christianity, many variations exist. The shape suggested is obviously a construction, not a description, and is persuasive only in light of a range of criteria. This shape provides a purpose or goal for creation—something we could not find in evolutionary history. From the paradigmatic story of Jesus we will propose that the direction of creation is toward inclusive love for all, especially the oppressed, the outcast, the vulnerable.[44]

This attempts to hold on to the normativity of the person of Jesus, while converting the claim to any finality or fixedness in the revelation in him into a claim for, again, Jesus' serving as the type to the greater antitype present in the divine life in all of creation. In addition, since McFague is able to retain classical Christianity's claim to God's purposes and goal for creation, she can reconstruct eschatological claims to fit the feminist narrative. That goal, stated in Ephesians 1:10 as "to unite all things in Him," becomes in McFague's work "inclusive love for all, especially the oppressed." This is done, with regard to Christology, via two specific moves:

> the first is to relativize the incarnation in relation to Jesus of Nazareth and the second is to maximize it in relation to the cosmos. In other words, the proposal is to consider Jesus as paradigmatic of what we find everywhere: everything that is is the sacrament of God (the universe as God's body), but here and there we find that presence erupting in special ways. Jesus is one such place for Christians, but there are other paradigmatic persons and events—and the natural world, in a way different from the self-conscious openness to God that persons display, is also a marvelous sacrament in its diversity and richness.[45]

Making Jesus the "paradigm," in McFague's terms, conflicts with the classical claim that Jesus is the unique "eruption" of God's presence of which all other eruptions are but instances or examples and against which they are to be compared and ultimately judged. What does this mean for how Scripture is read? In effect, it is another instance of the reversal of the flow of interpretation basic to classical reading of Scripture. While McFague wants to hold on to the centrality of the particularity of Jesus as the Gospels present him, she equally wants Scripture to be a resource and not a privileged norm, a *norma normata* but not a *norma normans*.

> Our first step, then, is to read the central story of Christian faith from the perspective of the organic model. The Christic paradigm must precede the cosmic Christ; the hints and clues for an embodied theology should arise from the particular, concrete insights and continuities of the tradition's basic story. This in no way privileges Scripture as the first or last word, but only as the touchstone text that Christians return to as a resource (not *the* source) for helping them to construct for their own time the distinctiveness of their way of being in the world.[46]

Since Jesus functions primarily as a paradigm, his theological significance can be relocated under the doctrine of creation as the cosmic Christ, the embodiment of God maximized in terms of creation and minimized in terms of the story of Jesus.

Allegorical Reconstruction: Christa and Christa-Community

The third model of addressing the reconstructive task is simultaneously an alternative to "letting go" of Jesus (as Carter Heyward said she could not do) and a solution to the problem of the potential oppressiveness of a male savior. One example of a feminist allegorical reconstruction of Christology is illustrated in "Christa," the female crucifix figure by the British sculptor Edwina Sandys. The Christ in female body hanging on the cross that was sculpted in 1975 for the United Nations' Year of the Woman, Christa was the source of much controversy after she was displayed in Lent of 1984 at Saint John the Divine Cathedral in New York City.[47] By now, of course, Christa has become a commonplace within feminist theology. She was originally greeted with both positive and negative reactions. Some reacted negatively to the woman's body on the cross, finding it sacrilegious. Others reacted negatively out of fear that she represented the glorification of women's suffering and death. Still other feminists, such as Carter Heyward, reacted positively to Christa: "She can represent for christian women precisely what the church has crucified with a vengeance, and what we must now raise up in our lives:the erotic as power and the love of God as embodied by erotically empowered women."[48]

Still, even Heyward in her general approval of the figure does have some hesitations. They are only marginally theological, however, tending to the practical side of theology, or the political side of the expedient, depending on how one views them. Heyward's worry here is that even Christa, if she is venerated in the same manner as is Jesus, could present the danger of idolatry, as feminist theologians accuse classical Christology of allowing:

> Like all religious symbols, Christa should always be transitional—an image to help keep us open and growing in our respect and love for erotically empowering women and men. We cannot get stuck on her as the redemptive image, even for those of us who are christians. To reify any one symbol is to give ourselves permission to stop growing and

changing. Christa is no one among us and never will be. She is no one child, woman or man. She is no one earthcreature, seacreature, skycreature.[49]

It is interesting here that Heyward acknowledges the non-narratival identity of Christa and that this should be part of her concern. However, this is not the main problem which worries Heyward about Christa; rather, the problem lies in normativity of the use of any one religious image or symbol.

Of course, Heyward is one of the bolder proponents of feminist theology, and one of the few who will admit openly and even rejoice in the discontinuities it presents with orthodox Christianity.[50] The discontinuity with orthodox Christology, then, is a badge of honor, for it signifies the very redemption of the orthodox versions of the Gospels from their destructive potential. But, as with orthodox Christology, Heyward wants to maintain the narratival specificity of the character Jesus within the Gospels. She understands this to be normative for Christian faith. The narratival specificity for Heyward, however, does not necessarily lead the Christian to proclaim the lordship of Christ, Jesus as the first fruits of the Resurrection of the dead, or his overcoming sin and death by his cross and rising. Instead, the character Heyward understands to be specifically narrated in the Gospel stories is, much more simply, one who knew and loved God:

> Christian faith must, I believe, point directly and particularly to the human life, faith, and teachings of Jesus as Christ, rather than simply to a free-floating symbol of what is valuable to us. . . . The Jesus story is about a person who knew and loved a God of justice. This is its particular message. This is its creative power. This is the only truly moral raison d'être for the Christian church, and a powerful and compelling one it is. They who have ears to hear, let them hear.[51]

As an alternative to suggesting a "Christa" figure to represent this "person who knew and loved a God of Justice," another example of allegorical reconstruction considers Jesus under the category "Christa-community," such as is suggested by Rita Nakashima Brock. She, like many mainline feminist theologians, understands traditional Christian focus on Jesus' role in Redemption to be misplaced, for she sees it as reflecting "an androcentric preoccupation with heroes."[52] Since she understands Christology to be "the logical explanation of Christian faith claims about divine presence and salvific activity in human life," she can easily engage in christological reflection without confining herself to the depiction of Jesus within the Gospel narratives, who apparently represents a larger reality than himself anyway (e.g., "salvific activity in human life").[53] Brock therefore suggests that, rather than engaging in some misplaced form of hero worship, we consider Christology under the rubric of community. Certainly, many strands of traditional Christianity understand the Holy Spirit to be powerfully present within the community of faith or that Jesus is present with the community in the eucharistic feast. This is not what Brock is suggesting, however. Instead, the community is itself the "healing center" of Christianity, such that the community is, in a sense, our true redeemer, if the word redeemer would even be appropriate here:

> In moving beyond a unilateral understanding of power, I will be developing a christology not centered in Jesus, but in relationship and community as the whole-making, healing center of Christianity. In that sense, Christ is what I am calling Christa/Community. Jesus

participates centrally in this Christa/Community, but he neither brings erotic power into being nor controls it. He is brought into being through it and participates in the co-creation of it. Christa/Community is a lived reality expressed in relational images. Hence, Christa/Community is described in the images of events in which erotic power is made manifest.[54]

Jesus, the character in the Gospel narratives, in effect becomes an allegorical marker for the Christian community, "of which Jesus is one historical part."[55] This is not to claim that Jesus the Christ is the sum of the individual members of the Christian community but that Jesus is one piece of the Christ, which itself is the Christa-community. What then becomes of the narrative moments of the Gospels, such as the Passion and Resurrection accounts? They, too, become allegorized:

> The death of Jesus reveals the brokenheartedness of patriarchy. His dying is a testimony to the powers of oppression. It is neither salvific nor essential. It is tragic. . . . The resurrection of an abandoned Jesus is a meaningless event. . . . The resurrection of Jesus is a powerful image of the need for solidarity among and with victims of oppressive powers. The resurrection affirms that no one person alone can overcome brokenness. Each of us lives in each other in Christa/Community. In caring for each other and in passionately affirming erotic power, we struggle on our journey to create spaces for it to flourish.[56]

This model, indeed, flourishes quite well entirely apart from the narrative context of the Gospels, not to mention the rest of the canon. Certainly, no claims to the authorizing of this model would need to appeal to the scriptures. This is, in principle, part of the appeal of the model.

These first three models of addressing the stumbling block which a male Jesus poses to feminist theologians involve creative reappropriation of themes present within the biblical narrative. The next model to be addressed in the following chapter takes its point of departure from historical-critical categories and research. Thus, while the previous models drew mainly on themes from the biblical narrative, we will see what historical reconstruction can offer feminist Christologies.

5

---◆◇◆---

FEMINIST CHRISTOLOGY AND
HISTORICAL RECONSTRUCTIONS

> The simplest and most basic meaning of the symbol of Goddess is the
> acknowledgement of the legitimacy of female power as a beneficent and
> independent power. A woman who echoes Ntosake Shange's dramatic state-
> ment, "I found God in myself and I loved her fiercely," is saying "Female
> power is strong and creative." She is saying that the divine principle, the
> saving and sustaining power, is in herself, that she will no longer look to
> men or male figures as saviors. The strength and independence of female
> power can be intuited by contemplating ancient and modern images of the
> Goddess.[1]

We saw in the previous chapter that the first three models of feminist reconstructions of Christology—internal apology, doctrinal relocation, and allegorical reconstruction—develop themes and motifs present in the biblical narrative. This
was apparent in, for example, the presentation of Jesus as a prophet (internal apology),
of Christ as agent in creation (doctrinal relocation), and of Christ's presence within
the community of faith (allegorical reconstruction). The fourth model of feminist
reconstruction to be considered in this chapter departs from these, insofar as it develops and furthers insights drawn from historical-critical scholarship. Here, we will
see the use of historical reconstructions of the "Hebrew Goddess" and of the figure
of Sophia within the Bible to reconstruct Christology for feminist purposes. In addition, we will find feminist uses of the historical-critical dichotomy of the Jesus of
history versus the Christ of faith for feminist reconstruction of doctrine.

Historical Reconstructions of the Feminine Divine, the
"Hebrew Goddess," and Sophia

Sophia, the English transliteration of the Greek word for "wisdom," is a theological
topic central to both Old Testament and New Testament. Old Testament Wisdom,
which, of course, influences New Testament discussions of Wisdom and its christological use, has been defined as the "practical knowledge of the laws of life and of
the world, based upon experience."[2] Feminist theologians have much material for
constructive work here, not only for the feminine figure occasionally represented by
Sophia within the Bible but also for the turn to experience as guide to wisdom. Sophia
has become an important theological construct over the past ten years in feminist

theology. On the more popular and pastoral level, Sophia made a much-debated appearance at the ReImagining Conference of 1993, which incorporated rituals, songs, and prayers to invoke her presence and blessing.[3] On the academic level as well, Sophia has been enjoying a swell in interest and discussion. Elisabeth Schüssler Fiorenza's earlier book *In Memory of Her* began to explore the possibilities of developing and expanding on Wisdom Christology in feminist theology, and one of her more recent books, *Jesus: Miriam's Child, Sophia's Prophet*, takes up Sophialogy as a central element in her project of a critical feminist Christology. In addition, the award-winning *She Who Is* by Elizabeth Johnson has brought Sophia into the theological spotlight.[4] In the field of biblical studies, the second volume of Elisabeth Schüssler Fiorenza's feminist commentary project, *Searching the Scriptures*, is almost entirely devoted to listening for the voice of Sophia in canonical and noncanonical writings.[5]

The forays into truly creative feminist theology that bear Sophia's name, such as those offered by Elisabeth Schüssler Fiorenza and Elizabeth Johnson, cannot be passed off as mere flights of imaginative fancy. While, of course, they make use of the imagination in theological reflection, the proposals they offer are also grounded in historical reconstructions of the feminine divine. Basic, then, to the work of such feminists who explore the possible uses of Sophia for Christology—and for the doctrine of God, as we shall see in chapter 6—is the scholarship of Joan Chamberlain Engelsman, Merlin Stone, Raphael Patai, and, to a certain extent, Elaine Pagels, to mention just a few names. In the field of archaeology, or archaeomythology, the work of Marija Gimbutas also intersects religious investigation of Sophia and goddess cults. Before examining the feminist theological uses of Sophialogy in reconstructing Christology and the doctrine of God, we will therefore review some of the historical theses which undergird the later theological work.

Merlin Stone's book, *When God Was a Woman*, first published in 1976, provides a basis on which some of the arguments for the reclaiming of the suppressed Sophia-goddess are built, implicitly or explicitly. Stone proceeds on the basis of the assumption that early historic periods of human development show evidence of goddess worship and proposes that such goddess worship was then suppressed by the monotheism of Judaism and Christianity:

> The Great Goddess—the Divine Ancestress—had been worshipped from the beginnings of the Neolithic periods of 7000 BC until the closing of the last Goddess temples, about AD 500. Some authorities would extend Goddess worship as far into the past as the Upper Paleolithic Age of about 25,000 BC. . . . Most significant is the realization that for thousands of years both religions existed simultaneously—among closely neighboring peoples. Archaeological, mythological and historical evidence all reveal that the female religion, far from naturally fading away, was the victim of centuries of continual persecution and suppression by the advocates of the newer religions which held male deities as supreme.[6]

Goddess worship, argues Stone, is therefore closer to the "original" human religious impulse. Relying on the assumption that the oldest is the best, Stone's theory of a goddess cult which preceded male-deitied cults has been used by feminists to critique traditional monotheistic religions. The critique often argues that, having unjustly stamped out the first human religious impulses simply because the divine was figured in feminine terms, the traditional monotheistic religions are morally inferior to the goddess cults. Here, the victim, that is Goddess, comes out the moral victor even if the religious failure. Tangentially supporting this idea is the archaeomythological theory of Marija Gimbutas, which posited a pre-Indo-European civilization in Neolithic Europe. This civilization, Gimbutas claimed, was matristic, egalitarian, communal and peace loving, artistic, and primarily goddess worshiping.[7]

Raphael Patai, whose book, *The Hebrew Goddess*, contributes to the debate over the feminine divine within Judaism in particular, makes a similar case. He suggests that, insofar as Judaism is a community rather than a politically structured institution, such as the Roman Catholic Church, the very fact of the presence of the Goddess within the Hebrew Bible necessitates that she be seen as a valid presence within Judaism. That is, belief in the Goddess is simply a minority belief within a range of equally valid ancient Hebrew views of God. The Goddess is therefore, according to Patai, not to be seen as an externally imported pagan phenomenon, but the "Hebrew Goddess":

> In contrast to the Roman Catholic faith with its single body, the Church, Judaism has never developed a monolithic structure which could superimpose its authority upon all Jewish communities in the many lands of their diaspora. . . . No such unity exists in Judaism, nor has it ever existed, with the possible exception of a brief period when the Great Sanhedrin exercised central authority in Jerusalem. . . . The feminine numina discussed in this book must, therefore, be considered part of the Hebrew-Jewish religion, whether they were admitted into the "official" formulation of the faith or accepted only by the simple people, against whose beliefs and practices the exponents of the former never ceased to thunder.[8]

The fact that the Hebrew Goddess may have been suppressed in the biblical canon, as Ackerman points out is the case with the Queen of Heaven in Jeremiah, is all the more reason to remember her as a lost voice within the ancient Hebrew faith.

The general view of Stone, Patai, and others that the original goddess cults were squelched by monotheistic worship thus links the demise of the goddess with sexist power plays of the cult of the male Yahweh. The goddess is oppressed by the authorities of male-deity cults and is the unhappy, innocent victim of the Hebrew God in particular. Thus, even in the very rise and origin of Jewish and Christian faith, patriarchy is shown to be a controlling factor. The Jewish and Christian faiths are thus cast as potentially (at the very least) "irredeemably patriarchal."

Based in part on Merlin Stone's thesis, Joan Chamberlain Engelsman's influential book, *The Feminine Dimension of the Divine*, first published in 1979, then applies the Jungian categories of the archetype and the collective unconscious to interpret what she sees to be the existence, repression, and subsequent reemergence of the divine feminine in Western Christian theology. According to Jungian psychology, archetypes such as mother, the anima, and the maid are structures of the collective unconscious, and as such they will always seek expression regardless of the conscious sanctioning or inhibiting of their expression. These archetypes emerge in part, according to Engelsman, in the feminine divine. Using the results of contemporary biblical scholarship, she points to underlying traditions of the feminine divine, such as those of Sophia, which were woven into the biblical material and formed some of the basis for the New Testament's Christologies. Sophia began, according to Engelsman's theory, as a personified hypostasis of God and grew in importance for the Hebrew faith from the fourth to the first century B.C.E. At this high point, says Engelsman, Sophia's power was similar to that of any Hellenistic goddess. The latent divine feminine expressed in Sophia was then repressed in the Hebrew scriptures, according to Englesman, by being subordinated to Yahweh as his firstborn of all creation.

Englesman's theory continues, however, to argue that Christian theology begins to allow for a reemergence of the divine feminine insofar as Jesus is identified as Sophia. This is not a happy circumstance for Sophia, however, because for the most part Jesus eclipses her by absorbing her within his male Messiah figure. Engelsman refers to key New Testament texts, particularly in Paul, Matthew, and John, to illustrate how this (hypothesized) repressed figure apparently reemerges. She then points to the work of the second-century theologians Justin Martyr, Origen, and Clement, in which this reemergence continues. The reemergence of the oppressed feminine dimension of the divine becomes especially problematic, however, says Englesman, with the Arian controversy. If Jesus and Sophia (Wisdom) are one, but Sophia is argued to be less than God as the firstborn of all creation (so the Arians held of Jesus), then Jesus-as-Sophia is less than God. In an attempt to reject Arian Christology, then, "orthodoxy" tends, according to Engelsman, to repress further the divine feminine. Insofar as Jesus' identification with Sophia was fuel for the subordinationist Christology opposed by the orthodox wing, Sophialogy was rejected.

Indeed, central to the debate over the supposed "suppression" of the feminine divine is the contention that not only Arianism but also other "heretical" movements were kindly disposed to females, whether as human or divine agents. Because of this supposed benign stance toward women, the "orthodox" deemed such movements heretical to protect patriarchal claims, hierarchies, and power structures. This notion is given credence by the highly popular work of Elaine Pagels, who lauds the gnostic movements as being more favorable to the feminine than the patriarchal "orthodox." Her popularly acclaimed work on gnosticism has provided an academically credible grounding for the belief that women were treated more equally in gnostic Christianity than they were in orthodox circles. Just how adequate her depiction is of gnosticism, however, is a matter of no small debate. Pagels comes to her thesis regarding the beneficence of gnosticism toward the feminine, both human and divine, in part via the (implicit) assumption that a relatively uncomplicated, one-to-one correspondence obtains between views of God and views of humanity. She then links this assumption with the observation that in many gnostic circles God was imaged in both male and female terms:

> In simplest form, many gnostic Christians correlate their description of God in both masculine and feminine terms with a complementary description of human nature. . . . Gnostic Christians often take the principle of equality between men and women into the social and political structures of their communities. The orthodox pattern is strikingly different.[9]

However, it has been pointed out that there is no clear evidence (1) that gnostic Christians understood God to be equally male and female and (2) that this divine equality translates into the sociological realm.[10] It cannot be stated without qualification that the gnostic writings affirm both the masculine and the feminine, whether

human creatures or divine agents. The gnostic writings, themselves far from a monolithic corpus, also abound in antifemale statements that make the "problematic" New
Testament passages about women pale in comparison to their own misogyny. For
example, we find in the *Gospel of Thomas* the following misogynistic words on the lips
of Peter and Jesus: "Peter said to them, 'Let Mary leave us, because women are not
worthy of the Life.' Jesus said, 'Look, I shall guide her so that I will make her male,
in order that she also may become a living spirit, being like you males. For every
woman who makes herself a male will enter the Kingdom of Heaven'" (*Gospel of
Thomas* 114). Pagels also notes other texts which contradict her thesis, for example,
from the *Book of Thomas the Contender* of the Nag Hammadi texts, "Woe to you who love
intimacy with womankind, and polluted intercourse with it," and from *Dialogue of the
Savior*, in which Jesus warns the disciples to "destroy the works of femaleness."[11] These
statements do not serve to uphold what Pagels considers a "principle of equality
between men and women." Far less can it be proven that they take this principle
"into the social and political structures of their communities" as Pagels contends.[12] In
fact, as Daniel Hoffman points out, only one stream of Valentinianism actually believed
that the supreme god was a dyad, in contrast to Pagels's thesis about divine gender
equality in gnostic thought:

> Only within [this one strand of Valentinian thought] would it be possible to refer to
> "God the Father/God the Mother," since other references to the Mother in the Nag
> Hammadi texts or Church Fathers refer to a female aeon within the Pleroma, or to some
> other female deity lower in hierarchy than the highest God and Father of the universe
> in Gnostic thought.[13]

As Hoffman convincingly demonstrates, to assume a more benign regard for the female sex in Gnosticism seems to require bracketing some of the evidence. In addition,
Pagels's thesis itself can, indeed, backfire when one uses it to attempt to secure for
women a more powerful and active role in religious life. For example, crediting
women's religious equality to gnosticism has fueled arguments against women's ordination on the basis of its linkage with heretical movements.[14] The argument can and
has been used against women, even when the intent is the opposite.

Englesman, then, follows a logic similar to that of Pagels's theory about the "oppression" inflicted on the feminine-divine cults by patriarchal orthodox detractors.
This is clear in her suggestion that it was the Arian controversy which undermined
sophiological Christology:

> Certainly Sophiology became an undertow, dragging Christ away from any true equiva-
> lence with God [the] Father. Thus, what promised to be such a fruitful addition to
> Christological thinking proved to be disastrous. In fact, the danger of misunderstanding
> the relationship between Father and Son seemed to increase the more Sophiology was
> used as a basis for Christology. Had Sophia been recognized in Jewish writings as co-
> equal with Yahweh, the opposite would have been true: then the identification of Christ
> with Sophia would have reduced the tendencies toward subordinationism. Since this was
> not the case, the early church fathers eventually had to redefine their Christology by
> abandoning all reference to Jesus as the incarnate Wisdom of God. This redefinition
> amounts to a second repression of Sophia. The feminine dimension of the divine was
> initially repressed by ascribing her attributes to Jesus. During the second and third cen-

turies, Wisdom returned as a more overt component of Christology until it became apparent that her status was a severe handicap to the development of a trinitarian Christianity. At this point Sophia was re-repressed in orthodox circles and disappeared from the Western theological tradition. . . . Thus, in many ways, it is possible to characterize the Arian controversies as Sophia's revenge. The theft of her attributes, powers and functions now contaminated Christology by casting Jesus in the same relationship with God the Father that she had been confined to by the scrupulous monotheism of the Jews.[15]

It is orthodox Christianity which therefore wipes out (or "represses" in psychoanalytic terms) what Engelsman considers the positive contributions of Sophialogy to Christology.[16]

Engelsman believes that the expression of the feminine dimension of God, which struggled throughout the millennia to surface in the collective unconscious, is now returning to our collective unconscious via the feminist movement and its analogues within modern theology. She acknowledges the debt of this return to the thought of Nietzsche and Feuerbach and marks the full impact of the repression in Western Christianity of the divine feminine with the dogma of the Assumption of the Virgin Mary (1950) and the rise of the feminist movement in the 1960s. These moments act, in Engelsman's view, as the eye-opener to the extent of the repression of the feminine divine and therefore signal its potential reemergence. The collective unconscious can now engage in the psychological work it had been trying to do all along: to project à la Feuerbach but, in this case, to project the feminine divine:

> Why this has happened now is probably as unanswerable a question as why the feminine was repressed in the first place. It may very well be, as psychotherapists suggest, that both are the result of psychic necessity. If that is true, there is little point in either congratulating ourselves for our current insight or in blaming those in the past for their repressive attitudes. What does seem necessary is to explore and evaluate the new gestalt which now seems to be emerging.[17]

According to Engelsman, the repressed Sophia reemerges in the collective unconscious, as will any Jungian archetype, according to the theory. The feminine divine itself reemerges in the specific doctrinal loci of Mariology, ecclesiology, and Christology. Engelsman predicted that the areas of systematic theology which will be affected by what appears to be this nascent shift in theological symbolism will be the doctrine of the Trinity, the nature and scope of evil, Mariology, anthropology, and the apophatic dimension of spirituality and theology. It is interesting to note that on this score her theory has shown itself capable of predicting the current trends in theology.

Not all feminist theologians, however, follow Engelsman's Jungian theory of repression, even those who are deeply committed to the tasks of feminist theology.[18] For example, another way of exploring the "reemerging" of the suppressed feminine divine is to see the biblical canon itself as the vehicle which allows for and encourages this reemergence. This is, in part, the view of Gail Paterson Corrington. She notes that Job shares with other traditional Jewish Wisdom teaching the belief that Wisdom as part of the deity is present at creation and thus preexists the created order. Here she can point to Proverbs 8:22–31 and the Prologue to the Gospel of John. She notes that in Job 28 Wisdom is portrayed not as an independent agent but as an attribute of God, even an object or creature generated by God. It is with Proverbs, according to

Corrington, that "wisdom takes on the personification that is suggested by its gram-matical gender: 'It' (wisdom) becomes 'She' (Wisdom)."[19] It is thus the scriptures themselves which lean toward the emergence of Sophia, and the reemergence of Sophia can therefore be furthered by careful examination and rereading of biblical texts. This is simply to point out that, whether or not we accept Engelsman's theory, we can nevertheless argue for the presence of the feminine divine within the biblical canon itself.

Sophia in Feminist Theology

The "prophetic" vision first proclaimed by Engelsman is now seeing confirmation in the work of feminist theologians such as Elisabeth Schüssler Fiorenza and Elizabeth Johnson. Both of these Roman Catholic scholars, the former trained in biblical studies and the latter in theology, engage in constructing theologies which uphold the values of feminism by examining the relationship between Jesus and the biblical Sophia. According to Johnson, Sophia is the remedy for the damage caused by patriarchal claims about Jesus' exclusive identity as Son of the Father:

> The christology of Jesus Sophia shatters the male dominance carried in exclusive language about Jesus as the eternal male Logos or Son of the Father, enabling articulation of even a high incarnational christology in strong and gracious female metaphors. . . . [The con-fession that Jesus Sophia is the Christ] also witnesses to the truth that the beloved com-munity shares in this christhood, participates in the living and dying and rising of Christ to such an extent that it too has a christomorphic character. Challenging a naive physi-calism which collapses the totality of the Christ into the human man Jesus, metaphors such as the Body of Christ (1 Cor. 12:12–27) and the branches abiding in the vine (Jn. 15:1–11) expand the reality of Christ to include all of redeemed humanity, sisters and brothers, still on the way.[20]

In the work of such theologians, we see the emergence of a "new paradigm" for theology which attempts via theological reflection on Sophia to undo what is seen to be the stranglehold of patriarchy on Christianity in particular.

Of course, it was not feminists who first "discovered" a Sophia-Christology in the New Testament. The allegedly "patriarchal" scholarship first focused attention on Jesus as Sophia.[21] New Testament scholarship has hypothesized (and broadly accepted, al-though a minority has challenged) that Q, or the sayings source, contains some of the oldest Jesus traditions. Within Q, traditions have been traced which depict the graciousness of God as divine Sophia, or divine Wisdom. The Gospel of Matthew goes as far as identifying Sophia with Jesus, while in Luke Jesus and John are depicted as the preeminent children of Sophia.[22] Thus, it is argued, the oldest traditions of the New Testament reflect this Sophialogy: "The earliest Christian theology is sophialogy. It was possible to understand Jesus' ministry and death in terms of God-Sophia, be-cause Jesus probably understood himself as the prophet and child of Sophia."[23] The language of Jewish Wisdom theology, it is claimed, in effect "baptizes" goddess lan-guage and uses it to speak of Yahweh himself. That is, Wisdom theology does not posit a second divine power to compete with Yahweh but takes up the language of pagan goddesses to speak of Yahweh, thus, in effect, subverting paganism.[24] Biblical Sophialogy, argue the proponents of Sophia, therefore is not "pagan" but uproots paganism, much as the Gospel of John's language world subverts gnostic theology: "Divine Sophia is Israel's God in the language and Gestalt of the goddess. . . . Goddess language is employed to speak about the one God of Israel whose gracious goodness is divine Sophia."[25] Biblical Sophialogy does not therefore threaten monotheism, as some of its detractors would argue. Feminist theology is not on thin ice in this respect.

Jesus, Prophet of Sophia

In one of her most creative works, *Jesus: Miriam's Child, Sophia's Prophet*, Elisabeth Schüssler Fiorenza develops the work begun in *In Memory of Her*, her investigations into the theological usefulness of Sophialogy. She does not simply attempt to trace a Wisdom Christology but builds one by using the traces available in the New Testament. This points to one of the most refreshing features of her work: she is one of the few mainline feminist theologians to claim openly the disjuncture between traditional reading of Scripture and her own feminist reading. She is not merely constructing according to the norms set by the tradition but attempting to build an entirely new paradigm. In fact, she rejoices in the differences between traditional reading of Scripture and her own, for they are the mark of the true feminist theologian:

> The image I want to suggest is that of the feminist theologian as troublemaker, as a resident alien, who constantly seeks to destabilize the centers, both the value-free, ostensibly neutral research ethos of the academy and the dogmatic authoritarian stance of patriarchal religion. Feminists can do so, I suggest, by rewriting and refashioning academic and ecclesial discourses from a critical feminist perspective of liberation. Feminist theologians should not situate their theological work on the boundaries and in the margins but should move it into the center of academy and religion. . . . In order to intervene effectively in malestream theoretical and theological practices, feminist discourses must become bilingual, speaking the languages the our intellectual-theological "fathers" as well as the dialectics of our feminist "sisters."[26]

Insofar as she claims that the feminist theologian is called to "troublemaking," Schüssler Fiorenza would clearly not agree about the inherent value of what we have referred to in this study as narrative reading. That is, she might well agree with us that feminist theology involves and, indeed, requires a non-narrative reading of the Bible, but she would differ insofar as she sees this as something to be celebrated rather than a cause for concern. However, it is not clear from her writing that the observations about the traditional reading of the Bible as narrative are part of her grid for understanding what she calls "malestream theology," her term for what we have been calling classical theology:

> Malestream theology insists that the Bible proclaims G*d as male and reveals his incarnation in the man Jesus of Nazareth and that such an assertion does not deny women's dignity and invaluable contributions to church and society. Rather, it simply upholds the particularity of G*d's historical revelation in Jesus Christ. To be a Christian requires one to believe that masculine G*d-language and the historical maleness of Jesus constitute ultimate revelation.[27]

Whether this is an adequate portrayal of "malestream" or classical theology is debatable. Indeed, what she seems to think reflects malestream theology is "the Christology of Jesus the great individual," which, to be sure, is an important element in modern Christologies but not in classical christologies.[28] In fact, Jesus-the-great-individual is representative of the Christology of specifically non-narrative theology. What is clear is that she believes a paradigm shift is needed and that the modes and norms of malestream theology and biblical studies cannot be allowed to govern the construction of the new paradigm:[29]

> Hence, its criteria of validation [of the reconceptualization of christological biblical discourses and Christian identity constructions] cannot be derived simply by observing the methodological procedures of biblical studies or by complying with the theological principles of dogmatics. Rather the theological criteria can be found in the embodied potential of text and intellectual frameworks to engender processes of interpretation and praxis that can transform kyriocentric mind-sets and structures of domination. In short, such a theological interest in the liberation of all wo/men must determine all the intellectual frameworks of biblical studies in particular and of christological studies in general and not simply those of feminist studies.[30]

If we are to understand fully the new paradigm presented in the work of Elisabeth Schüssler Fiorenza, it is important to hold in mind that she is not interested in simply digging up bits of evidence of a "feminist remnant tradition" as though then displaying these bits within the existing framework of Christian theological discourse would lead to emancipation of women and men from the entrapment of kyriocentric patriarchal theology. Rather, she engages in "feminist historical reconstruction," which involves a constructive task not within the embrace of the more descriptive task just described. The radicality of the task required points to the dangers inherent in tracing the Sophia traditions in Jewish Wisdom literature and in the New Testament. This literature was "shaped to serve the kyriarchal interests of elite men," and tracing anything within it is therefore potentially harmful to women.[31]

> In light of the overwhelming androcentric shape and kyriocentric framework of the texts that speak of Divine Wisdom, we must ask whether it is possible in a feminist exegetical-theological "alchemy" to transform such a figure clothed in kyriocentric language in a way that she can once again not only develop her freeing power in feminist theologies but also have a liberating function in emancipatory struggles for a more just world. How can we trace the submerged spirit of Divine Sophia in biblical writings in such a way that the theological possibilities offered by Wisdom, the Divine Woman of Justice, but never quite realized in history, can be realized? How can we reconstitute this tradition in such a way that the rich table of Sophia can provide food and drink, nourishment and strength in the struggles for transforming kyriarchy?[32]

This makes it clear that Schüssler Fiorenza wants to bring into being something that once existed only in nuce, to pull back the tradition and start over from the point at which Sophia was suppressed and subverted, as a knitter who realizes a stitch has been dropped must unravel and start again. In spite of the need for unraveling, which will require that our hands touch this kyriarchal fabric and thus potentially be stained by it, Schüssler Fiorenza nevertheless values the emancipatory power potentially available through these traditions to express "the need of women for a powerful divine savior figure."[33]

In order to do this constructive critical work, she retraces the theological roots of Wisdom in postexilic Jewish circles in Egypt, in the Apocalyptic literature, and in the writings of Qumran. In effect, this undoes the usual scholarly division between Wisdom and Apocalyptic, via which liberation and feminist theology could play Wisdom as the tradition of male elites off against Apocalyptic as the tradition of the poor and oppressed. After tracing Jewish Wisdom traditions, Fiorenza finds that it is easier to see that a "submerged theology of Wisdom, or sophialogy, permeates all of Christian Scriptures."[34]

She locates two strands of Sophialogy that intertwine at times in the New Testament. One presents Jesus as the prophet of Sophia, and the other identifies him as divine Wisdom (while an intermediary stage identifies the Logos with divine Wisdom). Both strands show signs, according to Schüssler Fiorenza, of succumbing to pressure from patriarchal norms in the introduction of father-son language.[35] On the basis of evidence in Matthew 11:25–27, she argues that "the introduction of father-son language into early Christian sophialogy is intrinsically bound up with a theological exclusivity that reserves revelation for the elect few and draws the boundaries of communal identity between insiders and outsiders."[36] Sophialogy is thus distorted and muffled by the kyriarchal relationship between the Father and the Son. This becomes pronounced, according to Schüssler Fiorenza, in the Gospel of John, which otherwise could have served well to make clear the sophialogical significance of Jesus:

> By introducing the "father-son" language in the very beginning and using it throughout the Gospel, the whole book reinscribes the metaphorical grammatical masculinity of the expressions "logos" and "son" as congruent with the biological masculine sex of the historic person of Jesus of Nazareth. The Fourth Gospel thereby not only dissolves the tension between the grammatical feminine gender of Sophia and the "naturalized" gender of Jesus but also marginalizes and "silences" the traditions of G*d as represented by Divine Woman Wisdom. In so doing, the christological language of the Gospel opens the door to a kind of philosophical/ontological theological reflection that is now able to merge the *biological* masculine gender of Jesus and the *grammatical* masculine gender of Logos, Son, and Father.[37]

And here is the problem. That traces of Sophialogy are obscured is bad enough from the point of view of the feminist biblical theologian, but the confusion of the biological gender of Jesus and the grammatical gender of the nouns Logos, Son, and Father furthers the damaging effects of kyriarchal thought. Schüssler Fiorenza refers to this phenomenon as the "naturalizing" of the grammatical masculinity of the nouns.

She links this naturalizing of the grammatical masculinity of the nouns Logos, Son, and Father with what she considers a Christian "amnesia" for the metaphoric quality of language. These have resulted, she argues, in an analogous inability to hear the grammatical femininity of the noun Sophia as metaphorical. This is highly problematic for the feminist theologian, for Schüssler Fiorenza is representative of other feminist theologians in claiming the metaphoricity of the language we use to speak of God:

> G*d-language is symbolic, metaphoric, and analogous because human language can never speak adequately about divine reality. . . . If language is not a reflection of reality but

rather a sociocultural linguistic system, then the relationship between language and reality is not an essential "given" but is constructed in discourse. This is especially true when language speaks about divine reality since divine reality cannot be comprehended in human language. The inability to comprehend and express who G*d is prohibits any absolutizing of symbols, images, or names for G*d, be they grammatically masculine, feminine, or neuter. Such an absolute relativity of theological G*d-language demands, to the contrary, a proliferation of symbols, images and names to express a humanly incomprehensible divine reality. If language is a sociocultural convention and not a reflection of reality, then one must theologically reject the ontological identification of grammatical gender and divine reality as well as grammatical gender and human reality.[38]

This view fits with the Feuerbachian theory of religious language as describing the projection of our deepest desires and needs, for it is "constructed in discourse" and requires a creative impulse toward a "proliferation of symbols" to express that which is "humanly incomprehensible." It also reflects the Kantian dichotomy between the noumenal and the phenomenal, for "human language can never speak adequately about divine reality" because "divine reality cannot be comprehended in human language."[39] This fits nicely with the feminist critique of patriarchal God language, taming the language, reducing its power. Since language is a social construct to begin with, it needs to be socially reconstructed. We are not "stuck" with the masculine imagery for God, because no God language can be "absolutized." It is this, taken to its logical extreme, which renders the claim that Jesus is the Son of God to be idolatrous.[40] To reintroduce Sophialogy and metaphoricity of religious language into theology, argues Schüssler Fiorenza, will allow a subversion of the entire patriarchal thought world of the New Testament:

> I find the early "Jesus messenger of Sophia" traditions theologically significant because they assert the unique particularity of Jesus without having to resort to exclusivity and superiority. In contrast to Jewish and Christian Apocalyptic traditions, the Wisdom tradition values life, creativity, and well-being in the midst of struggle. These elements— open-endedness, inclusivity, cosmopolitan emphasis on creation spirituality, and practical insight—have been especially attractive not only to feminists but also to Asians engaged in Christological reflection.[41]

Indeed, contra Engelsman's approach, the earliest Christian sophialogical categories for reflection do not seem to suggest a masculine-feminine gender dualism at all, for the masculinity of Jesus is not at issue in the earliest strands of Sophialogy. Instead, the earliest Christian Sophialogy takes a "theological" view, according to Schüssler Fiorenza. Here it is interesting that she assumes a distinction between a "theological focus" and a focus on the man Jesus, with his concomitant characteristics of masculinity, Jewishness, and so on. This is exactly, as we shall see later in this chapter, what Martin Kähler argued against: for the biblical witness, reflection on the man Jesus is indeed by definition theological.[42] Schüssler Fiorenza sees the fact that the earliest Sophialogy of the New Testament tends to focus on Jesus without recourse to gender dichotomy as one of the positive aspects of Sophialogy. The extent to which such traditions, when pulled out of their canonical framework, serve to exacerbate the dichotomy between the Jesus of history and the Christ of faith remains to be seen.

Elizabeth Johnson takes the constructive task further into the realm of systematic theology proper in her She Who Is. Sophialogy becomes theologically useful for Johnson for some very concrete reasons, and it allows several themes of feminist thought to come to the fore. First, a concern for the whole cosmos is already built into the biblical Wisdom traditions, and this, in turn, orients Christology outward, as she says, "beyond the human world to the ecology of the earth, and indeed, to the universe, a vital move in this era of planetary crisis."[43] Because planetary wholeness and health, a feminist value, is upheld by Wisdom traditions, Sophialogy will be useful to feminist theology. Second, in their concern for the global and the cosmic over against the local and the particular, biblical wisdom traditions can allow and even foster an open and nonjudgmental ecumenical perspective which respects other religious paths.[44] This, too, is more compatible with feminist values than the classical Christian distinction that there is "no salvation outside the church." Third, biblical wisdom traditions stress that "the passion of God is clearly directed toward the lifting of oppression and the establishing of right relations."[45] This concern for the oppressed is a value which runs throughout liberation theologies, in general, and feminist theology, in specific. Fourth, Sophialogy allows for the integration of women's experience into theological reflection. Johnson, like Schüssler Fiorenza, sees this as the opportunity for a major paradigm shift in theology:

> For theology as an academic discipline, it is clear that placing women's experience at the center of inquiry and pressing toward transformation of oppressive symbols and systems are occasioning an intellectual paradigm shift. There is new data at hand, which prevailing theory cannot account for, making the search for a new configuration of the whole essential. This is not minor tinkering with the discipline but an effort toward major reshaping of theology and the religious tradition which gives rise to it.[46]

Because modern theology in general, especially since Schleiermacher, has tended to give pride of place to human experience in theological reflection, feminist theology here is not breaking radically new ground. However, it is argued that what is distinct here—and, therefore, indeed revolutionary—is that in feminist theology it is not human experience in general but the incorporating of women's experience, "long derided or neglected in androcentric tradition, as an essential element in the theological task." As was pointed out earlier, the inclusion of women's experience in theological reflection has been a hallmark of feminist theology, and with Sophialogy we see this working itself out clearly. While Johnson, like many other feminist theologians, notes that women are pluriform and therefore their experience is as well, the specific kind of experience she refers to is the experience of conversion:

> Thus women's awakening to their own human worth can be interpreted at the same time as a new experience of God, so that what is arguably occurring is a new event in the religious history of humankind. . . . In myriad ways women are newly involved in experiencing and articulating themselves as subjects, as active subjects of history, and as *good* ones. Given the negative assessment of women's humanity under patriarchy, this self-naming has the character of a conversion process, a turning away from trivialization and defamation of oneself as a female person and a turning toward oneself as worthwhile.[47]

This experience, then, is specifically religious but is integrally bound to women's emancipation as they come to claim agency and active subjectivity. We see then how a redefinition of conversion for feminist purposes trades on the thesis of Valerie Saiving, which we explored in chapter 3, that women's sin is not prideful self-assertion but self-abnegation. This experience of conversion thus "has the fundamental character of hope, even hope against hope."[48] Because of women's conversion experience, argues Johnson, "new language about God is arising, one that takes female reality in all its concreteness as a legitimate finite starting point for speaking about the mystery of God."[49] Here the importance of Sophia becomes clearer. Not only does Sophialogy promote the feminist values of inclusivity, openness, ecological stewardship, and the like but also it allows women to name the divine in terms that validate their own subjectivity and agency as never before.

In addition, and directly relevant to feminist Christology, Johnson understands Sophialogy, much as does Schüssler Fiorenza, to allow a reconceptualization of the doctrine of the incarnation:

> What does it mean that one of the key origins of the doctrines of incarnation and Trinity lies in the identification of the crucified and risen Jesus with a female gestalt of God? Since Jesus the Christ is depicted as divine Sophia, then it is not unthinkable—it is not even unbiblical—to confess Jesus the Christ as the incarnation of God imaged in female symbol. Whoever espouses a wisdom Christology is asserting that Jesus is the human being Sophia became; that Sophia in all her fullness was in him so that he manifests the depth of divine mystery in creative and graciously saving involvement in the world. The fluidity of gender symbolism evidenced in biblical Christology breaks the stranglehold of androcentric thinking that circles around the maleness of Jesus. Wisdom Christology reflects the depths of the mystery of God and points the way to an inclusive Christology in female symbols.[50]

According to this argument, reconstructing Christology in female "symbols" as Johnson says is important not only for women but also indeed for our very confession of God. For Johnson as for many feminist theologians, Christology which focuses on a male Christ alone is tantamount to idolatry:

> Any representation of the divine used in such a way that its symbolic and evocative character is lost from view partakes of the nature of an idol. Whenever one image or concept of God expands to the horizon thus shutting out others, and whenever this exclusive symbol becomes literalized so that the distance between it and divine reality is collapsed, there an idol comes into being. Then the comprehensible image, rather than disclosing mystery, is mistaken for the reality. Divine mystery is cramped into a fixed, petrified image. Simultaneously, the religious impulse is imprisoned, leading to inhibition of the growth of human beings by the prevention of further seeking and finding.[51]

Reconstructing Christology is therefore necessary, lest heresy and idolatry be embraced. The logical outcome of this, of course, is the reconstruction of the doctrine of the Trinity, a reworking of the first four centuries of Christian theology, which Johnson takes up and which we shall consider in chapter 6.

Sophia: Is She Good for Us?

The advantages accrued to feminist theology in bringing in Sophia for consideration are many. By following the tracings of Wisdom traditions in the Gospels, Sophialogy can present a view of Jesus which neatly dovetails with feminist interests, values, and concerns. This Jesus is inclusive, egalitarian, and non-sexist:

> The Palestinian Jesus movement understands the ministry and mission of Jesus as that of the prophet and child of Sophia sent to announce that God is the God of the poor and heavy laden, of the outcasts and those who suffer injustice. As child of Sophia he stands in a long line and succession of prophets sent to gather the children of Israel to their gracious Sophia-God. Jesus' execution, like John's, results from his mission and commitment as prophet and emissary of the Sophia-God who holds open a future for the poor and outcast and offers God's gracious goodness to all children of Israel without exception. The Sophia-God of Jesus does not need atonement or sacrifices. Jesus' death is not willed by God but is the result of his all-inclusive praxis as Sophia's prophet.[52]

Here we have the God of the oppressed, the God of justice, the God of inclusive praxis. We even have the added benefit for the feminist paradigm that there is no specific focus on a bloody atonement, which feminist consciousness tends to reject as abusive:

> Along with other forms of political and liberation theology, feminist theology repudiates an interpretation of the death of Jesus as required by God in repayment for sin. Such a view today is virtually inseparable from an underlying image of God as an angry, blood-thirsty, violent and sadistic father, reflecting the very worst kind of male behavior. Rather, Jesus' death was an act of violence brought about by threatened human men, as sin, and therefore against the will of a gracious God. It occurred historically in consequence of Jesus' fidelity to the deepest truth he knew, expressed in his message and behavior, which showed all twisted relationships to be incompatible with Sophia-God's shalom.[53]

As regards the Gospels, one does not even need the Passion narratives at all. Since Q has no such narratives and Sophialogy is found within the Q traditions, the Passion narratives are, in theory, expendable to this kind of feminist Christology. This means that a feminist Sophialogy of this sort will not need to reckon in any narratival way with the cross. Instead of representing an instrument of execution from the turn of the Common Era, the cross can symbolize "a challenge to the natural rightness of male dominating rule."[54] This theological vision, even if it were not named under the feminine Sophia, is a near-perfect representation of feminist theological values.

While it is clear that equating Jesus with Sophia allows us to speak of him—and of the doctrine of incarnation and even of the Trinity—in feminine terms, what is less clear is just how helpful that actually is for women. Some have questioned how "usable" the Sophia traditions are for feminist theological building up of the sisterhood of women.[55] Indeed, some have noted that Elaine Pagels's gnostic Sophia in effect simply reinscribes patriarchal stereotypes of women. She is therefore not an unequivocally positive figure for women but remains ambivalent, bringing on as she does the Fall.[56] One could link Sophia's ambivalence vis-à-vis women with her emergence from a nonnarrative reading. In an autobiographical aside, Angela West implicitly does just this:

> As my acquaintance with scripture deepened I came to doubt—like, but totally unlike Daphne Hampson—that this faith which the Jewish and Christian scripture bear witness to was something that could be "cleaned up" in order to make it suitable for feminist requirements. I began to suspect that it might be us who would need to clean up our

thinking before the faith which these scripture testify to can make any real sense to us. For perhaps Sophia was not quite as we had fashioned her—and she too had her scandalous particularity. Scripture makes clear that she does not give herself to all those who profess a love of wisdom, by only those who follow her along particular paths. In our justifiable excitement to reclaim her, we seemed to have forgotten to reclaim her opposite number—Dame Folly (Prov. 9:13–18). We were apt to assume that women have had not part in the folly and sin that is part of Christian tradition, that had rendered it "exclusive." We defined in advance what we considered to be an acceptable presence of women in scripture. . . . But Sophia, speaking through the scriptures, tells us that those who are wise in their own eyes will not be able to find her. It seems she has ordained that those women or men who approach her with their own neat schemes for how justice is to be done on earth will not find her.[57]

Here, West is pointing out how a non-narrative Sophia contradicts the narrative Sophia, at which point the jig is up, so to speak, for a non-narrative Sophia turns out to look more like Dame Folly. Whether or not Sophia is "good" for women, the question remains about the use of the biblical narrative in reconstructing the doctrine of God in sophialogical terms. While a functionalist view may find the sophialogical approach marginally (if at all) helpful, this is because of the more properly theological assessment that such Sophialogy uses a non-narrative hermeneutic. That is, it allows and indeed insists that we step outside the larger biblical narrative. It depends upon the non-narrative reading of the Gospel narratives, such that Jesus is not a character within a larger story but a symbol for a feminist ideal. Gail Corrington points this out as she examines the question of the usefulness of female savior figures in a Christian theological context:

The difficulty inherent in seeing Isis as a female savior figure is that, in comparison with the Christian savior, she is not incarnate in any particular historical personage; this is true no matter how much she is viewed as incarnate in and embodying women, particularly in the female life cycle. This "difficulty" is of course created only when one views Isis as a savior from a particular Christian perspective.[58]

Likewise, in Christian Sophialogy, Sophia is incarnate only in the particular historical personage of Jesus, the man from Nazareth. But this is exactly what Sophialogy wishes to avoid in redescription, the male from Nazareth. Thus, "Sophia" becomes a cipher for a "virtual reality," a character who has no narrative identity. Indeed, she is narratively proscribed, which according to the feminist narrative is explained via the powers of patriarchal silencing, as we saw illustrated in Susan Ackerman's reading of the Jeremiah passages in chapter 2.

However, if one is to enter the narrative world created by the biblical stories, that narrative world has a different explanation for the proscription of the feminine divine where she is proscribed: Yahweh alone is God. Of course, here is the beauty of Sophialogy: Sophia does not claim to usurp worship from Yahweh, but rather she is Yahweh incarnate. Jesus points to her reality, thereby obscuring himself. In effect, Jesus becomes a John the Baptist figure, a forerunner who erases his own tracks so that feminists can follow the One who comes, the One greater than he, Sophia.

Historical-Critical Reconstruction and the
Jesus of History versus the Christ of Faith

Implicitly underlying many of the reconstructions of a Sophia Christology, such as that considered here, is the modern dichotomy between the Jesus of history and the Christ of faith. This dichotomy developed in eighteenth-and nineteenth-century theology and biblical criticism and forms the bond of intellectual and spiritual unity between feminist theologians and scholars of the "historical Jesus," such as those of the Jesus Seminar. Even while most feminist theologians would not want to engage in the construction or use of dichotomies, this particular dichotomy serves them well. However, according to narrative interpretation, such a splitting of the Jesus of history from the Christ of faith is theologically impossible.

The distinction between the Jesus of history and the Christ of faith arguably begins with Reimarus's attack on the Gospels as a "tissue of lies" which the church had woven to cover up what he claimed was the reality of a failed religious leader. Reimarus assumed, as many still do, a validity to the distinction between the "Jesus of history" and the "Christ of faith." In other words, a Jesus as he really was can be unearthed from the sedimented layers of Christian confession imposed on him in the New Testament record and subsequent theology. It was this Jesus of history which Reimarus assumed he had found.

Reimarus's writings on this topic were published anonymously after his death, between the years of 1774 and 1778, by Lessing, the famous theologian of the "ugly ditch." The last two portions of the seven "Wolfenbüttel Fragments," as Reimarus's writings were called, concern the life of Jesus. According to Reimarus, the apostles understood Jesus during his earthly life to be the temporal Messiah longed for in the Jewish scriptures, as did, indeed, Jesus himself. Reimarus, so it seems, attributed the "messianic secret," yet to be "discovered" by Wrede, to the historical Jesus as a countersuggestion which served to spread the word about the Messiah. But after Jesus' death, the disciples turned him into a spiritual Messiah with little resemblance to the earthly Jesus. They concocted this "new system" out of fear of disgrace at having followed a failed messiah, and out of lust for money. Indeed, lust for money and power, according to Reimarus, "is the real mighty wind (of Pentecost) that so quickly wafted all the people together. This is the true original language that performs the miracles" (2.60). Reimarus anticipates the discovery of the problem of the "delay of the parousia," arguing that since the apostles were, in fact, disappointed in their hope in Jesus as temporal Messiah, they changed their story about him to relieve their cognitive dissonance. Thus, according to Reimarus, the evangelists are not to be trusted as historians, which is nevertheless how they present themselves.

This view of Jesus, the disciples, and earliest Christianity, which results in the dichotomy of the historical Jesus and the Christ of faith, carries with it assumptions about Christian reception and interpretation of the Old Testament. According to Reimarus, Jesus adds no new doctrine to Judaism, but the evangelists report his teachings and deeds as, in fact, doing just this. Here Reimarus again makes an observation ahead of his time, that the Gospels are theologically motivated writings. Reimarus's understanding of the evangelists as "liars" in effect accuses the church of a marked tendency toward the Marcionite slippery slope. He argues that the church views Jesus as bringing a message totally foreign to the Old Testament. The church understands Jesus to introduce a better righteousness, which is discontinuous with the Old Testament, and to admit the correctness of the Pharisees' view of salvation, which they have learned from the pagans and not from the traditions of Israel. According to Reimarus, the church's understanding is that the Old Testament contributes nothing positive to Jesus' message, and Jesus' message is the sole content of theology (or "religion").

In contrast to this view of the church's understanding of Jesus, Reimarus himself emphasizes the "Jewishness" of Jesus. Pointing to Matthew 5–7, Reimarus argues that, contrary to the church's later understanding, Jesus did not intend to abolish the Jewish law. Instead, he upheld it and freed it of the later additions (i.e., oral Torah), which smothered it with hypocrisy. While Reimarus's method would therefore appear to offer a greater role to the Old Testament in that the discontinuity between Old and New is drastically diminished, it does not actually do so in practice. "Religion" is reduced to Jesus' intentions and message, and while it is coincidentally continuous with the Old Testament, the Old Testament itself serves no discrete theological function. For Reimarus, the only part of the canon which does serve a theological function is that from which we can reconstruct the message and intention of Jesus as distinct from the accretions of the church's theologizing about the Christ of faith. We find in much of Reimarus's thought in the "Fragments" that which overlaps with modern theology in general and feminist theologies in particular.

Over a century later, several critiques devastated the distinction between the Jesus of history and the Christ of faith. One of these was by Martin Kähler, who exposed the problem of the sources for historical Jesus research. First published in 1892, his lectures on the topic appear in English under the title The So-Called Historical Jesus and the Historic Biblical Christ. One of Kähler's contentions is that we do not possess adequate sources to reconstruct the life and teachings of Jesus because the Gospels are not intentionally objective reports. The confessional nature of the sources makes it impossible to cull the Jesus as he actually was from the reports about the Christ of faith. The Gospels are isolated reports with little external corroborating evidence, and they tell mainly of the shortest and latest period of Jesus' life. In fact, according to Kähler, the Gospels are "passion narratives with extended introductions." While Kähler can understand the interest in the person of Jesus, he sees such research as reading the Bible against the grain. Yet the quest continues as though Kähler, not to mention Schweitzer and Wrede, had never made a contribution to the debate.

Insofar as historical-critical methodology was at its inception fueled by a passion to liberate the truth of the biblical texts from the distortions of tradition accreted to them (Schweitzer acclaimed historical criticism as the "struggle against the tyrany of dogma"), historical Jesus research is a quintessentially Protestant undertaking, even though Roman Catholics now take part in such research. Feminist theologies share with historical criticisms of all kinds this "struggle against the tyrany of dogma."

However, the two categories of the "Jesus of history" and the "Christ of faith" are so thoroughly intermingled in the New Testament that they cannot be separated. This is what Kähler was saying, and it is why Frei speaks of the Gospel narratives as "history-like." Because the New Testament witness is a post-Resurrection phenomenon, there is no getting behind its faith or "bias" back to Jesus as he actually was. Jesus as he was is portrayed as the Christ and therefore the object of faith. This does not mean we must accept him as the object of our faith in order to understand the New Testament narratives. We may justifiably choose to reject acting upon the New Testament's portrayal of Jesus as the Christ, and we still may indeed have grasped the meaning of the text correctly. But the fact that the Gospel texts function as thoroughly integrated historical and theological witness is undeniable. According to narrative interpretation, we have, in fact, no grounds as Christians to speak of the Christ of faith as though he were separable from Jesus as he was. The Christ of faith is an "idea," a concept, but Jesus is a character depicted within a narrative, a narrative which makes totalitarian claims about his significance for human life and death. Not only do we have no grounds to speak of a Jesus of history versus a Christ of faith but also we have no place speaking of Jesus as a "concept" or "idea" or "consciousness" or "metaphor," as though he represented something other than or apart from himself, like some allegorical pointer. Indeed, when Jesus points to the God of Israel, he does so by pointing to his hands and his side. This is another way of recognizing that the New Testament narratival witness to Jesus, whose identity is portrayed in the fit between his intention and action, follows closely the Old Testament rendering of the identity of the God of Israel in its fit between character disclosure and plot. This is the literary observation which undergirds the Christian theological claim that Jesus is "God incarnate."

Feminist Uses of the Dichotomy

The use of the dichotomy of the Jesus of history and the Christ of faith appears in much of feminist Christology, whether it is openly acknowledged or not as a conceptual crowbar to separate the christic contents from the historical nutshell. Here is just one example of a feminist theologian's open embracing of this dichotomy:

> Christ, as a redemptive person and Word of God, is not to be encapsulated "once-for-all" in the historical Jesus. The Christian community continues Christ's identity. As vine and branches Christic personhood continues in our sisters and brothers. In the language of early Christian prophetism, we can encounter Christ *in the form of our sister* [italics hers]. Christ, the liberated humanity, is not confined to a static perfection of one person two thousand years ago. Rather, redemptive humanity goes ahead of us, calling us to yet incompleted dimensions of human liberation.[59]

Here Jesus functions more as a symbol of liberated humanity than as a character within a specific narrative. Here the choice is not for the historical Jesus, or even for the narrative Jesus, but rather for the Christ of faith who then becomes liberated humanity. Thus, even when feminist scholars declare that such dichotomies as that between the Jesus of history and the Christ of faith are no longer useful, they often operate with such a logical distinction anyway.[60] This is apparent also in the following quote from Elizabeth Johnson's critically acclaimed work: "In particular, when Jesus' maleness, which belongs to his historical identity, is interpreted to be essential to his redeeming christic function and identity, then the Christ serves as a religious tool for marginalizing and excluding women."[61] The driving of a wedge between the "historical identity" of Jesus and his "redeeming christic function and identity," I would argue, functions analogously to the dichotomy between the Jesus of history and the Christ of faith.

While materially feminist Christologies and the work of the Jesus Seminar are clearly different, formally the logic with which they operate is quite similar. Feminist Christologies of this type tend to want to reduce Jesus' maleness in theological significance, thereby allowing more of a focus on the Christ of faith, which is more interesting for the feminist project because maleness does not need to be a defining factor in discussions of the Christ of faith. The man Jesus of Nazareth thus becomes the external wrapping which contains the "mystery prize" of the Christ of faith. The feminist task here is to seek a new package that is more appropriate for holding the contents. In an inverse project, the Jesus Seminar focuses on what presumably can be determined about the container, and this is used to reconfigure the contents. Both projects, however, are under the faulty assumption that Jesus of Nazareth can somehow be isolated or separated from "the Christ of Faith."

We saw this to be the case in the example we considered from Sallie McFague's work in the last chapter. That is, we might say that for McFague, the "Christic paradigm" functions analogously to the figure of the "historical Jesus." She claims that this figure must precede—whether logically or chronologically, it is not clear—the "cosmic Christ." This "cosmic Christ" seems to be analogous to the "Christ of faith" in some senses but is given greater universalistic and immanentistic dimensions than are usually attributed to the Christ of faith. The reason that the Christic paradigm must precede the cosmic Christ, it seems, is because of McFague's commitment to and interest in "embodiment." To uphold and affirm life in the body, which is McFague's overriding goal, one must find a theological place for the historical Jesus, or at least the embodiment of God in Jesus' story. However, at the same time, McFague wants to maintain this character Jesus, and the scriptures that narrate him, as "touchstones" and not "final arbiters of truth." This necessitates reconstructing Jesus in terms of "paradigm" or type, which allows for the immanentistic and universalistic claims which McFague wants to make, and which she sees as necessary to wholeness for the feminist and ecological projects:

> What does Christian faith, and especially the story of Jesus, have to offer in terms of a distinctive perspective on embodiment? What is the shape that it suggests for God's body, the universe, enlivened by the breath of God's spirit? . . . The story of Jesus suggests that the shape of God's body includes all, especially the needy and outcast.[62]

In an attempt to counter the accusations from radical feminists about the "irredeemably patriarchal" nature of Christianity, Patricia Wilson-Kastner also makes implicit use of this dichotomy in constructing her Christology.[63] For her, one of more vexing questions which feminist theology must seek to answer is how the first four centuries of Christianity could have metamorphosed the "egalitarian Jesus" of history, who accepted women as equal to men, into an "exclusivistic Christ" of faith, who, according to Wilson-Kastner, the church increasingly proclaims as a "figure of male excellence."[64] However, she claims, the fact that Jesus was a male is as irrelevant to his significance for Christian faith as was his Jewishness or the fact that he lived at the turn of the Common Era. What is important about Jesus, according to Wilson-Kastner, is that he is the incarnation of the eternal Word of God:[65] "The incarnation, passion, resurrection of Christ, and the sending of the Spirit are not acts of an exclusive or oppressive God. No one can deny that Jesus the Christ was a male person, but the significance of the incarnation has to do with his humanity, not his maleness."[66] However, Wilson-Kastner claims that the search for the "Jesus of history," as a distinct character from the "Christ of faith," is not of great importance for her theological position, for she claims that "finally, one must conclude that all of the biblical material offers different and developing perspectives on one Christ, incarnate in Jesus of Nazareth, who still lives in the cosmos and in the church."[67] This curious denial of interest in the dichotomy between the Jesus of history and the Christ of faith is, in this case, an assertion of the importance of the dichotomy. That is, Wilson-Kastner first acknowledges that the Jesus of history is not what really matters and so sets him aside and focuses on what does really matter, namely, the Christ of faith. This assumes that one can, indeed, separate the two figures in the first place.

Indeed, feminist theologians as different from one another as Patricia Wilson-Kastner, Carter Heyward, and Elizabeth Johnson can rely on the distinction between the Jesus of history and the Christ of faith in order to reimage Jesus.[68] This itself comes back to the central problem of Jesus' maleness. The Jesus of history was a male Jew, while the Christ of faith becomes a more nebulous figure, seemingly at our disposal to be shaped as a potter works with clay. The question can even be raised and answered positively as to whether Jesus could have become incarnate as a woman:

> Could God have become a human being as a woman? The question strikes some people as silly or worse. Theologically, though, the answer is Yes. Why not? If women are genuinely human and if God is the deep mystery of holy love, then what is to prevent such an incarnation? But taking for granted the implicit inferiority of women, Christian theology has dignified maleness as the only genuine way of being human, thus making Jesus' embodiment as male an ontological necessity rather than a historical option. Owing to the way christology has been handled in an unthinking androcentric perspective, Jesus' maleness has been so interpreted that he has become the male revealer of a male God whose full representative can only be male. As a package, this christology relegates women to the margins of significance.[69]

Theologically, the answer can be Yes to the question Johnson raises if one has first implicitly accepted the validity of the distinction between the Christ of faith and Jesus of history and determined that the Jesus of history is the shell to be disposed of surrounding the Christ of faith nutmeat. Of course, Johnson is not questioning the bare fact that Jesus himself was a male. Rather, for her the "historical identity" of Jesus is fundamentally a problem because of the way it has been construed by the tradition so as to "stifle the gospel" and to exclude women. The logical conclusion we can draw is that for Johnson, Jesus' historical identity is, to say the least, less important than his identity as the Christ of faith:

> But that good news is stifled when Jesus' maleness, which belongs to his historical identity, is interpreted as being essential to his redeeming christic function and identity. Then the Christ functions as a religious tool for marginalizing and excluding women. Let us be very clear: the fact that Jesus of Nazareth was a male human being is not in question. His sex was a constitutive element of his historical person along with other particularities such as his Jewish racial identity, his location in the world of first-century

Galilee, and so on, and as such is to be respected. The difficulty arises, rather, from the way Jesus' maleness is construed in official androcentric theology and ecclesial praxis.[70]

Any focus on the maleness of Jesus, in effect, stifles the good news of the gospel, according to Johnson. In addition, it threatens the very salvation of women and, in turn, the salvation of all humankind:

> Given the dualism which essentially divorces male from female humanity, the maleness of Christ puts the salvation of women in jeopardy. The Christian story of salvation involves not only God's compassionate will to save but also the method by which that will is effective, namely, by plunging into sinful human history and transforming it from within. The early Christian aphorism, "What is not assumed is not healed" sums up the insight that God's saving solidarity with humanity is what is crucial for the birth of the new creation. As the Nicene creed confesses, "et homo factus est" ("and was made [hu]man"). But if in fact what is meant is "et vir factus est" ["and was made a man"], if maleness is essential for the christic role, then women are cut out of the loop of salvation, for female sexuality was not assumed by the Word made flesh.[71]

This is one of the greatest obstacles for many feminist theologians to overcome: if Jesus was male, can he save women? Indeed, Rosemary Radford Ruether has asked this question point-blank, with a questionable response.[72] Yet, even as male, Jesus can be seen to be the embodiment of the self-emptying, the very kenosis, of patriarchy:

> In the light of this history Jesus' maleness can be seen to have a definite social significance. If a woman had preached compassionate love and enacted a style of authority that serves, she would have been greeted with a colossal shrug. Is this not what women are supposed to do by nature? But from a social position of male privilege Jesus preached and acted this way, and here lies the summons. The cross, too, is a sturdy symbol of the "kenosis of patriarchy," the self-emptying of male dominating power in favour of the new humanity of compassionate service and mutual empowerment.[73]

For these feminist theologians, the historical identity of Jesus is less important for the life of faith than his identity as the incarnate Word and Christ of faith. How can this be assessed in such a way that feminist theology can move forward rather than simply tear down or complain about traditional Christologies? For Johnson, the "key elements of a feminist christology" are the Resurrection, wisdom Christology, and the biblical symbol of the body of Christ.[74] Ellen Wondra would agree formally as regards Jesus' maleness, but whereas Johnson would speak in terms of theological loci, Wondra emphasizes Jesus' inclusive, self-giving love:

> Jesus' being male has revelatory importance only because of the meaning of maleness in patriarchal history and culture. The fact that Jesus' relations with others were self-giving, inclusive, reciprocal or mutual, cooperative and just stands against the patterns and conventions of patriarchy, which operate to the benefit of men of dominant groups and to the detriment of women and other marginalized persons.[75]

All of these elements allow distance to be placed between the male Jesus and the "mystery" of the Christ figure. This, it is often claimed, follows the tradition of apophatic theology, in which the unspeakable mystery of God is emphasized.[76] The extent to which this actually follows the apophatic tradition in theology has been questioned, most notably by Verna Harrison.[77] The appeal to the apophatic tradition, whether warranted or not, functions to allow the transference of the consideration of Jesus' incarnation to the community and thus can be used to help downplay the difficulties posed by Jesus' maleness. Instead of the focus on the body of Jesus on the cross, the image of the community as the body of Christ can aid feminist theological claims to equality.[78] This is an important move to make, especially for a Roman Catholic who hears from the magisterium that women cannot be ordained because they do not share the very masculinity of Jesus and his immediate disciples and thus cannot serve to represent Christ. Indeed, Johnson claims that the present discussion of the maleness of Christ has arisen because of the church's shortcomings in its witness, and that in a more just church the necessity even to dwell on Jesus' masculinity would not even arise.[79]

Along the lines of Johnson's critique here and the use of the dichotomy of the Jesus of history and the Christ of faith, a penetrating and illuminating related set of questions is raised by Teresa Berger. She notes that, throughout world Christianity, there is a tendency to condone inculturation of the gospel; that is, Jesus is often represented by a black figure in African churches, the Holy Family represented as Asians in churches in the Far East, and so on: "It is worth thinking about why we have become so accustomed to a Black Christ figure or a Campesino on the cross or a Chinese Holy Family as legitimate forms of the inculturation of the Gospel—while a female Christ child in the manger or woman on the cross appear to many of us as incomprehensible or unacceptable."[80] If, asks Berger, the Jewishness of Jesus is not threatened by portraits of him as either black or Asian, then why is it not possible to accept an inculturated portrait of Jesus as female? Unfortunately, her questions were not addressed by the magisterium or, rather, were addressed by ensuring that she was denied teaching posts at Catholic universities in Europe.[81] Here is an example of a lost opportunity on the part of the magisterium to engage an interesting and important set of questions, and the lost opportunity on the part of those universities which sought Berger's teaching skills. It is hard to explain the series of events, as she recalls them in her article, as motivated by anything but sexism.[82] The set of questions she raises could have been quite fruitfully addressed by discussing, for example, the quote from Rahner which Berger uses to legitimate her inquiry: "Why do we accept the mediator to be a man but not a woman? Our answer will have to be that the maleness of the mediator is ultimately irrelevant for his universal significance as Saviour. It is simply part of the contingent particularity . . . which the eternal Word of God had to take upon itself."[83] This quote, of course, points to the non-narrative interpretation which guides Rahner's theological inquiry. As for the question of why inculturation in terms of race is not threatening to the incarnation while that in terms of gender is, one can imagine Barth, for example, responding that the creation narratives point to a more central differentiation in the human creature, that of sex: "male and female created He them." This differentiation distinguishes the human creature from all of the other creatures God had previously created, which were all created "according to their kind." The distinction between male and female is also tied in the narrative presentation to the comment that "in the image of God He created them." Thus, part of the mark of being human is to be created male and female, in the image of God.

Racial distinctions are, according to the narrative presentation, less central to the category of humanity and are only brought into the story after the Fall and expulsion from the Garden of Eden.

In any event, these questions are fascinating and deserve far more treatment than either the magisterium apparently gave them or the present project can afford. What is significant, from the point of view of narrative interpretation, is Berger's comment that "I am not concerned with an exact portrait, but rather with a symbol. That this symbol has to be formed in response to historical events and must in some way correspond to them, is a basic theological principle which I accept. What interests me however, is where the boundaries of the correspondence lie."[84] From the point of view of narrative interpretation, there is no discrete or systematically accessible gap between symbol and exact portrait, between historical events and theological principle. Thus, we might go as far as to say that the insights drawn from narrative interpretation would suggest that the masculinity of Jesus may be more important—not soteriologically but in terms of the narrative—than Johnson, Berger, and Rahner give credit for here.

We have seen the noteworthy attempts made by many feminists of the Christian faith at rescuing the gospel from the radical feminist charge of Christianity's supposedly "irredeemably patriarchal" nature. Like Bultmann, these feminists intend to remove the unnecessary scandals which would cause people to stumble over Jesus, while remaining true to the scandal which cannot be avoided. Feminist theologians and Bultmann alike share a passion for apologetics, certainly a passion with which the Christian can, at the very least, be sympathetic. However, we have seen the difficulties of apologetics conducted on the basis of an extra-narratively derived explanatory framework.

Jesus' Maleness Reconsidered

As we noted earlier in this chapter, Martin Kähler pointed out more than a century ago that the nature of the Gospels, which are our sources for understanding who Jesus was, makes it clear that there is no "Christ-figure" apart from Jesus as he is depicted in the Gospels. It is a logical impossibility and conceptual error to claim that we can strip away the church's confessional accretions from the historical nuggets in the Gospels and come up with a "Jesus as he actually was." The Jesus of history, if by the phrase we mean the earthly Jesus, is the Christ of faith: there is no splitting one from the other.

When such a project is claimed to be possible, what results is usually a Jesus of history who looks very much like his reconstructors, as Schweitzer noted almost a hundred years ago in his *Quest of the Historical Jesus*. This is just as true now as during the "Old Quest," when we were offered portrait after portrait of a blond-haired, blue-eyed Aryan Jesus. Now late-twentieth-century American academicians depict Jesus as a revolutionary antiestablishment sophist, and, using similar logic with different results, feminist scholars propose portraits of a female Christ figure. However, the Gospel writers depict Jesus as a male Jew, which brings us full circle back to the feminist offense.

Although most feminists have been shown to respond to the offense by denying the theological importance of Jesus' masculinity, this is, I would argue, counterproductive. Instead, I would claim that Jesus' maleness is indeed significant, at least when understood narrativally. My claim here is not based on a political or logistical warrant. That is, I am not claiming that Jesus had to be a man because no one would have listened to a woman in Jewish culture at the turn of the Common Era.[85] Neither am I basing the claim on the logic of feminist discourse itself, such as in the argument that Jesus had to be a male because while "Jesus the man turns things upside down, Jesa the woman would always have been at the bottom."[86] Nor is the claim based on the type of argument that is used in traditional Catholic circles against the ordination of women, that Jesus' masculinity is crucial for the imaging of Christ in the priesthood.[87]

Instead, the claim about the importance of Jesus' maleness is a specifically theological claim based on the logic of narrative reading of the scriptures. While it makes sense to say that Jesus' maleness is an accident in the technical philosophical sense, the narrative context, such as it is, would not allow a female savior. This may sound dangerously sexist, but it is protected from this fate by the doctrine of the last things. That is, Christian eschatology alone undercuts any possibility that such a statement could uplift the male over against the female and logically disallows male "lording" over female within the body of Christ.

Classical Christology claims Jesus to be the Son of God and the son of Mary, fully divine and fully human. Since humans are born (except in the rarest cases) with the physical and hormonal makeup which mark us as either males or females, being human means being either male or female. Few feminist theologians, as we have seen, want actually to deny Jesus' maleness. But they do want to deny that his being male is related to his soteriological significance. However, since Jesus was a Jew who fulfilled the promises to Israel and offered up once and for all the perfect sacrifice, he had to be male. If he were not male and a Jew—indeed, a free Jewish male—how could the baptismal promise of Galatians 3:27–29 have been granted? "For as many of you as were baptized into Christ have put on Christ. There is neither Jew nor Greek, there is neither slave nor free, there is neither male nor female; for you are all one in Christ Jesus. And if you are Christ's then you are Abraham's offspring, heirs according to the promise." The three sets of opposition in Galatians 3:28—Jew-Greek, slave-free, male-female—correspond to the categories in which Jewish election is cast. God freely bestows his grace on a male, Abraham, and on his descendants. And the religiously observant male Jew praises God everyday for making him male and not female, Jewish and not Gentile. In the conservative prayerbook, though apparently not in the orthodox prayerbook, he adds the thanksgiving that God has made him free and not a slave like his ancestors in Egypt. These are arguably even in Jesus' day the marks of Jewish election.[88] In Galatians, Paul is saying that what has happened in Jesus has turned this election on its head: now in the new "time zone" inaugurated by Jesus' Resurrection, there is no distinction in God's electing grace between Jew and Gentile, slave and free, male and female.

Therefore, the remedy to the feminist offense at Jesus' masculinity is already found within the logic of the Christian biblical narrative in the conjunction of Christology with its distinctive eschatology. The New Testament understands Jesus' Resurrection to be the eschatological event par excellence. According to the New Testament, his Resurrection forms the linchpin between two time zones, if you will: Jesus is the first fruits of the general resurrection, for in his rising from the dead, the end of the ages has dawned. The neglect of classical Christian eschatology present in some of modern theology may, indeed, influence feminist Christologies, insofar as most feminist theology is a subset of modern theology.[89] Yet it is precisely classical Christian eschatology which is both the basis of any biblically grounded feminism and the remedy to antifeminism.

Because in Jesus the end of the ages has dawned, even the relationship between male and female has taken a radical turn, and the fallen order has become the New Creation. In the time zone inaugurated by the Resurrection of Jesus, the curse of Genesis 3 has been lifted. Most feminist theologians have not sufficiently dealt with the implications of this. In Genesis 3:16, we hear God's words to Eve following the disobedience in the garden: "your desire shall be for your husband, and he shall rule over you." The male's rule over the female is one among many of the results of their disobedience to the Creator. Humanity had been created good, indeed, in the words of Genesis 1:31: "behold, it was very good!" but after the first theological conversation in the garden and the consequent disobedience to the will of God, everything is cursed. But in Jesus Christ, as Paul says in 2 Corinthians 5:17, we have been made new creatures, "the old has passed away, behold, the new has come."

And this, indeed, is the only reason why it makes no sense theologically to block the ordination of women solely on the grounds that they are not male. To assume that men can represent Christ more easily or fully than women is in itself a theological error, somewhat analogous to the feminist confusion that women cannot be saved by a male savior.[90] The ordination of women is not a "justice issue"; it is a christological issue and therefore an eschatological issue. But one can come to these conclusions only from a standpoint internal to the narrative. Once one has stepped outside the narrative, one has effectively abandoned the tools by which the problem of sexism can be addressed.

Thus, we have seen how the fourth model of feminist christological reconstruction, which uses historical-critical assumptions and conclusions, depends also on a non-narrative reading of Scripture. Whether explicitly or more often implicitly, feminist theologies can build on the literature which unearths the Goddess as well as that which uses the distinction between the Jesus of history and the Christ of faith. They cannot be faulted for using the same methodologies as those used in the academy at large. Their weakness, however, like that of the methodologies in the academy, is based on a non-narrative logic. We turn now to an examination of an extended use of Sophia in feminist reconstructions of Christian doctrine in the doctrine of the Trinity.

6

FEMINIST TRINITARIAN
RECONSTRUCTIONS

In the previous chapter, we saw how some feminist reconstructions of Christology made use of historical-critical tools and, in particular, historical research into feminine representations of the divine. In this chapter, we will consider the extension of this reconstructive work into the doctrine of the Trinity and its application in the church's liturgy and sacramental life. At this point, feminist theology takes on the practical task of reshaping not only the church's theology but also its worship.

Sophia in Trinitarian Dress

Elizabeth Johnson pushes Sophialogy further than did Elisabeth Schüssler Fiorenza by using it to reconstruct a feminist doctrine of the Trinity. Indeed, Johnson is the first to explore this ground. Taking up Rahner's axiom that the "economic trinity is the immanent Trinity," Johnson centers in on the notion of the relationality of God inherent in the doctrine of the Trinity. Like other feminists who have claimed the doctrine of the Trinity as a feminist theological ally for its focus on relationality, an aspect of human life valued and upheld in feminist thought, Johnson grasps the usefulness of the doctrine of the Trinity for the feminist theological project: "Being in communion constitutes God's very essence."[1] God's relationality is of the essence of God and not simply an attribute, "accident," or afterthought.

Again, as we saw was the case for Schüssler Fiorenza, Johnson considers Sophialogy to be theologically promising not simply because of the link with a female name and feminine-gendered noun, Sophia, but because of the deeper implications its thought world holds for the wedding of key feminist themes and Christian theology.[2] Indeed, the sophialogical depiction of God allows for the lifting up and affirming of women's experience and women's embodiedness:

> To see the world dwelling in God is to play variations on the theme of women's bodiliness and experience of pregnancy, labor and giving birth. Correlatively, this symbol lifts up precisely those aspects of women's reality so abhorred in classical Christian anthropology—the female body and its procreative functions—and affirms them as suitable metaphor for the divine. More than suitable in fact, for they wonderfully evoke the mystery of creative, generative love that encircles the struggling world, making possible its life and growth in the face of the power of nonbeing and evil. . . . To see God and the world existing in a relationship of friendship, each indwelling the other, has deep affinity with women's experience.[3]

Here we find traces of essentializing of "women's experience" in the assumption that women intuitively know the "mystery of creative, generative love" in their very embodied potential for "pregnancy, labor and giving birth." In any event, the fact that the Wisdom traditions can be used to uplift and validate women's bodily realities as depicting the creative activity of God is important for Johnson as she takes up Sophialogy in her consideration of the doctrine of the Trinity.

In her feminist Trinitarian reflection, Johnson proceeds on the assumption that the three hypostases of the Trinity each transcend the categories of gender. Since they each cannot be bound by the designations of "male" and "female," according to Johnson, each hypostasis may, in fact, be spoken of in female terminology as equally as male.[4] Because of the social ills caused by the oppression of women and the quasi deification of men which has been supported by masculine God-language, however, Johnson asserts that it is necessary to use female terminology for the hypostases of the Trinity. She therefore uses the designations of Mother-Sophia, Jesus-Sophia, and Spirit-Sophia to speak of the three persons of the Trinity, while reversing the usual order such that the first person is spoken of last and the last as first: Spirit-Sophia, Jesus-Sophia, and Mother-Sophia.

This seems most fitting for someone who understands Christianity non-narratively. That is, Christianity is seen to be a subspecies of the greater class known as "religion," and religions as a general class are understood to express religious experience. They thus "thematize . . . [grace] in narrative and ritual, thereby clearly focussing on the Spirit's deeds of drawing all creation toward the holiness of God."[5] Narrative becomes the exterior and secondary clothing for the interior and primary "experience" which it "thematizes." Prior to narratival thematization is experience of the Spirit's grace, which itself is the starting point for theological reflection. One therefore need not start with the narratival depiction of Jesus and work from there to the doctrine of the Trinity. Thus Johnson starts with the Spirit whom we experience. A narrative approach, however, would seem to require the opposite move, as does most classical Trinitarian theology.

Johnson thus offers the name for the Godhead SHE WHO IS, which she says is a "feminist gloss" on Exodus 3:14, in which God reveals the divine name to Moses as "I AM who I AM."[6] The warrants for Johnson's use of SHE WHO IS instead of HE WHO IS, ὁ ὢν, itself which is derived from the divine self-naming in Exodus 3:14, are designated to be linguistic, theological, existential, spiritual, and political:

SHE WHO IS: linguistically this is possible; theologically it is legitimate; existentially and religiously it is necessary if speech about God is to shake off the shackles of idolatry and be a blessing for women . . . Spiritually, SHE WHO IS, spoken as the symbol of ultimate reality, of the highest beauty and truth and goodness, of the mystery of life in the midst of death, affirms women in their struggle toward dignity, power, and value. It discloses women's human nature as *imago Dei*, and reveals divine nature to be the relational mystery of life who desires the liberated human existence of all women made in her image. In promoting the flourishing of women SHE WHO IS attends to an essential element for the well-being of all creation, human beings and the earth inclusively. Politically, this symbol challenges every structure and attitude that assigns superiority to ruling men on the basis of their supposed greater godlikeness.[7]

Again, the warrants for the suggested name are not based on a narrative reading of Scripture but on the practical functions of the name for validating and affirming the experience of women as able to image the divine. That is, SHE WHO IS is taken up for theological consideration because of what it has to offer, what it does for us, how it improves our lives. No one would want to reject the value of something that could improve life. However, the logic of such warranting is much the same as that for a consumerist society. Similar warrants are used, for instance, in advertising a new and improved product. Indeed, here for feminist theology, the new and improved product is not yet fully developed, but the hope is that someday it will be, and that the use of feminine-gendered language for the deity will allow the improved product's development and marketing. While retaining the use of the traditional terms, God/He, may be an "interim strategy," according to Johnson, until such a time that the language of God/She will serve to generate "new content for references to deity in the hopes that this discourse will help to heal imaginations and liberate people for new forms of community."[8]

It is at this point that the logic begins to become circular and doubles back on itself. Previously, Johnson had implied that language is a reflection of prelinguistic or prethematic experience. This would lead one to believe that language refers to a reality beyond itself or, rather, before or prior to experience. If the religious reality is truly prelinguistic, presumably once it is thematized or put into language, this will not change it or add anything new, since the thematization or linguistic expression is only secondary and exterior. Now, however, Johnson wants to propose language which she claims will generate new content or new experience. However, this is exactly what religious language *cannot* do if it expresses a prelinguistic reality or experience. Indeed, she argues, if we do not construct language which will generate new content, Christianity may wither and fade as a result: "If the idea of God does not keep pace with developing reality, the power of experience pulls people on and the god dies, fading from memory. Is the God of the Jewish and Christian tradition so true as to be able to take account of, illumine, and integrate the currently accessible experience of women?"[9] Feminist theology is thus the savior of Christianity for the contemporary moment. This "salvation" requires that we construct new religious language that will mediate the same prelinguistic experience that is mediated in the traditional but patriarchal and thus ultimately defeating religious language. How does one determine, however, that the same prelinguistic reality or experience is mediated by the new language? Here is the "wiggle room" created by the claim to prelinguistic experience in which feminist theology can construct new language. Johnson then claims that such new language can actually add to our (prelinguistic) experiential knowledge of God. By expanding our library of metaphors for God, says Johnson, we will learn something about the divine.

> One effective way to stretch language and expand our repertoire of images is by uttering female symbols into speech about divine mystery. It is a complex exercise, not necessarily leading into emancipatory speech. An old danger that accompanies this change is that such language may be taken literally; a new danger lies in the potential for stereotyping women's reality by characterizing God simply as nurturing, caring, and so forth. The benefits, however, in my judgment, outweigh the dangers. Reorienting the imagination at a basic level, this usage challenges the idolatry of maleness in classic language about God, thereby making possible the rediscovery of divine mystery and points to recovery of the dignity of women created in the image of God.[10]

But how can new language which simply reclothes the same prelinguistic religious experience actually teach us anything, especially anything new? This conceptual knot seems, indeed, impossible to untangle.

Of course, it must be quickly stated that Johnson is not alone in being caught in this conceptual knot but is in good company among modern religious thinkers. For example, she draws on Tillich in her understanding of the function of religious language. This itself is compatible with Engelsman's use of Jungian repression and re-emergence of religious archetypes. Johnson uses both Tillich and Jungian thought (as did Tillich) to back up her statement that the nature of symbols for the divine is plastic, whereas the symbols themselves are not. That is, symbols grow from the "collective unconscious" and "cannot be produced intentionally."[11] In our day, the collective unconscious is shifting, and the patriarchal symbols are no longer capable of mediating divine mystery: "Women's religious experience is a generating force for these symbols, a clear instance of how great symbols of the divine always come into being not simply as a projection of the imagination, but as an awakening from the deep abyss of human existence in real encounter with divine being."[12] The claim is that something deeper is at work here than merely consciously and imaginatively reinventing religious symbols. On the level of the cultural or collective unconscious, we find emerging the need to express or project the feminine divine. Of course, where Johnson would differ from Engelsman is clear, for Johnson is not interested in a "feminine dimension" of the divine. Rather, the female deity is "the expression of the fullness of divine power and care shown in a female image," not simply a way of accessing God's maternal or feminine side.[13] Indeed, because God, as ultimate mystery, can be spoken of equally well or poorly with male or female terminology, feminine symbols and language are, in practice, superior to masculine, for they will break through the "idolatrous fixation" on the masculine.[14]

Again, however, we find ourselves in a logical quandary. How do we develop new religious language if it operates on the level of the collective unconscious and cannot be consciously imagined, "cannot be produced intentionally," as Johnson says? How do we encourage the emergence of religious language which will aid our flourishing if we do not consciously participate in its development and generation? Certainly

Johnson has engaged her conscious, imagination-driven productive creativity with her suggestions of SHE WHO IS, Spirit-Sophia, Jesus-Sophia, and Mother-Sophia. Where is the Archimedean point at which we move the religious structures of our collective unconscious? She admits, in effect, that no such Archimedean point exists and that this project is, in fact, "unrealizable in actual life," but that constructing such religious language is "not an end in itself." It is, however, an "essential element in reordering an unjust and deficiently religious situation."[15]

Of course, it hardly needs to be articulated that such a view of religious language necessitates a revision of the traditional claims to Scripture's "revealed" nature. Johnson does not backpedal here but openly states that this is the case. In fact, she sees the claim to Scripture's revelation to be the "brake on the articulation of divine mystery in the light of women's dignity."[16] Once the claim is granted that Scripture is revealed, argues Johnson, then the attendant claim is made that scriptural language cannot be changed or inclusivized. According to Johnson, holding to a propositional view of revelation disallows the very project in which she is engaged: "in this perspective, the church has no option in the light of women's pressing experience but to continue to repeat the pattern of language about God in the metaphor of ruling men."[17] She therefore finds the understanding of revelation on the symbolic or metaphoric rather than verbal level to be more compatible with her project. Revelation seems not to be, therefore, on the level of the metanarrative. That is, the reality of the divine life is not presented only in the overarching biblical narrative, the center of which is the Gospel stories about Jesus. Here is an example: "The woman with the coin image [the parable in Luke 15:4–10], while not frequently portrayed in Christian art due largely to the androcentric nature of the traditioning process, is essentially as legitimate a reference to God as is the shepherd with his sheep."[18] No mention is made that in other parts of the canon Jesus refers to himself as the Good Shepherd, or that Isaiah, the Psalms, and other texts speak of God as shepherding the people of Israel. This could, presumably, undercut her statement that the woman with the lost coin is "as legitimate a reference to God as is the shepherd with his sheep." God as shepherd appears throughout the scriptures, whereas God as a woman seeking a lost coin appears once. Of course, "legitimacy" for references to God cannot be based on frequency alone, both for Johnson and for the tradition in which she stands. However, to point to Jesus's self-reference as the Good Shepherd, for example, would not necessarily trump Johnson's proposal here, since presumably she could argue that the canon itself is understood as the "traditioning process," which is "androcentric" and therefore suspect as an authority.

Since the notion of "revelation" on the narrative level seems therefore to be suspect, Johnson locates it instead on the symbolic and metaphorical level. Indeed, one of the many points of convergence between Johnson and Schüssler Fiorenza, and many other feminist theologians as well, is the claim that religious language is symbolic and metaphorical:

> It is not necessary to restrict speech about God to the exact names that Scripture uses, nor to terms coined by the later tradition. So long as the words signify something that does characterize the living God mediated through Scripture, tradition and present faith experience, for example, divine liberating action or self-involving love for the world,

then new language can be used with confidence . . . The reality of God is mystery beyond all imagining. So transcendent, so immanent is the holy mystery of God that we can never wrap our minds completely around this mystery and exhaust divine reality in words or concepts.[19]

Again, we see the implicit appeal to what is claimed to be an apophatic element. As has been pointed out, however, such a claim about religious language can be, in fact, a misconstrual of apophatic theology in service of an ideological end.[20] That is, the claim that God is ultimate mystery does not mean for the apophatic tradition that the words of Scripture are therefore inadequate in addressing or depicting God.

Of course, the classical doctrine of the Trinity does, indeed, paint a picture of a God to whom relationality within God's very being and to all of creation is a defining factor. Certainly, this is a fitting judgment. In addition, we find the attraction for Johnson toward the doctrine of the Trinity in its congruence with her (implicitly) essentialist understanding of women's nature: here is a doctrine that speaks to the experience of women. Because, as Johnson says, "women typically witness to deep patterns of affiliation and mutuality as constitutive of their existence and indeed of the very grain of existence itself," the doctrine of the Trinity can help reach, validate, express, and confirm what women instinctively know in the depths of their being, contrary to the way patriarchal "classical theism" has undervalued and stifled this pattern of relationality that women inherently bear.[21]

It is here that we find, especially throughout her consideration of the doctrine of the Trinity, that Johnson appears to be reacting negatively to a quasi-Deist understanding of God, which she then reads back into what she calls "classical theism." This God of "classical theism" (who looks very much like the Deist God, the watchmaker who sets the works running and then steps back) is judged inadequate. This God is not intimately involved in the world, is fundamentally distant and unrelated, and ultimately does not meet the standards of feminism. However, the argument from the standards set by feminism is not the only way we could reasonably reject this depiction of God. We could just as easily argue, for example, in agreement with Johnson but on a different basis, that the Deist depiction of God is inadequate because it does not take fully into account the biblical narratival depiction of God. Arguing on the basis of Scripture's narrative would allow an internally fit and logically sound rejection of what Johnson sees as classical theism, without the need to bring in the warrants from feminism that rely on essentialist notions of women's identity. This would be an advantage to her, because presumably the detractors whom she wants to convince may not agree with her as to the inherent value of feminist values but would agree with her on the importance of remaining true to the depiction of the God intimately concerned for creation in the biblical narrative, as well as tradition.

Instead of pointing to the biblical narratival depiction of God to fortify and correct the "classical theist" cum Deist position against which she reacts, Johnson reaches for a panentheistic understanding of God to clear away the deficiencies of the depiction of classical theist-Deist's "unrelated" God. She is quick to point out that she is not opting for pantheism and that she wants to retain the distinction between God and creation that is dissolved in pantheism. To emphasize God's intimate connection with creation, she finds panentheism useful:

Here is a model of free reciprocal relation: God in the world and the world in God while each remains radically distinct. The relation is mutual while differences remain and are respected. . . . If theism weights the scales in the direction of divine transcendence and pantheism overmuch in the direction of immanence, panentheism attempts to hold onto both in full strength.[22]

How successful Johnson is in maintaining the distinction between God and the world is a matter for discussion. However, she finds what she considers to be an adequately panentheistic depiction of God in the biblical Wisdom traditions.

Johnson's call for a revised doctrine of the Trinity, with its corresponding revised names for each person of the Trinity—Spirit-Sophia, Mother-Sophia, Jesus-Sophia— is creative and breaks new ground. It may become the Trinitarian formula of choice for future feminist revisions for liturgical language. Many such revisions have been offered, to be sure, but they usually lack the theoretical underpinnings and theological work which Johnson provides in *She Who Is.* The following section deals with such revisions, including the objections to the traditional formula and to other suggestions made for its revision. Many of these revisions have, in fact, already been incorporated in liturgies of some of the major Christian denominations in the United States.

Liturgical Reconstructions of the Trinitarian Formula

Feminist reconstructions of the doctrine of the Trinity such as that of Elizabeth Johnson have had an impact on the worship of the church. Almost every mainline denomination in the United States has seen hymnals, prayerbooks, psalters, and/or lectionaries altered to reflect feminist inclusivizing of language for humanity and for the divine. Proposals have been set forth to alter the traditional Trinitarian formula, "in the name of the Father and of the Son and of the Holy Spirit," to make the language which names God in worship less exclusively masculine in gender. This has then been brought into liturgical forms such as prayers, lectionaries, hymnody, and sacraments. The arguments in favor of altering the traditional Trinitarian name charge that masculine naming of God at best does not disallow and at worst leads to the church's valuing of the male over against the female, which, in turn, supports the sexism of the broader culture. But how is the Christian community or communities to determine whether the formula can be changed? Following William Christian's model, such communities, in attempting to answer such questions, would appeal to their sources and principles or rules for adjudicating. This would require consideration of (at least) the following: what is the provenance and the significance within Christian discourse of the name "Father, Son, and Holy Spirit"? How do we know and name God? How, why, and according to whose authority do we invoke God's presence and blessing?[23] Such questions do need to be addressed because several charges against the traditional Trinitarian formula and against the church's baptism in that name, as well as several alternatives to the formula, have been raised by feminist theologians. We turn now first to the objections to the traditional formula and then to some of the proposed alternatives.

Sexism of God the Father

Most of the complaints leveled at the traditional Trinitarian formula center around the term "Father." The masculine term "Son" is not usually deemed as problematic as is the term "Father," for if one is willing to accept the humanity of Jesus, as we have seen, one is generally logically committed to accepting that he was male. However, as we saw in the previous chapter, this does not always follow in practice, despite the logic. Since classical Christian theology never claims for the first person of the Trinity physical attributes of masculinity, the charge is made that calling the first person "Father" is "sexist." While the term "Holy Spirit" poses even fewer immediate problems than does "Son" for reasons which should be obvious, the entire formula comes under scrutiny as both saturated with sexism and perpetuating it within the life of the church.

While the debate about sexist language is relatively new, the confusion between nominal gender and sexuality within the Godhead is not a new phenomenon and reflects a misconstrual of Christian confession.[24] The very changing of the language of worship (e.g., where "Father" becomes "Creator" or simply "God") implicitly sanctions such a misunderstanding and in essence concedes to this charge that "Father" God is male.[25] It is also charged that the very process by which the doctrine of the Trinity was articulated was itself sexist and elitist. That is, according to the argument, since the only ones "making" the doctrinal statements were those of the church hierarchy, the voices of lesser degree, especially the women, were not heard. Of course, this does not take into account the influence of the *sensus fidelium*, which moved conciliar definitions to give the "stamp of approval" to confession which had been long and widely held within the church.

Metaphor and the Trinitarian Name

Some feminists take issue with those who maintain that "Father, Son, and Holy Spirit" is God's proper name.[26] That is, they claim that "Father, Son, and Holy Spirit" is not a name but a series of metaphors. The implication ends up being that the traditional formula, "I baptize you in the *name* of the Father, and of the Son, and of the Holy Spirit" signifies "I baptize you in the *metaphor* of the Father, and of the Son, and of the Holy Spirit." According to this view, "Father, Son and Holy Spirit" is neither a divinely revealed name nor ecclesiastically produced but a metaphorical representation of or reference to the Deity. Along with this argument often comes the claim that God is ultimate mystery, Wholly Other, entirely unknowable. Since our language is inadequate to the task of speaking of God, so the argument goes, all language we use to speak of God is metaphorical, as we saw was the case for Elizabeth Johnson.[27] A possible corollary to this may claim, but does not necessarily have to claim, that all language for God is socially constructed. It follows from this claim that we are free to construct new metaphors when the old die out.

Of course, to assume that language for God is, at some level, divinely given, even while enfleshed by cultural forms, puts the Christian who claims that it is also sexist and therefore potentially harmful in a terrible bind. If we understand the language and the story which describe the Holy One of Israel as divinely given, even through and in its cultural conditioning, and if we then charge this language with sexism, the logical conclusion is that the God who gives such a gift is either sexist (in which case no true feminist worth her salt would worship such a God, as is the claim of Mary Daly and Daphne Hampson), or that this God gives noxious gifts, or both. This problematic conclusion is often avoided by feminist theologians in their implicit assumption that God-talk is not at any level divinely given but is in toto culturally created. This, however, departs radically from traditional Christian claims about knowledge of God and the nature of Scripture, insofar as it leaves aside almost entirely any attempt to negotiate or refashion claims to God's speaking through Scripture.[28] Again, we found this to be the case with Elizabeth Johnson.

Sexism Denies the Power of the Gospel

This charge links the assumptions of the two previous claims with a revised understanding of the sacrament of baptism itself. The most articulate expression of this position is the doctoral dissertation of Ruth Duck, a feminist theologian best known for her inclusive-language hymns: "Images that reflect cultural gender biases contradict conversion to new life in egalitarian community and subvert openness to the gifts of the Spirit. The formula must be revised; the Trinitarian formula presently used is not adequate to serve as the theological and liturgical center of the rite of baptism."[29] Drawing her understanding of metaphor from the writings of Ricoeur, Black, and Wheelwright, Duck posits that, in metaphor, meaning emerges from the tension arising from the use of two terms which are both like and unlike each other.[30] Meaning created by a metaphor cannot be paraphrased or put into other words since metaphors create meaning through a specific association of interaction of two terms.[31] A major logical inconsistency in Duck's argument emerges at this point, for the assertion that metaphors are untranslatable does not square with her insistence on the "translatability" of the "metaphor" Father, Son, and Holy Spirit. Since each hearer will have his or her own associations for the terms juxtaposed by the metaphor, Duck argues, a metaphor maker or user cannot control how the metaphor will be received.[32] This means that the "meaning" of the metaphor is, for the most part, out of the hands of its user and in the ears of the listener or reader.

While Duck acknowledges that traditional understandings of God insist that God is beyond the confines of the categories of sexuality and physicality, she argues that people often nevertheless assume that God is masculine because of the largely masculine language used to name God. If we assume that God is masculine, so the argument goes, we violate the commandment, "You shall not make for yourself a graven image." That is, we invoke an idol of our own making. Instead of suggesting that we attend more closely to our catechizing in order that such mistakes are not made, she suggests, instead, that we change our language and, ultimately implicitly, the story we tell in that language.

According to Duck's feminist reinterpretation of the sacrament, baptism signifies a conversion to new life in the egalitarian community of the body of Christ. Basing her understanding on the work of Sallie McFague, Duck says that dying with Christ in baptism means participating with Jesus Christ in living in "radical identification with all . . . the needy, the outcast, the oppressed," and rising with Christ means "knowing God as a permanent presence empowering the fulfillment of all creation."[33] However, even a casual reading of Romans 6, 1 Corinthians 15, and Colossians 2 points to the "thin" quality of Duck's description of the Christian sacrament of baptism even while what she does offer in itself is not thereby objectionable.[34] According to her definition, the traditional baptismal formula, "in the name of the Father, Son, and Holy Spirit," allegedly reflects patterns of sexism and gender bias and contradicts the egalitarian newness of life of the community of the baptized and its new ethical orientation.[35] To charge, as does Duck, that the "sexism" of the formula denies the freedom of baptism in fact requires a thin description of the sacrament.

The Doctrine of the Trinity Is Not Biblical

The claim that the doctrine of the Trinity is not biblical is based in the first place on the assumption that that which is authoritative is that which can be demonstrated to be "biblical."[36] Just what it means to be "biblical," however, must be demonstrated before one can reasonably claim that since the doctrine of the Trinity is not biblical, we need not be wed to it. Ruth Duck implicitly assumes that that which is "biblical" is confined to those words or concepts which are contained on the pages of the Bible.[37] From this point of view, it does, indeed, appear that the doctrine of the Trinity is not "biblical" in this strict sense. The fact that Athanasius withheld reproach from those semi-Arians who could not accept the homoousios on the basis of its nonbiblical origin could serve as an indicator for a catholic patience with the likes of Ruth Duck on this matter.

While it may seem that the only obvious way to define "biblical" is that which appears on the pages of the Bible, for the orthodox patristic writers, that which counts as "scriptural" and therefore authoritative (the key notion behind the term "biblical here") encompasses that which is argued, inferred, or construed on the basis of the biblical witness read within the guidelines of the rule of faith. This, as is apparent by the general acceptance of the term homoousios, is true whether or not the concepts, titles, or formulae are actually contained on the pages of Bible itself.[38]

When the Bible is used as "source" in Duck's sense, a mine of concepts which can be employed at will without a canonically internal discrimination as to what constitutes centrality, we present-day readers have equal footing with the biblical writers to name and describe God. We may therefore generate, so the argument goes, new metaphors which are "equivalent" to those in the biblical source.[39] This is not to say that the Bible is not revelatory; the metaphors in the Bible can, indeed, "reveal God's nature." The distinction is that this "revealing" of God's nature is not unique or limited to the canonical witness.[40] Since content of God's nature is described through metaphors, instead of via characters whose identities are displayed in the concrete interplay of action and intention, that which is described ("God") can be separated from that which describes it (the narrative structure) as the grain can be separated from the husk that contains it. This, as we have seen, is one of the hallmarks of non-narrative reading of the Bible.

Thus the reader is free to construe Scripture not as a holistic, overarching story whose main characters are Israel and its God but as a collection of concepts or images, and the authority of these concepts is assessed on the basis of historical priority, facticity, and/or verifiability. Therefore, since the baptismal formulae often regarded by historical critics to be the oldest bear only the name of Jesus, Duck argues that the traditional trinitarian baptismal formula is not the only possible name in which Christians may be baptized.[41] Likewise, Duck notes that the historical reliability of the risen Christ's commission to baptize in the name of the Father, Son, and Holy Spirit is not supported by scholarly evidence. Hence, she argues, Matthew 28:19 cannot be used as an authoritative dominical injunction to necessitate baptism only in the name of the Father, Son, and Holy Spirit. Reading Scripture as source which can be historically sifted for nuggets of "fact" thus aids Duck in overturning what she sees to be the hegemony of the traditional baptismal formula:

> Persons who accept historical-critical scripture scholarship would find it difficult to support the idea that the trinitarian baptismal formula must be used because it represents the words of Jesus. . . . Clearly, the idea that we must baptize with the formula "In the name of the Father . . ." because of its presence in Matthew 28:19b is not adequately supported by the evidence.[42]

While Duck may be correct that contemporary critical biblical scholarship cannot fully support the sole use of the traditional baptismal formula, neither can such scholarship argue against it. To assume that the theories of historical-critical scholarship could play such a role is to place far too much confidence in the "objectivity" and conclusiveness of the methods. According to the methods of most historical Jesus research, the words of the risen Lord preserved for us by the canonical witness are not within the bounds of investigation: research on the "historical Jesus" tends to stop at the crucifixion. To be a thorough going historical-critic at this point, one would not claim any such confidence regarding the words of the risen Lord.

Ecumenicity, Catholicity, and Truth

All of these arguments are especially vulnerable to the objection raised by the matter of ecumenicity: the sole element which all Christians have in common is baptism by water in the name of the Father, Son, and Holy Spirit. To threaten this feeble but blessed tie which binds our hearts in one accord may finally be too much to ask of ecumenically minded mainline denominations. The baptismal formula cannot be changed, say those who oppose the alternative proposals, without broad ecumenical consensus if such baptisms are to be recognized by the church universal.

However, the bolder proponents of changing the formula do not accept any such pleas for Christian unity on the basis of ecumenicity, for they argue that the truth (such as they conceive of it) is more important than any unity based on a distortion of the gospel. For example, Duck notes the following: "I do not advocate waiting for ecumenical consensus before seeking alternatives to the traditional baptismal formula. . . . Christian unity' that accepts patriarchal ideology is fraudulent; for in patriarchal systems, unity is based on domination, subordination and violation, and not on the mutual relations of love proper to Christian unity."[43] This attitude veils provincialism and insensitivity to other Christian communions. In the field of anthropology, such a judgment might be called "ethnocentric." However, the feminist objection here is extremely important and often neglected in the "for the sake of ecumenicity, let's put this one off" plea: if we claim to speak about truth, no amount of compromising to appease is appropriate. Certainly, the truth of the gospel must be proclaimed despite its reception, positive or negative. The question, however, remains: whose version of "truth" is a convincingly adequate presentation of the truth of the gospel of Jesus Christ?

Because of these objections to the Trinitarian formula, several alternative triadic formulae have been suggested for use in Christian baptism. So far as I am aware, no one has yet proposed Elizabeth Johnson's Spirit-Sophia, Mother-Sophia, and Jesus-Sophia, for use in baptism, but this may not be long in coming. The alternatives vary widely in their degree of proximity to biblical language, and some attempt to retain the Trinitarian formula's compact, pithy nature, while others have rich imagery and abundant turns of phrase.[44]

Creator, Redeemer, Sustainer

An alternative frequently suggested is the triadic formula "Creator, Redeemer, Sustainer."[45] However, even some feminist Christians interested in changing the baptismal formula understand it to be inadequate, insofar as it overdistinguishes the three persons of the Trinity.[46] For example, Christian confession understands creation to be the work of the Father in the Son by the power of the Holy Spirit; the works *ad extra* of the Trinity are not divided. This is implicit in the claim that "in him [Jesus] all things were created, in heaven and on earth, visible and invisible" (Col. 1:16). The fact that the Nicene creed borrows the language from this very verse about Jesus to speak of the *Father* underscores the point: "We believe in one God, the Father Almighty, maker of Heaven and Earth, of all that is, visible and invisible." To suggest, then, that "Creator" equals "Father" is to misrepresent Christian confession, split off the persons of the Trinity one from the other, and divide the Godhead much as in the manner of Marcion. Again, to suggest that "Redeemer" equals "Son" and that "Sanctifier" equals "Holy Spirit" can only cause confusion, for classical Trinitarian confession understands the entire Godhead to operate in redemption and sanctification. Predicates never serve as grammatical subjects.

In addition, the formula "Creator, Redeemer, Sustainer" does not adequately link the God whom it names to the personal God depicted in the biblical narrative. One could, in theory, witness a baptism in the name of the Creator, Redeemer, and Sustainer and quite possibly not recognize this name to refer to the God of the Bible who called a specific people named Israel and who sent a male Jew named Jesus to be Israel's Messiah. At the very least, the baptismal formula used by Christians should allow us to make clear to ourselves and to the world our confession of the One to whom we belong. "Creator, Redeemer, and Sustainer" does not adequately fit this criterion.

Fountain, Offspring, Wellspring

Ruth Duck, in her turn, suggests that we restore the threefold questioning recorded in Hippolytus's *Apostolic Tradition*, which incorporated within the baptismal rite a combination of the recitation of the rule of faith and an examination of the baptismal candidate.[47] Whereas the *Apostolic Tradition* recorded the use of the Trinitarian name, Duck suggests changing the name while retaining the form of threefold questioning:

Do you believe in God, the Source, the fountain of life?

I believe.

Do you believe in Christ, the offspring of God embodied in Jesus of Nazareth and in the church?

I believe.

Do you believe in the liberating Spirit of God, the wellspring of new life?

I believe.

After each response, the water would be administered. Duck claims that she retains the triadic form but not the Trinitarian name for reasons of theological integrity.[48] She feels that her alternative is an improvement over "Creator, Redeemer, Sustainer," insofar as it describes more fully the relationship between the first and second persons of the Trinity. She also regards her use of "fountain," "offspring" and "wellspring" to express without functional metaphors the relationships between the persons of the Trinity. She also appreciates the use of such metaphors related to water, which she feels are particularly appropriate to baptism and are more "lively than the overused Father-Son metaphor."

Duck has offered a truly creative solution. Certainly, we can appreciate her use of traditional sources and her honest attempt to remain faithful to some form of Trinitarian confession, if not to the Trinitarian name. Two problems, however, remain: the lack of clear biblical warrants for her use of "Fountain, Offspring, and Wellspring," combined with the highly historicist objection to the Matthean formula, and the tenuous account within her liturgy of the intra-Trinitarian relationships. While she wants to avoid the highly "condensed" nature of the Trinitarian formula, her less concentrated version does not say as much. Thus, her argument ultimately confirms what she would like to set aside: that the Trinitarian name is shorthand, a picture that paints a thousand words. Her suggestion for alternative baptismal liturgy simply cannot express with its almost fifty words what "I baptize you in the name of the Father, Son, and Holy Spirit" denotes in concentrated form.

Abba, Servant, Paraclete

Gail Ramshaw takes the important step of acknowledging that all Trinitarian knowledge of God stems from our knowledge of Jesus Christ.[49] Of course, she is recasting what Athanasius tried to point out to the Arians, that "He who calls God Father names

Him from the Word . . . the title Father has its significance and bearing only from the Son."[50] Ramshaw therefore begins her consideration of an alternative Trinitarian formula with the term "Son" and offers us as an alternative "Servant." She chooses Servant because it takes up the imagery of the Isaiah servant songs, of Jesus' washing the disciples feet, healing the sick and feeding the hungry, and atoning for the sin of all humanity through his sacrifice on the cross. Then she moves to the first person of the Trinity and offers as a possible alternative to "Father" the term "Abba", which is, of course, the Aramaic word for "Father" used by Jesus in his agony in Gethsemane in Mark 14:36, and used by Paul in Galatians 4:6 and Romans 8:15. The alternative for "Spirit" that Ramshaw offers, Paraclete, is simply the Greek term used for the figure Jesus promises to send when he "goes to the Father." [51] While it is not clear from Ramshaw's essay why one would need an alternative to the term "Spirit," in her later book *God Beyond Gender*, she comments on the catechetical harm wrought by liturgical art:

> In the church I attended as a child, the massive chancel mural depicted the Father as a bearded old man, the Son as a long-haired young man bare to the waist, and the Spirit as an ermine-cloaked and hooded figure with a shining hand upraised. Someone once suggested to me that my entire scholarly career is in reaction to that mutual.[52]

Such tidbits of biographical information may help the reader better understand the author but only serve to strengthen the suspicion that what is needed is not a change in language but, rather, better catechesis and liturgical art. Nevertheless, Ramshaw points to what she sees as an advantage to this alternative formula in its multilingual, multicultural representation of the faith in its combined use of Aramaic, Latin, and Greek, three languages of some of the earliest Christian communities.

While Ramshaw explicitly states that "Abba, Servant, Paraclete" is not intended to replace the Trinitarian formula ("That Trinity language can be discarded is not true: Father-Son-Spirit language is normative for Christian orthodoxy"[53] she does suggest that "such a model can complement our normative imagery of the triune God."[54] However, her prayer for the feast of the baptism of our Lord and her doxology and blessing replace "Father, Son, Holy Spirit" with "Abba, Servant, Paraclete." It is ultimately not clear how comfortable Ramshaw feels with "orthodoxy" here, and one wonders if she might prefer to say that at times "orthodoxy" and "inclusivity" may be mutually exclusive alternatives.[55]

Of Whom, through Whom, in Whom

Ramshaw also briefly mentions the possibility, "recalling Augustine, to baptize 'in the name of the Triune God, from whom, through whom, and in whom all things exist, now and forever.' "[56] This again, like her "Abba, Servant, Paraclete," is a truly creative attempt to struggle with Trinitarian theology while searching for an alternative triad for the Trinitarian name. Whereas "Abba, Servant, Paraclete" was an attempt to find within biblical language a resource for alternative triads, this proposal looks to tradition as resource, specifically here to Augustine's *On Christian Doctrine*. There, Augustine states: "For it is not easy to find a name that will suitably express so great excellence, unless it is better to speak in this way: The Trinity, one God, of whom are all things, through whom are all things, in whom are all things."[57] Augustine echoes here Romans 11:36, the benediction which concludes Paul's three-chapter discussion of the faithfulness of God in his dealings with Israel. Paul himself is stressing the unity of God, as he does in a similar statement in 1 Corinthians 8:6. It is this stress on the oneness of God (not a concern for the "sexism" of the Trinitarian name or for the sacrament of baptism at all) which Augustine is picking up in Paul's statement. This becomes clearer when Augustine's statement is read in context, for he has said immediately prior to the quote which Ramshaw picks out: "The true objects of enjoyment, then, are the Father and the Son and the Holy Spirit, who are at the same time the Trinity, *one Being*, supreme above all, and common to all who enjoy Him, if He is an object, and not rather the cause of all objects, or indeed even if He is the cause of all." Clearly, therefore, Augustine was not suggesting that "of Whom, through Whom, in Whom" is a preferable replacement for "Father, Son, and Holy Spirit". He was simply trying to point out that the words "Father, Son and Holy Spirit" do not signify three distinct "objects" to be "enjoyed" but rather name the one triune God who is the cause of all objects which we use and thereby the only true "object" of our "enjoyment."

In any case, even though she may misrepresent Augustine here, Ramshaw nevertheless does present an interesting possibility. Here is a triad which is biblical, insofar as it is found within the Pauline corpus and is present throughout the church's liturgical traditions. Since the phrase "Triune God" itself is not a *name* at all, into which we can baptize as even Ramshaw understands, she adds the prepositional triad, which has a Trinitarian ring to it. This does not solve the problem, however, because prepositional phrases are not usually names, and nowhere in Scripture or tradition are these prepositional phrases deemed a replacement for the Trinitarian name "Father, Son, and Holy Spirit." Because of this, the prepositional triad does not adequately name the deity into whom Christians are baptized. The same criticism thus applies here as was mentioned with regard to Creator, Redeemer, and Sustainer: it does not specify personally the God of the Bible, who called Israel into covenant and who sent a male Jew named Jesus to be Israel's Messiah.

Mother, Lover, Friend

This triad offered for our consideration by Brian Wren, the well-known inclusive language hymnist, is the furthest removed from either traditional or biblical language and theology. Wren credits his triad of metaphors, "Mother, Lover, Friend," to feminist theologian Sallie McFague.[58] Since Wren's work is a popularization of academic feminist theological ideas and not a systematic theology itself, he does not even begin to suggest that "Mother, Lover, Friend" is an alternative triadic formula to the Trinitarian name. Instead, he uses each of the three "models", as well as many others, independently and interchangeably. His hymn "Bring Many Names" is a good illustration of the Wrenian technique: images and metaphors and similes are brought together without apparent concern to theological or even thematic logic. The effect is kaleidoscopic; the hymn washes over its singers many possible ways of speaking of and imagining

God, such that one's understanding of God is broadened and challenged. Because of this, many of Wren's hymns function as catechesis rather than doxology: the intention is to teach the congregation more than it is to praise any specific deity. To be sure, most hymns do indeed function in both respects, as catechesis and doxology, but since Wren is self-consciously engaged in a reformation, his main concern is to educate the laity in the newly reformed doctrine and confession. One need only consider his polemic against the very notion of grace as being "hierarchical" to sense the direction of the reformation he proposes.[59]

Father, Son, Holy Spirit: One God, Mother of Us All

The alternative which merits the most serious attention is the formula developed for use at Riverside Church in New York City by James F. Kay, now homiletician at Princeton Seminary. Augmenting the traditional Trinitarian name is the phrase "One God, Mother of Us All," the appellation "Mother" being appropriated from the use of Julian of Norwich. Kay acknowledges that he framed this formula by way of compromise "to preserve trinitarian signification, to protect the ecumenical validity of baptisms administered at The Riverside Church, and to satisfy sufficiently feminist demands that had earlier led the pastor to employ a novel formula that was a doctrinal disaster."[60]

In 1982, the pastoral staff at Riverside, then led by William Sloane Coffin, had decided to "inclusivize" the language of the baptismal formula and began administering baptisms in the name of "God the Creator, Christ the Redeemer, and the Holy Spirit, our Constant Companion." Christopher Morse of Union Theological Seminary voiced his objection, mentioning his concerns to James F. Kay, who was at the time one of Morse's doctoral students at Union. The parish staff was angry at Morse's "hairsplitting"(!) and challenged him to offer a better alternative. Kay then did just this, combining Julian's use of "Mother" for Christ with the insight from the axiom that the works ad extra of the Trinity are undivided. On this basis, so the argument goes, we can call the Godhead itself "Mother."

Kay's assessment of Riverside's original "inclusivized" version of the baptismal formula is perceptive; it was, indeed, a theological disaster. And, if one feels challenged by the feminists in the pews to make some changes in language, his revised Riverside formula may be the best alternative. But the question remains whether Kay's suggestion in the end only serves to make catechetical and theological matters worse. That is, does the addition of "One God, Mother of Us All" not give the impression to the Mr. and Mrs. Murphy of the congregation that, indeed, God the Father is a male in need of a female companion? Doesn't this just confirm the stereotypes one is trying to overturn? Again, one remembers Gail Ramshaw's reaction to the art in her childhood church: what was needed there, and here as well, is not a few more pictures or an extra metaphor here and there, but better catechesis. Changing words or tacking on phrases may not be the best way to do this.

Of course, baptism in any name other than that of the Father, Son, and Holy Spirit is a grievously communion-dividing issue. Rebaptism or conditional baptism has been and will continue to be required by the church universal where such baptism have taken place, for they are not Christian baptisms from the perspective either of the scriptural witness or the ecumenical catholic Christian faith.[61] Ultimately, however, the arguments for retaining the Trinitarian name for God presented here are not based on ecumenism, a misplaced sense of nostalgia, or an odd belief in the magical efficacy of the Trinitarian formula. Rather, "Father, Son, and Holy Spirit" is the only shorthand we have which expresses the canonical identity of Jesus Christ, his relation to the God of Israel, the salvific nature of his work, and the identity of the church called forth in his name. Unless and until another is thoughtfully worked out and ecumenically agreed upon, it is the name for the God into whom we baptize in Christian baptism. The burden of proof rests on those who do not believe that this is a proper name for God. Those who object to the name Father, Son, and Holy Spirit must examine whether they, in fact, want to name a god other than the Holy Trinity.

We have seen in this chapter some of the creative work of feminist theologians with regard to the doctrine of the Trinity and to alternative Trinitarian formulae. This is one of the key points at which feminist work has engaged the worship life of the church, and feminist theology has leapt off the written page and into the prayers and hymns of the people. The constructive work we have seen here, however, has been, for the most part, non-narrative, relying for its understanding of God primarily on feminist arguments about what counts as sexist and only secondarily on the narrative depiction of the God of the Bible. This is not to say that these reformulations are not "christian." Neither are they "unbiblical." They are, simply, less narratival in their depiction, naming and address of God.

CONCLUSION
Changing of the Gods?

I believe in God
who created woman and man in the image of God,
who created the world
and entrusted the care of the earth
to both sexes.

I believe in the totality
of the redeemer,
in whom there is neither Greek nor Jew
neither slave nor free, neither man nor woman,
for we are all one in redemption.

I believe in the Holy Spirit,
the feminine Spirit of God
who gave us life like a mother bird,
and bore us
and covers us
with her wings.[1]

What, then, happens to the biblical narrative in feminist theological interpretation? How do the parts of the biblical narrative relate to the whole, and the whole to the believers, both as individuals and as a community? As this creed illustrates, the shape of the whole Christian story begins very subtly and slowly to shift in much of mainline feminist theological reconstructions. The concrete individuality of each narrative moment of that story dissolves, along with the shifting whole. This indicates what we

128

outlined in chapter 1 as a non-narrative reading of the Christian scriptures, in distinction to a narrative reading.

In chapter 2, we found that the hermeneutical presuppositions on which mainline feminist theologies tend to base their reconstructions of Christian doctrine allow for a fundamental repatterning and narrative decontextualizing of the story. In chapter 3, we saw how this affected the doctrine of sin, such that the Fall story could be translated in terms of a fall into patriarchy and women's sin could be fundamentally abstracted from and distinguished over against men's sin. In chapters 4 and 5, we discovered how mainline feminist theologies can alter the identity of Jesus as he is presented in the Gospels of Christian Scripture: rather than showing how he belongs to a particular configuration of events, those of the life of Israel before God and Jesus' own earthly life, mainline feminist theologies have offered us a new narrative setting into which Jesus may be fitted. In chapter 6, we noted that the doctrine of God has relied on a refitting of the narrative pieces of the Christian story, such that a reconstructed doctrine of the Trinity can emerge.

If these observations are correct, it puts mainline feminist theologies in a position of self-contradiction. In theory, mainline feminist theologies exult in the contextual and relational; however, in practice, they are in fact an example of non-narrative reading and thus non-contextual and a-relational in this sense. Consider the following quote regarding the fundamental relational aspect of narrative understanding:

> the sort of understanding gained from narrative does not abstract from the concrete individuality of that which is understood. Narratives depict events ' . . . as elements in a single and concrete complex of relationships. Thus a letter I burn may be understood not only as oxidizable substance but as a link with an old friend. It may have relieved a misunderstanding, raised a question, or changed my plans at a crucial moment. As a letter, it belongs to a kind of story, a narrative of events which would be unintelligible without reference to it.' [. . .] Narratives help us understand events by locating them within larger meaningful patterns . . . [this] configurational understanding is the sort of understanding provided by a narrative. Within a narrative, an event ceases to be an isolated monad and becomes a part of the whole.[2]

Such relationality and contextuality is exactly what mainline feminist theological interpretation of Christian Scripture does not offer us with regard to the biblical narrative depiction of God, in spite of its best intentions for wholeness. Indeed, we have seen how mainline feminist Christologies abstract from the concrete particularity of the Christian story.

Mainline feminist theologies, therefore, rely not on configurational understanding, which "organizes episode, event, and character into meaningful patterns without systematically abstracting from their individuality in the way that general laws do," but rather rely on what we might call disfigurational understanding.[3] This, as we have seen, is the goal of much of mainline feminist theology, to disfigure, destabilize, and reconfigure the narrative, which itself is claimed to be so thoroughly stained with patriarchy that no alternative besides disfigurement remains.

We have seen that some feminist theologies, insofar as they represent non-narrative theology, assume that the character of the biblical text is such that we can indeed have the "subject matter" of the Bible without the stories, that the biblical narratives do not mean what they say, and that there is a gap between the representation and the represented. To assume this is to undo the logic of belief with which the canonical Gospels themselves operate, as well as that exhibited in the classical hermeneutic.[4] That is, it dismantles not merely the interpretive practices of reading Christian Scripture but the entire web of logically interdependent narrated moments which together form the meta-narrative of the Christian canon.

First, we saw that mainline feminist theology, as a subset of modern Christian theology, takes on the extra-narratival claims of the feminist movement and feminist theorists. In the case of mainline Christian feminist theologies, the extra-narratival claims of feminism are usually deemed to be true and, as such, are taken into the body of doctrines considered authentic doctrines. A way to explain this phenomenon is to point out that many feminist theologians tend to assume a T/R-A pattern of connecting truth and authenticity in the governing doctrines. That is, for mainline feminist theology, the extra-narratival claim of feminism, for example, the obviously valid claim that "women deserve equal pay for equal work," is understood to be true and *therefore* on par with authentic Christian doctrine. The claims of feminism are then granted the status of governing doctrines, which place the biblical depiction of God at a secondary level of authority.

This distinction underscores the inherent conceptual instability in many feminist theological reconstructions. As we saw in chapter 1, the T/R-A pattern allows all truths to be absorbed into the community's body of doctrines as authentic doctrine, and the community of faith is thereby bound to teach them. This conceptual instability, of course, has little to do with the specific nature of feminist extra-narratival claims but rather has its roots in the implicit pattern with which authentic doctrine and truth are related. Feminist theologies may be able to build stronger and internally less inconsistent ways of relating authentic doctrine and truth claims, but they will first need to grapple with the internal logical difficulties which, despite their best efforts, undermine their project because of the pattern which applies.

While mainline feminism does appear to operate with an implicit T/R-A schema of relating truth to authenticity, we have seen that biblical feminism implicitly adopts the pattern A/T-R for its governing doctrines. Can biblical feminism then point the way for a new and stronger Christian feminism? For biblical feminists as for mainline feminists, the extra-narratival claim of feminism, such as "women deserve equal pay for equal work," is taken to be true, but for biblical feminists and those who adopt an implicit A-T/R pattern for their governing doctrine, such claims are not necessarily granted the status of an authentic doctrine, much less a governing doctrine. This is because the A-T/R pattern of relating truth to authenticity allows for the possibility for truths external to the religious system. The theological sources allow the acceptance of these extra-narratival claims as truths without absorbing them as authentic doctrine, either primary or governing. They may be accepted, but this does not necessarily have to be the case. Even if they are not accepted as authentic doctrine, they can be theologically explored as truths apart from the immediate religious framework.

Another way to describe this is to say that when mainline feminists allow feminist extra-narratival claims to become governing doctrine, the logic of how to relate truth and authenticity flips or reverses from that of the classical pattern of the world religions. Here is the doctrinal analogue to the hallmark practice in modern biblical interpretation which Frei pointed to: the reversal of the direction of interpretation.

Mainline feminist Christian theologies tend to be internally unstable and logically inconsistent because the T/R-A pattern of their governing doctrines tends to force them to accept such a multiplicity of truths as authentic doctrine that what counts for authentic doctrine becomes incoherent. The pattern of connecting truth to authenticity can thus pull them toward post-Christian confession through the acceptance as true those claims which at best question and at worse contradict classic points of Christian confession. Biblical feminist Christian theologies, by contrast, embodying as they do the A/T-R pattern, tend to be more consistent at holding to the biblical narrative depiction of God. While biblical feminist work may have a greater success rate at remaining recognizably Christian than does some mainline feminist work, it tends to do less "political" work. Many biblical feminists are still struggling with equality of women in ministry rather than forging fresh doctrinal tools as the mainline theologians are attempting.

However, we noted two mainline feminist theologians whose work proved exceptions to this pattern, Sarah Coakley and Mary Grey. Examples from their work were mentioned in chapter 3 as fitting the narrative pattern, unlike most mainline feminist theologies, and yet they both are actively engaged in feminism as a means of social change. In addition, Angela West has served in chapters 3 and 5 as an example of a narrative but socially progressive feminist. "Narrative" therefore does not equal "socially conservative."[5]

While feminist theology has become, over the course of the last twenty years, quite popular, it has nevertheless received criticism from the scholarly guild and from some of the mainline denominations. Up until very recently, there has been a only a trickle of critique in the form of scholarly publication. However, the critique evidently has been enough to cause the feminist theological guild anguish and concern. Indeed, one of the recent annual meetings of the American Academy of Religion had an entire session devoted to discussing the "backlash" against feminism, particularly in the theological and religious studies guild. Backlash is understood as:

> a powerful counterassault on the rights of women of all colors, men of color, gay, lesbian, and bisexual persons, working-class persons, poor persons, and other less powerful groups both in the U.S. and abroad. In Faludi's words, "backlash [is] an attempt to retract the handful of small and hard-won victories that the feminist movement did manage to win for women. This counterassault is largely insidious: in a kind of pop-culture version of the Big Lie, it stands the truth boldly on its head and proclaims that the very steps that have elevated women's position have actually led to their downfall. . . . [This reaction] has been set off not by women's achievement of full equality but by the increased possibility that they might win it."[6]

With regard to our initial consideration of narrative interpretation and the logic of relating truth and authenticity, we can sketch in broad strokes the types of critique of feminist theology thus far as follows: Of the instances of backlash, two broad types follow the A-T/R, that is, the narrative pattern. In one of these, the extra-narratival claims of feminism are deemed false, and in the other they are deemed true, but in neither are the extra-narratival claims elevated to the place of governing doctrine. The first is represented by such writers as Susan Foh, who rejects even the most innocent of "biblical feminism," and Manfred Hauke.[7] The second type of critique is represented by some biblical feminists and by Susanne Heine, among others, who often represent mainline feminism and yet tend toward a narrative approach.[8] Both of these types tend to fit the narrative interpretive logic and on this basis critique mainline feminist theology. A third critique of feminist theology follows instead the T/R-A pattern and deems the extra-narratival claims of feminism to be true, but the authentic doctrine of the classical Christian faith to be false. Examples of this critique include Daphne Hampson and Mary Daly.[9] This critique is consistently non-narrative and (purposefully) post-Christian. This serves to show that critique of feminist theology does not always come from the "narrativists" but from non-narrativists as well. Being critical of mainline feminist theology does not depend on one's adopting a narrative approach.

Any woman who does identify herself as a feminist will want to work to avoid the losses which could be incurred, as Letty Russell says, by any backlash resulting from our actually winning something like equality. However, part of being a powerful woman is to refuse to let others speak or think for her, whether that be the male establishment or the feminist counterestablishment. To critique feminist work can itself be a form of feminist work, which can serve ultimately to strengthen it. However, in the present climate, any work which uncovers potential flaws in a feminist theologian's methodology or constructive work tends to be understood as backlash, a dangerous and reproachable betrayal.

Nevertheless, I will venture an assessment of mainline feminist theologies. Most mainline feminist theologians, sharing as they do the direction of hermeneutical flow with the final critique here, that is, the non-narrative flow, would probably find themselves quite close ideologically and theologically, if they were consistently and courageously honest, to Mary Daly and Daphne Hampson. As it is, however, mainline feminist theology tends to occupy a mediating position, attempting to "redeem" Christianity and purge it of its patriarchy while remaining within the fold.

As regards the logic of belief versus the logic of coming to belief, we find that mainline feminist theologians tend to favor the logic of coming to belief. That is, they are engaged in an apologetic task rather than a properly dogmatic task. An example of the attempt to engage in the dogmatic task while, in fact, doing apologetics can be found in the title of the well-known essay by Rosemary Radford Ruether which poses the question, "Can a Male Savior Save Women?"[10] The question as to whether a male savior can save women is implicitly posed as though directed toward the cultured despiser who finds a datum which is incidental to Christian confession, that is, the very maleness of Jesus, to be problematic. For the narrative reader of Scripture, however, the question itself is a priori ruled out by the logic of belief, for to call Jesus "savior" means that he, by definition, *saves all* who call upon his name. The intent, however, is noble: to "apologize" or to make more palatable the claims of Christianity to those outside the faith, particularly here, feminists.

As Frei claimed, so mainline feminist theology bears out, that when the logic of coming to belief wins out over the logic of belief—that is, extra-narratival versus internal description—the narratives about Jesus (if they are to remain meaningful, and all Christian theologians want to claim they do remain meaningful in some way) must be made to refer to some subject matter other than a man named Jesus presented to us in the interplay between plot and character development in the Gospels. So, the way the narratives were deemed meaningful for Schleiermacher was that they mediated to us Jesus in his "God-consciousness." For Bultmann, the narratives mediated "existential encounter" with Jesus. For Elizabeth Schüssler Fiorenza and Elizabeth Johnson, who follow in Schleiermacher's and Bultmann's steps, we have seen that the narratives can mediate "Sophia," while for Rita Nakashima Brock it can be "Christa-community." Here again we see the congruence between non-narrative reading and feminist hermeneutics:the concern for apologetics and drawing in the "cultured despiser" of Christianity, bleeds through to the task of dogmatics.

As an apologetic project, mainline feminist theology then is simply in good company among modern theologies. That is, mainline feminist theologians are not engaged in any radically new task at all when read in the light of other modern theology, which also exchanges the logic of belief for the logic of coming to belief, or, in other words, the task of dogmatics with that of apologetics. It is rather ironic that some of the same scholars who were quick to accept the theology of Bultmann and Tillich should so vociferously and energetically reject the theology of feminists. Certainly, this is yet another example of sexism rearing its ugly head. If one can accept modern theology, one should have no problem with feminist theology, unless it is, indeed, a matter of patriarchal assumptions about what "counts" and does not "count" as matters worthy of theological reflection.

However, my objection to mainline feminist theology does not entail a denial of the validity of most of the feminist claims about the nature of patriarchy and the oppression of women. The validity of many of these feminist claims seems to be as obvious as the doctrine of original sin, which is to say, as plain to me as daylight. They may be extra-narratival claims, arising as they do from within another field of discourse. After all, this is exactly what feminist theologians have been saying, that the church has not spoken and acted on behalf of women as it should have for all of these centuries and that the critique must be brought from the outside. However, now that the extra-narratival claims of feminism are being considered by Christian communities, many are proving to convince us as true claims. The problem is that mainline feminist theology's lack of narratival reading, linked to the confusion between the tasks of dogmatics and of apologetics, can lead into the position of radical discontinuity with the legacy of the Reformers and most of their predecessors, both Roman Catholic and Eastern. It is precisely the feminist affinity for modern theology's non-narrative reading which can displace the tradition's broad consensus about the authority of Scripture and the biblical depiction of God and can misshape the classically conceived web of belief. However, this is exactly what mainline feminist theologians want. Let me be clear that I am not recommending that we leave theology as it is, as it always has been, as though it were engraved on tablets of stone. This is neither desirable nor possible. However, if we do not respect the holistic narratival depiction of the biblical God, there is no compelling reason for us to claim as true or even as noteworthy any of the remnant details presented to us in that depiction.

There are, however, degrees of variation within both the narrative and non-narrative approaches, just as there are within the theological approaches and outcomes of mainline feminist theologies. As a way of attempting to point out the differences among some of the writers we have considered as examples, we might venture the following conclusions. If we were to consider theological approaches as concentric circles, with the center point focusing on the "Christian story," we might note an array such as the following. First, occupying the outer edges of the circle, beyond the penumbras of Christianity, we would find self-acclaimed pagan and post-Christian feminist theology, represented by the well-known Wiccan thealogian, Starhawk, and Naomi Goldenberg, who coined the term "thealogy." We might also find there Daphne Hampson and Mary Daly. Closer toward the center, but still beyond the penumbra as they themselves would claim, are Jewish feminist theologians, represented here by Judith Plaskow. These then are post- and non-Christian writers.

But how are we to understand those theologians who claim to be Christian and yet seem to offer reconstructions of the Christian story which are only barely recognizable as such? Openly antiorthodox, anticatholic, antitradition, they occupy a still-penumbral position in the circle only slightly closer to the center point than the self-proclaimed non-Christians. At this area in the circle, we would find voices such as Carter Heyward and Rita Nakashima Brock. Elizabeth Schüssler Fiorenza may also be seen to occupy this area of the circle, insofar as she, while remaining a Catholic, openly seeks to destabilize orthodoxy. These writers propose theological positions which are inconsistent with large parts of the Christian story. They are well aware that the positions they propose, or historic analogues of it, have been rejected by Catholic Christianity, but they are eager nevertheless to hold and to teach the positions they propose. This we might call anti-narrativalist.

Less bothersome to classical Christianity but still problematic are those who offer versions of the Christian story which are internally inconsistent. That is, elements of the reconstructed story contradict parts of the classical Christian story such that a fundamental incoherence results. Closer still toward the center than anti-narrativalists, these theologians hold and teach reconstructions of the Christian story, parts of which implicitly contradict or countermand other areas of the Christian story. They may be unaware that this is the case. This area within the circle we might call penumbral narrativalist, that is, in the shadows between coherence with the biblical narrative and material contradiction of (at least) parts of it. As we saw, Elizabeth Johnson and most of the mainline feminist theologians occupy this penumbral narrativalist area.

Still closer toward the center of the circle, sharing territory with a "generous orthodoxy," are most of the narrativists. Among the feminist theologians, we found that certain samples of the work of mainline feminists Mary Grey and Sarah Coakley presented in chapter 3 and of Anne Carr in chapters 2 and 4 are among the narrativists. In addition, we noted that biblical feminists such as Elaine Storkey tend to be narrativists.[11] This serves to show that not all mainline feminist theologians are in the penumbras of the circle and that mainline and biblical feminists can indeed share aspects of thought.

If George Lindbeck is correct that the thesis of narrative interpretation may be as important in our day as was the homoousios was to the fourth century, and if my analysis of these few feminist theologies is adequate as regards this thesis, does this, then, mean that most of feminist theology, being as it is either non-narrativalist or penumbral narrativalist, counts as "heresy"? After all, the routing out of heresy was, in part, a result of the creation of the term homoousios in the fourth century, with the exception of Athanasius's unwillingness as Lindbeck reminds us, to cast in the role of heretics those who could not accept the homoousios because of its absence in the

Bible. Are non-narrative readers ipso facto heretics? This question we might answer in the negative. After all, Augustine did say that "not all error is heresy."[12] Would we, however, agree that much of non-narrative theology and, with it, much of mainline feminist theology and, indeed, most of modern theology, is in error? How the churches will respond to that remains to be seen. A much smaller and more manageable question asks which pattern is more appropriate to Christian theology. If we agree with Frei that the type of interpretation which is more appropriate to Christian Scripture and theology is description rather than explanation, we may in the end have a limit beyond which we cannot reconstruct Christian doctrines, beyond the biblical-narratival description of the God of Israel. However, within that limit, there is great potential for fresh theological work. Non-narratival feminist theology may unmask much of modern theology in this respect.

Ultimately, we are left with the question which sparked the debate between Daphne Hampson and Rosemary Radford Ruether: can feminism and Christianity coexist?[13] Hampson, of course, argues in the negative, while Ruether argues in the positive. Is there a place for feminists in a Christian church? Clearly, the answer is yes, because there are plenty of feminists in plenty of Christian churches. There is clearly an overlap between the claims of the gospel and some of the claims of feminism. The question which interests me is this: can there be narrative feminists in a Christian church, and, if so, what would their theology look like?[14] We have seen some hints of this, but since feminist theology is a comparatively young discipline, we have yet to see developed examples. As we saw in chapter 3, a narrative consideration of sin can lead to a feminist reconstruction of the doctrine of sin which presents women as powerful and wise while still affirming sin as personal as well as structural. If we were to consider a narrative feminist Christology, what might this look like? My own suggestions grind to a halt here, in the words of Denise Riley. This work is for a future project. One possibility might be to reflect on what the incarnation means within the narrative: what does it mean for Jesus to have been incarnate of a women without the physical intervention of a male, especially within the life of Israel where the male is religiously so important? It would seem that there are many possibilities, and this is just one suggestion for a rich field waiting to be worked. That field, though, for the narratival feminist, will not be without a perimeter, a discernible and flexible border which will shape feminist reconstructions of Christian doctrine.

NOTES

PREFACE

1. See, for example, Kari Elisabeth Børresen, *Subordination and Equivalence: The Nature and Role of Women in Augustine and Thomas Aquinas* (Washington, D.C.: University Press of America, 1981); Beverly Mayne Kienzle and Pamela J. Walker, eds., *Women Preachers and Prophets through Two millenia of Christianity* (Berkeley, Calif.: University of California Press, 1998); Patricia Wilson-Kastner, et al., *A Lost Tradition: Women Writers of the Early Church* (Washington, D.C.: University Press of America, 1981); and Mary D. Pellauer, *Toward a Tradition of Feminist Theology: The Religious Social Thought of Elizabeth Cady Stanton, Susan B. Anthony, and Anna Howard Shaw* (Brooklyn: Carlson, 1991).

2. Mary Hayter, *The New Eve in Christ: The Use and Abuse of the Bible in the Debate about Women in the Church* (London: SPCK, 1987); Aïda Besançon Spencer, *Beyond the Curse: Women Called to Ministry* (Nashville: Thomas Nelson, 1985).

3. See for this Rita M. Gross, *Feminism and Religion: An Introduction* (Boston: Beacon Press, 1996).

4. For a biblical feminist approach to this, see Catherine Clark Kroeger, Mary Evans, and Elaine Storkey, eds., *Study Bible for Women: The New Testament* (Grand Rapids: Baker Books, 1995).

INTRODUCTION

1. Naomi R. Goldenberg, *Changing of the Gods: Feminism and the End of Traditional Religions* (Boston: Beacon, 1979), 10.

2. Certainly, by this point in the late twentieth century, we can cease arguing over what counts for "classical Christian theology." Let us stipulate for the purposes of this book that it refers to Christian thought and practice in accord with the claims about the Trinity and about Christ's two natures made at Nicaea and Chalcedon. See George Lindbeck's use of the term "classical hermeneutic" in "Post critical Canonical Interpretation," in *Theological Exegesis: Essays in Honor of Brevard S. Childs*, ed. Christopher Seitz and Kathryn Greene-McCreight (Grand Rapids:

Eerdmans, 1999), pp 26–51. See also his description of this as reading the Bible as a "Christ-centered narrationally and typologically unified whole in conformity to a Trinitarian rule of faith" in George Lindbeck, "Scripture, Consensus, and Community," in *Biblical Interpretation in Crisis*, ed. Richard John Neuhaus (Grand Rapids: Eerdmans, 1989), 77.

3. Catherine Mowry LaCugna, "Review of *Speaking the Christian God: The Holy Trinity and the Challenge of Feminism*," *Pro Ecclesia* 3 (1994): 114–16; Alvin F. Kimel, ed., *Speaking the Christian God: The Holy Trinity and the Challenge of Feminism* (Grand Rapids: Eerdmans, 1992); Alvin F. Kimel Jr., "It Could Have Been . . . ," *Pro Ecclesia* 3 (1994): 389–94.

4. LaCugna, "Review of *Speaking the Christian God: The Holy Trinity and the Challenge of Feminism*," 114.

5. Ibid.

6. Ibid., 116.

7. Kimel, "It Could Have Been . . . ," 389.

8. Ibid.

9. Ibid., 391–92.

10. Ibid., 393.

11. Ibid., 394.

12. George A. Lindbeck, "Reflections on Trinitarian Language," *Pro Ecclesia* 4 (1995): 261.

13. LaCugna, "Review of *Speaking the Christian God: The Holy Trinity and the Challenge of Feminism*," 116; Kimel, "It Could Have Been . . . ," 394.

14. LaCugna, "Review of *Speaking the Christian God: The Holy Trinity and the Challenge of Feminism*," 114; Kimel, "It Could Have Been . . . ," 393.

15. Kimel, "It Could Have Been . . . ," 393.

16. Lindbeck, "Reflections on Trinitarian Language," 263.

17. As regards the term "Yale School," cf. Kevin J. Vanhoozer, *Biblical Narrative in the Philosophy of Paul Ricoeur: A Study in Hermeneutics and Theology* (Cambridge: Cambridge University Press, 1990), 184, n. 30: "The 'Chicago School' includes a New Testament scholar (Norman Perrin), a philosopher of religion (Ricoeur) and a theologian (Tracy). The 'Yale School' is made up, appropriately enough, of three theologians (Frei, Lindbeck, Kelsey). By referring to 'schools' I mean only to highlight an informal connection." I find it interesting that Vanhoozer has left out the names of Brevard Childs (Old Testament), Wayne Meeks (New Testament), Paul Holmer (philosophical theology), and William Christian (philosophy of religion), who were "informally connected" to the "Yale school" and who may have made the Yale School more competitive in his eyes with Chicago. However, Vanhoozer favors Ricoeur.

18. Lindbeck, "Reflections on Trinitarian Language," 264.

19. Margot Badran has coined the phrase "gender activists" to refer to women who do not identify themselves as feminists per se but who struggle for women's rights. While the term arose from her work for women's rights in the context of Islamic fundamentalism in Egypt, its usefulness in the context of the Western women's movement points to an underlying conflict over the goals and strategies of feminism. Margot Badran, "Gender Activism: Feminists and Islamists in Egypt," in *Identity Politics and Women: Cultural Reassertions and Feminisms in International Perspective*, ed. Valentine M. Moghadam (Boulder, Colo.: Westview, 1994), 211–21.

20. See, for example, Manfred Hauke, *God or Goddess? Feminist Theology: Where Does It Lead?* trans. David Kipp (San Francisco: Ignatius Press, 1995); and Manfred Hauke, *Women in the Priesthood? A Systematic Analysis in the Light of the Order of Creation and Redemption*, trans. David Kipp, (San Francisco: Ignatius Press, [1986] 1988).

CHAPTER ONE

1. For example, just some of the applications of narrative for theology: Garrett Green, ed., *Scriptural Authority and Narrative Interpretation* (Philadelphia: Fortress, 1987); Frank McConnell, ed., *The Bible and the Narrative Tradition* (New York: Oxford University Press, 1986); Stanley Hauerwas and L. Gregory Jones, eds., *Why Narrative? Readings in Narrative Theology* (Grand Rapids: Eerdmans, 1989); David Ford, *Barth and God's Story: Biblical Narrative and the Theological Method of Karl Barth in the Church Dogmatics* (Frankfurt: Peter Lang, 1981); George Stroup, *The Promise of Narrative Theology* (London: SCM, 1981); Michael Goldberg, *Theology and Narrative: A Critical Introduction* (Nashville: Abingdon, 1982); Gerard Loughlin, *Telling God's Story: Bible, Church and Narrative Theology* (Cambridge: Cambridge University Press, 1996); William C. Placher, *Narratives of a Vulnerable God: Christ, Theology, and Scripture* (Louisville, Ky.: Westminster/John Knox, 1994); Gabriel Fackre, *The Christian Story: A Narrative Interpretation of Basic Christian Doctrine* (Grand Rapids: Eerdmans, 1978); and Darrell J. Fasching, *Narrative Theology after Auschwitz: From Alienation to Ethics* (Minneapolis: Augsburg, 1992).

2. Just to mention a few titles. Paul Nelson, *Narrative and Morality* (University Park: Pennsylvania State University Press, 1987). David M. Gunn and Danna Nolan Fewell, *Narrative in the Hebrew Bible* (Oxford: Oxford University Press, 1993); James W. Aageson, *Written Also for Our Sake: Paul and the Art of Biblical Interpretation* (Louisville, Ky.: Westminster/John Knox, 1993); Richard L. Eslinger, *Narrative and Imagination: Preaching Worlds That Shape Us* (Minneapolis: Fortress, 1995); Kevin J. Vanhoozer, *Biblical Narrative in the Philosophy of Paul Ricoeur: A Study in Hermeneutics and Theology* (Cambridge: Cambridge University Press, 1990). Mark Allan Powell, *What Is Narrative Criticism? A New Approach to the Bible* (London: SPCK, 1993); David Rhoads and Donald Michie *Mark as Story: An Introduction to the Narrative of a Gospel* (Philadelphia: Fortress, 1982); Robert C. Tannehill, *The Narrative Unity of Luke-Acts: A Literary Interpretation* (Philadelphia: Fortress, 1986); and Paul Brockelman, *The Inside Story: A Narrative Approach to Religious Understanding and Truth* (Albany: State University of New York Press, 1992).

3. Hans W. Frei, *The Eclipse of Biblical Narrative: A Study in Eighteenth and Nineteenth Century Hermeneutics* (New Haven: Yale University Press, 1974); Hans W. Frei, *The Identity of Jesus Christ: The Hermeneutical Bases of Dogmatic Theology* (Philadelphia: Fortress, 1975). In addition to Hans Frei, the phrase "Yale School" sometimes includes Brevard Childs in Old Testament, Paul Holmer in philosophical theology, David Kelsey in systematic theology, George Lindbeck in historical theology, and Wayne Meeks in New Testament. Their predecessor, it is sometimes pointed out, was H. Richard Niebuhr, of the previous generation at Yale. It should be noted that many of the Yale School no longer teach at Yale, that when they did, they rarely considered themselves a school of thought and that they have questioned the applicability of the term to themselves. For example, see Hans W. Frei, " 'Narrative' in Christian and Modern Reading," in *Theology and Dialogue*, ed. Bruce Marshall (Notre Dame, Ind.: University of Notre Dame Press, 1990), 161; and Brevard S. Childs, *The New Testament as Canon: An Introduction* (Philadelphia: Fortress, 1982), 541–47. David Ford says that the marks of the Yale School are "emphasis on the unsubstitutable identity of Jesus Christ, rendered primarily in narrative form, as the main way of doing justice to Christian particularity" and "capacity to generate a generous orthodoxy hospitable to many different methods, philosophies, churches, anthropologies, cultures, periods, etc." David Ford, "Hans Frei and the Future of Theology" *Modern Theology* 8 (1992): 207

Newer scholars who now fall into the Yale School generally do not teach at Yale but many were themselves students of these scholars. They include Garret Green, Stanley Hauerwas, George Hunsinger, Bruce Marshall, William Placher, Kathryn Tanner and William Werpehowski. See the collection of essays on Frei's work in *Modern Theology* 8:2 (1992), with articles by George Hunsinger, John Webster, Walter Lowe, George P. Schner, Bruce D. Marshall, Paul Schwartzentruber, William Placher, and David Ford. For an account of the differences between the Yale and Chicago versions of "narrative theology," see Mark I. Wallace, *The Second Naiveté: Barth, Ricoeur and the New*

Yale Theology, Studies in American Biblical Hermeneutics 6 (Macon, Ga.: Mercer University Press, 1990). See my comments in the introduction, note 17.

4. "By [the Christian story] I mean the stories that make up the Christian Bible read as constituting a single comprehensive narrative" (Michael Root, "The Narrative Structure of Soteriology," *Modern Theology* 2 [1986]: 157, n.3).

5. Erich Auerbach, *Mimesis: The Representation of Reality in Western Literature,* trans. William Trask (Princeton, N.J.: Princeton University Press, 1953), 15–16. See also Frei, *The Eclipse of Biblical Narrative,* 3.

6. For an example of such tedious debates over Frei's stance on the Bible's factual referentiality, see the 1985 lectures given at Yale by Carl Henry and the response in Hans W. Frei, *Theology and Narrative: Selected Essays,* ed. George Hunsinger and William C. Placher (New York: Oxford University Press, 1993), 207–12. For those who, like Henry, are worried that Frei is (either intentionally or unintentionally) denying the necessity of Christian claims to factuality of the gospel accounts, the concern is evidence of a misunderstanding of Frei's project. See, for example, Frei, *The Identity of Jesus Christ,* 132ff; and Frei, "The 'Literal Reading' of Biblical Narrative in the Christian Tradition: Does It Stretch or Will It Break?" in *The Bible and the Narrative Tradition,* ed. Frank McConnell (New York: Oxford University Press, 1986), 62–63. See also Jeffrey Hensley, "Are Postliberals Necessarily Antirealists? Reexamining the Metaphysics of Lindbeck's Postliberal Theology," in *The Nature of Confession: Evangelicals & Postliberals in Conversation,* ed. Timothy R. Phillips and Dennis L. Okholm (Downer's Grove, Ill.: InterVarsity, 1996), 69–80. This last piece refers more directly to George Lindbeck but is useful on Frei as well.

7. Frei, *The Eclipse of Biblical Narrative,* 13–14.

8. Ibid., 16.

9. Of course, here Frei uses the term "history-like" and "realistic" much as Barth used the term *geschichtlich,* and "historical" is used much as Barth used the term *historisch.* The interpreters of Frei who have difficulty at this point might be helped by rereading Barth's discussions in which these terms play an important role. For example, see Karl Barth, *Church Dogmatics,* vol. 3.1, "The Doctrine of Creation," ed. G. W. Bromiley and T. F. Torrance (Edinburgh: T. & T. Clark, 1958), 3.1, 80ff.; and Karl Barth, *Die Kirchliche Dogmatik,* vol. 3.1, "*Die Lehre von der Schöpfung,*" (Zollilkon-Zürich: Evangelischer Verlag, 1945), 87 ff. For those interested in Frei's use of the terms "historicity," "factuality," and "mythic," see Frei, *The Identity of Jesus Christ,* chapters, 12 and 13.

10. This was particularly true of the biblical scholarship of the eighteenth and nineteenth centuries, the period with which Frei was mainly concerned here. Contemporary biblical scholarship is far more diverse than this statement would suggest, but the hermeneutical underpinnings nevertheless remain.

11. George A. Lindbeck, *The Nature of Doctrine* (Philadelphia: Westminster, 1984), 118; Frei, "The 'Literal Reading' of Biblical Narrative," 72.

12. Frei, *The Eclipse of Biblical Narrative,* 33, 36.

13. George Lindbeck, "Scripture, Consensus, and Community," in Biblical Interpretation in Crisis, ed. Richard John Neuhaus (Grand Rapids: Eerdmans, 1989), 75.

14. Frei, "The 'Literal Reading' of Biblical Narrative," 44–54.

15. Ibid., 46.

16. Ibid., 48.

17. Ibid.; John Dominic Crossan, ed., *Semeia 4: Paul Ricoeur on Biblical Hermeneutics* (Missoula, Mont.: Scholars Press, 1975), 127.

18. Frei, "The 'Literal Reading' of Biblical Narrative," 51, 57.

19. Ibid., 67.

20. Ibid., 73.

21. Ibid., 66.

22. Ibid., 71; Lindbeck, *The Nature of Doctrine.*

23. Frei, "The 'Literal Reading' of Biblical Narrative," 72.

24. This, and not the phrase "postliberal," which is Lindbeck's, more adequately describes Frei's hermeneutical approach. See Frei, "The 'Literal Reading' of Biblical Narrative," 60.

25. "One may want to claim that a notion similar to 'second naiveté' (though not necessarily isomorphic with it) is indeed meaningful, but not because it is part of, or justified by, any general theory" (Frei, "The 'Literal Reading' of Biblical Narrative, 60.) It will be remembered that Frei refers to Ricoeur's "second naiveté" as an "illusion, a verbal pirouette" (p. 57) and "a misleading term" (p. 60).

26. Basic to his approach here is the understanding that religions are like the language systems of cultures, bound to communal norms and rules. Frei, "The 'Literal Reading' of Biblical Narrative, 68–69.

27. Ibid., 72.

28. Ibid., 75.

29. Frei, *The Identity of Jesus Christ,* xiv.

30. Italics his; Frei, *The Identity of Jesus Christ,* 65. Because of his underlying adoption of Barth's particular use of the terms *geschichtlich* and *historisch,* Frei prefers the term "the depicted Jesus" to the term "historical Jesus," which itself is a category error (Frei, *The Identity of Jesus Christ,* 142).

31. The phrase "cultured despisers" is, of course, from Friedrich Schleiermacher, *On Religion: Speeches to Its Cultured Despisers,* trans. John Oman (New York: Harper & Row, 1958). Schleiermacher is one of the key apologists of Christianity in modern theology and in many ways is a precursor to feminist theology.

32. Frei, *The Eclipse of Biblical Narrative,* 129. He continues: "Usually, apologetic mediating theologians have accused their predecessors of wanting to 'prove' or 'secure' the Christian gospel (that saving truth for the human condition comes through Jesus Christ), while they themselves only wanted to indicate how it could be 'meaningful' to 'modern man'. . . . Notable instances of this procedure are the revolt of the nineteenth-century Christian liberals against the 'evidence'-seeking theology of the eighteenth century, the revolt of the so-called dialectical or neo-orthodox theologians against nineteenth-century liberalism in the 1920's, and contemporary arguments in favor of the meaningfulness of a specific Christian 'language game' among all the other language games people play."

33. There is also a narrower sense of "apologetics" compatible with a dogmatic approach thus defined. See William Werpehowski, "Ad Hoc Apologetics," *Journal of Religion* 66 (1986): 282–301.

34. Frei, *The Identity of Jesus Christ,* xi.

35. The best study which I have found on the status of historical arguments for the logic of belief and the logic of coming to belief is an unpublished dissertation by one of Hans Frei's former students, Richard H. Olmsted, "Christian Beliefs, History and Historical Study" (Ph.D. diss., Yale University, 1975).

36. Frei, *The Identity of Jesus Christ,* xii.

37. Ibid., 148.

38. Hans W. Frei, *Types of Christian Theology,* ed. George Hunsinger and William C. Placher (New Haven: Yale University Press, 1992), 159.

39. William A. Christian Sr., *Doctrines of Religious Communities: A Philosophical Study* (New Haven: Yale University Press, 1987).

40. Ibid., 1.

41. Ibid.

42. As George Lindbeck has pointed out, this distinction is somewhat like the Episcopal Church's decision in the Righter trial between "core doctrine" and what might be called "peripheral doctrine." George Lindbeck, SEAD Conference, "On Core Doctrine," Stamford, Conn.,

May 3, 1997. Ironically, for Christian's philosophical study, it is governing ("peripheral") doctrines which are significant; for the Episcopal Church, it is primary doctrine ("core doctrine") which is the more significant.

43. Christian, *Doctrines of Religious Communities*, 1–2.

44. Ibid., 2.

45. Ibid., 33.

46. "[Irenaeus] needs a framework for arguments on questions of the form: Is *s* a Christian doctrine? These questions cannot be argued unless there is some non-arbitrary way of dealing with them. They call for principles and rules to guide arguments and judgments. The following are some of the parts of the framework Irenaeus develops for dealing with such questions: *s* is not a Christian doctrine unless it is in accord with the Scriptures. Passages in the Scriptures, like passages in Homer, ought to be interpreted in their contexts [*Against Heresies* i, ix, 4]. Apostolic tradition confirms and amplifies what the Scriptures say. Bishops can be relied upon to preserve apostolic tradition. Now in *Against Heresies* it is clear that Irenaeus means to speak not just for himself but for his community. So he must be putting forward these principles and rules as Christian doctrines. And, since their function in the situation in which he speaks is to guide judgments as to whether something is a Christian doctrine or not, we might say of the framework as a whole that it is being proposed as a Christian doctrine about Christian doctrines" (Christian, *Doctrines of Religious Communities*, 12).

47. Some beliefs which are distinctively Christian (or Buddhist, etc.) may be "alien" in the sense of "not obligatory," for example, that Eve and Adam were buried under Golgotha.

48. Christian, *Doctrines of Religious Communities*, 73.

49. "[A]lthough alien claims, with respect to some community, are not doctrines of that community, it is not a part of the concept of an alien claim that an alien claim is inconsistent with doctrines of that community" (Christian, *Doctrines of Religious Communities*, 146).

50. Ibid., 68.

51. Ibid., 69.

52. Ibid., 74.

53. Ibid., 70.

54. Ibid., 71.

55. Ibid., 74.

56. "There seems to be a deep-seated tendency in the major religious communities to develop a comprehensive pattern of life, a pattern of life which bears on all human interests (and thus indirectly on the objects of those interests) and on all the situations in which human beings find themselves. Thus the pattern might order life as a whole. This aim might be adopted as a guiding principle embodied in a doctrine of a community about its doctrines: The community should develop a comprehensive pattern of life. Now if a community means to teach and nurture in its members a comprehensive pattern of life, so the objection would run, it cannot recognize limitations on the scope of its teachings. It would have to undertake to teach all truths whatever and all those courses of action which, in general or in some circumstances, are right. Otherwise the pattern of life it teaches would not be comprehensive" (Christian, *Doctrines of Religious Communities*, 186).

57. "If a religious community is an integral, perhaps a dominant, feature of a traditional society, there is a tendency for the community to claim that other features of the society including its laws, its arts, and its sciences derive from the sources of the community's doctrines. Hence there is a tendency to look on all the truths and right courses of action which are embodied in the society's institutions as authentic doctrines of the community, not as alien claims. In such situations there would be, in principle, no problems about the comprehensiveness of the pattern of life taught by the community. But this tendency does not always prevail.

At least in some periods of their histories, the major religious communities have found themselves in societies of a different type, societies in which secular interest, inquiries, and claims are important, if not indeed dominant. In such situations religious communities are under pressure to consider whether there may be truths and right courses of action which are not authentic doctrines of the community" (Christian, *Doctrines of Religious Communities*, 187).

58. An example of this is Karl Rahner's notion of the "anonymous Christian." See "Anonymous Christians," *Theological Investigations* 6 (London: Darton, Longmann and Todd, 1961–1992), 390–98; "Anonymous Christianity and the Missionary Task of the Church," 12: 161–78; "The Anonymous Christian," 14: 280–94; and "Jesus Christ in the Non-Christian Religions," 17: 39–50.

59. "Proposing negative valuations of secular alien claims is compatible with the position that there may be alien claims which are true or right" (Christian, *Doctrines of Religious Communities*, 202),

60. "A norm is introduced which may contrast with what has been taught in the past or what happens to be going on within the bounds of the community at present. It may be that at some point in its teaching activities the community was not, or is not, being true to itself" (Christian, *Doctrines of Religious Communities*, 81).

61. Ibid., 81.

62. Ibid., 146.

63. "It may happen in some particular historical situation that the mind of a community is not yet made up on some question. The time is not yet ripe for the community to speak clearly and firmly, even on questions which seem to fall within the bounds of its competence. At the time, the theoretical and practical implications of some proposition or some course of action have not yet been worked out. So it is not yet clear how it is relevant to the doctrines of the community and whether it is inconsistent or not with authentic doctrines of the community. These matters would have to be pondered, and sometimes the pondering goes slowly, especially when consensus is an important criterion of authenticity, or when a doctrine of some other religion or some secular claim introduces unfamiliar concepts or depends on unfamiliar procedures. The histories of religious communities show good reasons for tempering tendencies to give quick answers to complex questions. Hence at particular times it may be that just what a community is bound to teach on some topic is not yet clear to it" (Christian, *Doctrines of Religious Communities*, 185).

64. "The normative flavor of internal questions about doctrines and the answers they call for may be brought out further by considering some doctrines which advance consensus as a criterion of authenticity. For example, when Roman Catholic Christians ask whether some sentence has been accepted as a teaching of the church everywhere, always and by all, applying the rule of St. Vincent of Lerins, the scope of the question is often narrowed to focus on the fathers and doctors of the church. Similarly, when Sunni Muslims ask whether what is said in some sentence is a part of the ijmâ' (consensus) of the Muslim community, attention is focused on the mujtahids, those who have a right, in virtue of knowledge, to form a judgment of their own on the question at issue. In these cases it seems that a consensus of the community is not to be determined statistically by an unweighted count of the opinions of all the members. . . . Whatever the scope of a consensus is taken to be, it seems implausible that a religious community could teach and continue to teach that the authenticity of some doctrine can be determined from historical and sociological considerations alone" (Christian, *Doctrines of Religious Communities*, 19). This is similar to what George Lindbeck says of consensus: "The *consensus fidelium* is not to be confused with majority opinion nor with localized unanimity whose wider and enduring persuasiveness is uncertain. The consent that counts is that of the company of those whose lives cohere with the creed they profess, who are not swept

about by every wind of doctrine and who are prepared to die rather than dishonor the Name" (George A. Lindbeck, "Atonement and the Hermeneutics of Social Embodiment," *Pro Ecclesia* 5 (1996): 4.

65. This points to the instability of the position put forward in the Righter trial decision. In the Episcopal church, U.S.A. That is, while Bishop Righter may not have violated "core doctrine" ("primary doctrine" in Christian's terms by ordaining a "practicing" homosexual to the priesthood,) it appears that he may well have violated the principles and rules held, taught, and used by the Anglican communion for determining authentic doctrine and right practice.

66. Root, "The Narrative Structure of Soteriology."

67. Ibid., 147.

68. Ibid.

69. Wallace considers the readers whom I put in the category of "non-narrative" to be "impure narrative" readers. His distinction blurs what Frei was trying to point out. See Wallace, *The Second Naiveté*.

70. See my "We are Companions of the Patriarchs," *Modern Theology*. No pun is intended by the word patriarchy; it is simply Calvin's title.

71. John Calvin, *A Commentary on the Book of Genesis*, trans. John King (Grand Rapids: Baker, 1979), 66. I trust that readers will not take offense at my use of Calvin here; he could not help being male!

72. Here I will be using the terms "figural," "figurative," and "typological" interchangeably for all nonliteral reading. I will use the term "allegory" to signify this same phenomenon in the context of discussion where Calvin himself chooses this term. Following James Barr ("Typology and Allegory," *Old and New in Interpretation* [New York: Harper & Row, 1996]), I am not assuming an airtight distinction between allegory and typology, and I do not think that Calvin held such a distinction either.

73. Calvin, *A Commentary on the Book of Genesis*, vol. 2, 22–23.

74. Ibid, vol. 1, pp. 207–208.

75. Ibid, vol. 1, p. 298.

76. Ibid., vol. 2, 413–14.

77. Calvin does not use the specific phrase "simple sense" here, but he does use it elsewhere in opposition to such phrases as "uncertain speculations." It seems clear from the context that he does not claim to be adding anything to the text in offering this interpretation, and therefore we can assume that Calvin would not call this interpretation "uncertain speculation."

78. "Thus it has happened, that in striving earnestly to elicit profound allegories, they have departed from the genuine sense of the words and have corrupted, by their own inventions what is here delivered for the edification of the pious. But lest we should depreciate the literal sense, as if it did not contain speculations sufficiently profound, let us mark the design of the Holy Spirit" and "I abstain from those allegories which to some appear plausible; because, as I said at the beginning of the chapter, I do not choose to sport with such great mysteries of God" (Calvin, *A Commentary on the Book of Genesis*, vol. 2, 439, 451). Despite these comments, occasionally Calvin openly approved of a specific allegorical reading, such as in his discussion at Genesis 27:27: "The allegory of Ambrose on this passage is not displeasing to me. Jacob, the younger brother, is blessed under the person of the elder; the garments which were borrowed from his brother breathe an odour grateful and pleasant to his father. In the same manner we are blessed, as Ambrose teaches, when, in the name of Christ, we enter the presence of our heavenly Father: we receive from him the robe of righteousness which, by its odour, procures his favour; in short, we are thus blessed when we are put in his place" (vol. 2, 91).

79. Ibid., vol. 2, 113–14.

80. Ibid., vol. 2, 432.

81. Ibid., vol. 2, 428–29.

CHAPTER TWO

1. Frances Martin, *The Feminist Question: Feminist Theology in the Light of Christian Tradition* (Grand Rapids: Eerdmans, 1994); Linda Woodhead, "Spiritualising the Sacred: A Critique of Feminist Theology," *Modern Theology* 13 (1997): 191–212.

2. Esther D. Reed, "Whither Postmodernism and Feminist Theology?" *Feminist Theology* 6 (1994): 15–29. This is not to say that feminist theology does not have within its general stream currents of postmodern thought, which it clearly does have and is in the process of furthering.

3. R. R. Reno, "Feminist Theology as a Modern Project," *Pro Ecclesia* 5 (1996): 406. The following is typical of many feminist theologians: "The pervasive, profoundly patriarchal elements of Christianity have forced those of us who consider ourselves feminist and Christian to struggle intensely with our faith and our commitments to justice and wholeness." Rita Nakashima Brock, *Journeys by Heart: A Christology of Erotic Power* (New York: Crossroad, 1989), 50.

4. See Van A. Harvey, *Feuerbach and the Interpretation of Religion* (New York: Cambridge University Press, 1995). See also the helpful corrections to Harvey's misunderstanding of Barth's position on Feuerbach in Garrett Green, "Who's Afraid of Ludwig Feuerbach? Suspicion and the Religious Imagination," in *Papers of the Nineteenth Century Theology Group*, American Academy of Religion 1996 Annual Meeting, New Orleans, ed. Claude Welch and Daniel W. Hardy (Colorado Springs: Colorado College, 1996), 18–39. The thesis I am presenting here is quite similar to the one proposed in Garrett Green, "The Gender of God and the Theology of Metaphor," in *Speaking the Christian God: The Holy Trinity and the Challenge of Feminism*, ed. Alvin F. Kimel (Grand Rapids: Eerdmans, 1992), 44–64.

5. Green, "Who's Afraid of Ludwig Feuerbach?" 22; John Glasse, "Barth on Feuerbach," *Harvard Theological Review* 57 (1964): 72.

6. Karl Barth, *Theology and Church*, trans. Louise Pettibone Smith (New York: Harper & Row, [1928] 1962), 217.

7. Harvey, *Feuerbach and the Interpretation of Religion*, 6.

8. Ludwig Feuerbach, *The Essence of Christianity*, trans. George Eliot (New York: Harper & Row, 1957), 63; Mary Daly, *Beyond God the Father: Toward a Philosophy of Women's Liberation* (Boston: Beacon, 1973), 19.

9. Green, "The Gender of God," 48.

10. Quoted in Barth, *Theology and Church* (London: SCM Press, 1962), 223.

11. Barth, *Theology and Church*, 223.

12. Mary Daly, *Gyn/Ecology: The Metaethics of Radical Feminism* (Boston: Beacon, 1978).

13. B. A. Gerrish, "Feuerbach's Religious Illusion," *Christian Century* 114 (1997): 364.

14. Rudolf Bultmann, "New Testament and Mythology: The Problem of Demythologizing the New Testament Proclamation," in *New Testament and Mythology and Other Basic Writings*, trans. and ed. Schubert M. Ogden (Philadelphia: Fortress, [1941] 1984), 1.

15. Ibid., 3, 6.

16. Phyllis Trible, "Depatriarchalizing God in Biblical Interpretation," *Journal of the American Academy of Religion* 41 (1973): 30–48.

17. Gerda Lerner, *The Creation of Feminist Consciousness: From the Middle Ages to Eighteen-Seventy* (New York: Oxford University Press, 1993).

18. Ibid., 274.

19. Betty Friedan, *The Feminine Mystique* (New York: Dell, [1963] 1983); Simone de Beauvoir, *The Second Sex* (New York: Knopf, 1953).

20. Elizabeth Cady Stanton, *The Original Feminist Attack on the Bible: The Woman's Bible*, intro. Barbara Welter (New York: Arno, 1974).

21. Diana Fuss, *Essentially Speaking: Feminism, Nature and Difference* (New York: Routledge, 1989), xi.

22. This can be true even when the feminist theorist or theologian self-consciously attempts to incorporate both categories within her analysis, e.g., Serene Jones, *Cartographies of Grace: Feminist Theory and Theology* (Minneapolis: Fortress, forthcoming).

23. Fuss, *Essentially Speaking*, xii.

24. "Indeed, I have come to think even of the phrase 'as a woman' as the Trojan horse of feminist ethnocentrism" (Elizabeth V. Spelman, *Inessential Woman: Problems of Exclusion in Feminist Thought* [Boston: Beacon, 1988], x).

25. "The more universal the claim one might hope to make about women—'women have been put on a pedestal' or 'women have been treated like slaves'—the more likely it is to be false" (Spelman, *Inessential Woman*, 9).

26. Denise Riley, *Am I That Name? Feminism and the Category of "Women" in History* (Minneapolis: University of Minnesota Press, 1988), 98. "My aim . . . is to emphasize that inherent shakiness of the designation 'women' which exists prior to both its revolutionary and conservative developments, and which is reflected in the spasmodic and striking coincidences of leftist and rightist propositions about the family or female nature. The cautionary point of this emphasis is far from being anti-feminist. On the contrary, it is to pin down this instability as the lot of feminism, which resolves certain perplexities in the history of feminism and its vacillations, but also points to its potentially inexhaustible flexibility in pursuing its aims."

27. Indeed, it will be helpful for feminist theory as well, as is evident in the following extended quote. Our particular concern here, however, is feminist theology: "Equality; difference; 'different but equal'—the history of feminism since the 1970's has zigzagged and curved through these incomplete oppositions upon which it is itself precariously erected. This swaying motion need not be a wonder, nor a cause for despair. If feminism is the voicing of 'women' from the side of 'women,' then it cannot but act out the full ambiguities of that category. This reflection reduces some of the sting and mystery of feminism's ceaseless oscillations, and allows us to prophesy its next incarnations. . . . Does all of this mean, then, that the better programme for feminism now would be to minimize 'women'? To cope with the oscillations by so downplaying the category that insisting on either differences or identities would become equally untenable? My own suggestions grind to a halt here, on a territory of pragmatism. I'd argue that it is compatible to suggest that 'women' don't exist—while maintaining a politics of 'as if they existed'—since the world behaves as if they unambiguously did. So that official suppositions and conservative popular convictions will need to be countered constantly by redefinitions of 'women.' Such challenges to 'how women are' can throw sand in the eyes of the founding categorisations and attributions, ideally disorientating them" (Riley, *Am I That Name?* 112).

28. "Sometimes it will be a soundly explosive tactic to deny, in the face of some thoughtless depiction, that there *are* any 'women.' But at other times, the entrenchment of sexed thought may be too deep for this strategy to be understood and effective. So feminism must be agile enough to say, 'Now we will be 'women'—but now we will be persons, not these 'women' " (Riley, *Am I That Name?* 113).

29. Elisabeth Schüssler Fiorenza, "The Will to Choose or to Reject: Continuing Our Critical Work," in *Feminist Interpretation of the Bible*, ed. Letty M. Russell (Philadelphia: Westminster, 1985), 127, italics mine.

30. For a different view of patriarchy, its origins, and future, see Steven Goldberg, *Why Men Rule: A Theory of Male Dominance* (Chicago: Open Court, 1993).

31. Gerda Lerner, *The Creation of Patriarchy* (New York: Oxford University Press, 1986), 212.

32. Ibid., 38–39.

33. Ibid., 52–53. See also pp. 40, 42.

34. Ibid., 212.

35. Lerner, *The Creation of Patriarchy*, 214.

36. Ibid., 219.

37. "A literary canon, which defined itself by the Bible, the Greek classics, and Milton, would necessarily bury the significance and the meaning of women's literary work, as historians buried the activities of women. The effort to resurrect this meaning and to re-evaluate women's literary and artistic work is recent." Ibid., 225.

38. Ibid., 229.

39. Rita Nakashima Brock, Claudia Camp, and Serene Jones, eds., *Setting the Table: Women in Theological Conversation* (St. Louis: Chalice, 1995), 33–43.

40. See the operative comment by Elisabeth Schüssler Fiorenza: "a feminist critical hermeneutics of suspicion places a warning label on all biblical texts: *Caution! Could be dangerous to your health and survival*" (italics hers, "The Will to Choose or to Reject: Continuing Our Critical Work," 130.

41. Fiorenza, "The Will to Choose or to Reject," 126.

42. Carolyn Osiek, "The Feminist and the Bible: Hermeneutical Alternatives," in *Feminist Perspectives on Biblical Scholarship*, ed. Adela Yarbo Collins (Chico, Calif.: Scholars Press, 1985), 97.

43. Elisabeth Schüssler Fiorenza, *Bread Not Stone: The Challenge of Feminist Biblical Interpretation* (Boston: Beacon, 1984), 15ff.

44. See the helpful chapter in feminist hermeneutics in Bible and Culture Collective, ed., *The Postmodern Bible* (New Haven: Yale University Press, 1995), 245–70, which uses the categories of recuperation, suspicion, survival, and postmodern. See also Schüssler Fiorenza, *Bread Not Stone: The Challenge of Feminist Biblical Interpretation*.

45. To be sure, some of the feminist theologians whom I might classify in the following categories instead of this one do also understand the Bible to function as witness. This is true, for example, of Letty Russell, even though I would not classify her understanding of the Bible primarily in this category. While it is true that she states, "The particular interpretive key that assists me in continuing to give assent is the witness of scripture to God's promise (for the mending of creation) on its way to fulfillment," this is not the consistently overriding function she ascribes to the Bible. This may be the interpretive key to the Bible for her, but it does not seem to be her understanding of the Bible's primary function. Letty Russell, ed., *Feminist Interpretation of the Bible* (Philadelphia: Westminster, 1985), 139. The question which guides my analysis here is the primary function ascribed to the biblical texts by feminist theologians.

46. Bible and Culture Collective, *The Postmodern Bible*.

47. A contemporary example of this approach would be Marti Steussy; an analogue from the previous generation would be Charlotte von Kirschbaum, *The Question of Woman: The Collected Writings of Charlotte von Kirschbaum*, ed. Eleanor Jackson, trans. John Shepherd (Grand Rapids: Eerdmans, 1996). This definition is offered by June Steffensen Hagen, ed., *Gender Matters: Women's Studies for the Christian Community* (Grand Rapids: Academie Books, Zondervan, 1990), 19.

48. Elaine Storkey, *What's Right with Feminism?* (Grand Rapids: Eerdmans, 1986), 163.

49. See, for example, Gilbert Bilezikian, *Beyond Sex Roles: What the Bible Says about a Woman's Place in Church and Family*, 2d ed. (Grand Rapids: Baker Book House, 1997), and the extensive bibliography there, as well as Letha Scanzoni and Nancy Hardesty, *All We're Meant to Be*, 3d ed. (Waco, Tex.: Word, 1992), Storkey, *What's Right with Feminism?* and Patricia Wilson-Kastner, *Faith, Feminism, and the Christ* (Philadelphia: Fortress, 1983). The exceptions prove the rule. See, for example, Gracia Fay Ellwood, "God Is a Virgin Mother," *Reformed Journal* 26, no. 4 (1976): 19–22; and Virginia Ramey Mollenkott, *The Divine Feminine: The Biblical Imagery of God as Female* (New York: Crossroad, 1983).

50. Elizabeth Achtemeier, et al., "Women of Renewal: A Statement," *First Things* 80 (February 1998): 36–40.

51. Ibid., 137.

52. Gretchen Gaebelein Hull, *Equal to Serve: Women and Men in the Church and Home* (Tarrytown, N.Y.: Fleming H. Revell, 1987), 56.

53. See, for example, Schüssler Fiorenza, *Bread Not Stone*, 10: "Because the Bible is stamped by patriarchal oppression but claims to be the Word of God, it perpetuates an archetypal oppressive myth that must be rejected by feminists on the one hand and must be maintained over feminism by biblical religion on the other hand. The archetypal myth of the Bible as the Word of God has been challenged by historical-critical scholarship and has undergone significant modifications in the last centuries."

54. Lerner, *The Creation of Patriarchy*, 228.

55. "Womanism" is a term brought into currency in feminist theory by Alice Walker, *In Search of Our Mother's Gardens* (New York: Harcourt, Brace, Jovanovich, 1983), xi. It has been taken up into feminist theological circles to refer to the feminist theology done from the specific standpoint of African American feminists.

56. Susan Brooks Thistlethwaite, *Sex, Race, and God: Christian Feminism in Black and White* (New York: Crossroad, 1989).

57. Bible and Culture Collective, *The Postmodern Bible*, 230.

58. Rosemary Radford Ruether, *Sexism and God-Talk: Toward a Feminist Theology* (Boston: Beacon, 1983).

59. Elisabeth Schüssler Fiorenza, *In Memory of Her: A Feminist Theological Reconstruction of Christian Origins* (New York: Crossroad, 1983); Antoinette Clark Wire, *The Corinthian Women Prophets: A Reconstruction through Paul's Rhetoric* (Minneapolis: Fortress, 1990); Karen Jo Torjesen, *When Women Were Priests: Women's Leadership in the Early Church and the Scandal of Their Subordination in the Rise of Christianity* (San Francisco: HarperSanFrancisco, 1993).

60. Phyllis Trible, *Texts of Terror: Literary-Feminist Readings of Biblical Narratives* (Philadelphia: Fortress, 1984); Elisabeth Schüssler Fiorenza, *But She Said: Feminist Practices of Biblical Interpretation* (Boston: Beacon, 1992).

61. Trible, *Text of Terror*, 255.

62. Mieke Bal, *Lethal Love: Literary Feminist Readings of Biblical Love Stories* (Bloomington: Indiana University Press, 1987).

63. Pui-Lan Kwok, "Racism and Ethnocentrism in Feminist Biblical Interpretation," in *Searching the Scriptures*, Vol. 1, *A Feminist Introduction*, ed. Elisabeth Schüssler Fiorenza (New York: Crossroad, 1993), 103.

64. Margaret Farley, "Feminist Consciousness and the Interpretation of Scripture," in *Feminist Interpretation of the Bible*, ed. Letty M. Russell (Philadelphia: Westminster, 1985), 44.

65. For a consideration of the specific locus of revelation in feminist theology, see Esther Reed, "Revelation in Feminist Theology and Philosophy," in *Divine Revelation*, ed. Paul Avis (Grand Rapids: Eerdmans, 1997), 156–73.

66. Rosemary Radford Ruether, "Feminist Interpretation: A Method of Correlation," in *Feminist Interpretation of the Bible*, ed. Letty M. Russell (Philadelphia: Westminster, 1985), 115. See also this principle applied to the function and goal of worship: "[The goal of women-church] is not simply the 'full humanity' of women, since humanity as we know it is male defined, but women's religious self-affirmation, power and liberation from all patriarchal alienation, marginalization, and oppression" (Schüssler Fiorenza, "The Will to Choose or to Reject," 126.

67. Russell, *Feminist Interpretation of the Bible*, 143–44.

68. Linda Hogan, *From Women's Experience to Feminist Theology* (Sheffield: Sheffield Academic Press, 1995), 10.

69. Ruether, "Feminist Interpretation," 114.

70. Angela West, *Deadly Innocence: Feminist Theology and the Mythology of Sin* (London: Cassell, 1996), 65 (italics hers).

71. "The feminist claim to a kind of 'pure experience' is a denial of an aspect of human finitude—the vulnerability and dependence of human beings on their social and cultural environments. The use of women's experience in the sense of an unmediated experience and knowl-

edge of reality that will provide a sure foundation for the validity of feminist claims shows that feminists are not always consistent with their avowed desire to challenge the prevailing attitudes of our culture on what it means to be human. These feminists are still assuming a conception of a kind of human experience which transcends the uncertainty, vulnerability, and historicity of human finitude" (Tiina Allik, "Human Finitude and the Concept of Women's Experience," *Modern Theology* 9 [1993]: 74).

72. George Schner, "The Appeal to Experience," *Theological Studies* 53 (1992): 40–59.

73. One could also turn to other feminist scholars, such as Katharine Doob Sackenfeld, for a typology of feminist hermeneutics. See, e.g., Sackenfeld, "Feminist Uses of Biblical Materials," *Feminist Interpretation of the Bible*, ed. Letty Russell (Philadelphia: Westminster, 1985), 56.

74. Emily Cheney, *She Can Read: Feminist Reading Strategies for Biblical Narrative* (Valley Forge, Pa.: Trinity, 1996).

75. See, however, Celia M. Deutsch, *Lady Wisdom, Jesus, and the Sages: Metaphor and Social Context in Matthew's Gospel* (Valley Forge, Pa.: Trinity, 1996).

76. Ibid., 42.

77. Ibid., 43.

78. Ibid., 66.

79. Emily Cheney, *She Can Read*, 120.

80. Susan Ackerman, " 'And the Women Knead Dough': The Worship of the Queen of Heaven in Sixth-Century Judah," in *Gender and Difference in Ancient Israel*, ed. Peggy Day (Minneapolis: Fortress, 1989), 109.

81. Jeremiah 7:16–20 and 44:15–30, New Revised Standard Edition.

82. Ackerman, " 'And the Women Knead Dough,' " 117.

83. Ibid.

84. Ibid., 118.

85. Cheney, *She Can Read*, 123.

86. Aurelius Augustine, *The City of God*, in *The Nicene and Post-Nicene Fathers of the Christian Church*, ed. Philip Schaff and trans. Marcus Dods (Grand Rapids: Eerdmans, 1978), 11.19.

87. Aurelius Augustine, *On Christian Doctrine*, in *Nicene and Post-Nicene Fathers*, Vol. 2, ed. Philip Schaff and trans. John Shaw (Grand Rapids: Eerdmans, 1979).

88. Ibid., 15.7, 26, from the section written in 418.

89. Ibid., 1.36.40.

90. Ibid., 1.40.44.

91. E.g., Augustine, *The City of God*, 11.32. In fact, a diversity of interpretations is even useful as long as the translation itself is not wrong (Augustine, *On Christian Doctrine*, 2.12).

92. In order to (subdue) pride by toil and (prevent) a feeling of satiety in the intellect which generally holds in small esteem what is discovered without difficulty" (Augustine, *On Christian Doctrine*, 2.6.7).

93. Ibid., 2.6.8.

94. Cheney, *She Can Read*, 125.

95. Judith Plaskow, *Standing Again at Sinai: Judaism from a Feminist Perspective* (New York: Harper & Row, 1990); Susan Heschel, ed., *On Being a Jewish Feminist: A Reader* (New York: Schocken, 1983).

96. Plaskow, *Standing Again at Sinai*, 134–35.

97. Ibid., 135.

98. Reno, "Feminist Theology as a Modern Project"; Susanne Heine, *Christianity and the Goddesses: Systematic Criticism of a Feminist Theology* (London: SCM, 1987), 36.

99. Bible and Culture Collective, *The Postmodern Bible*, 225–26.

100. E.g., "Refusing to be regulated by the norms of patriarchal scholarship, feminist theorists have insisted on the desirability and inherent worth of a flexible, unstable position" (Linda Hogan, *From Women's Experience to Feminist Theology* [Sheffield: Sheffield Academic Press, 1995], 13).

101. Alicia Suskin Ostriker, *Feminist Revision and the Bible* (Oxford: Basil Blackwell, 1993).

102. Hans W. Frei, "The 'Literal Reading' of Biblical Narrative in the Christian Tradition: Does It Stretch or Will It Break?" in *The Bible and the Narrative Tradition*, ed. Frank McConnell (New York: Oxford University Press, 1986), 36–77.

103. Susannah Heschel, "Anti-Judaism in Christian Feminist Theology," *Tikkun* 5 (1990): 26–28; Katharina von Kellenbach, *Anti-Judaism in Feminist Religious Writings*, American Academy of Religion Cultural Criticism Series (Atlanta: Scholars Press, 1994); Judith Plaskow, "Christian Feminism and Anti-Judaism," *Cross Currents* 33 (1978): 306–9; Judith Plaskow, "Feminist Anti-Judaism and the Christian God," *Journal of Feminist Studies in Religion* 7 (1991), 99–118; Judith Plaskow, "Anti-Judaism in Feminist Christian Interpretation," in *Searching the Scriptures*, vol. 1, *A Feminist Introduction* ed. Elisabeth Schüssler Fiorenza, (New York: Crossroad, 1993), 117–29; Marie Therese Wacker, "Feminist Theology and Anti-Judaism: The Status of the Discussion and the Context of the Problem in the Federal Republic of Germany," *Journal of Feminist Studies in Religion* 7 (1991): 109–16.

104. As proposed by Lloyd Gaston, quoted by Kellenbach, *Anti-Judaism in Feminist Religious Writings*, 13.

105. Bernadette Brooten had also broached the topic: "Jüdinnen Zur Zeit Jesu," *Theologische Quartalschrift* 161 (1981), 280–85.

106. Plaskow, "Feminist Anti-Judaism and the Christian God," 101; Kellenbach, *Anti-Judaism in Feminist Religious Writings*, 40–41.

107. Plaskow, "Anti-Judaism in Feminist Christian Interpretation," 117.

108. Leonard Swidler, "Jesus Was a Feminist," *Catholic World* 212 (1971): 177–83; Virginia Ramey Mollenkott, *Women, Men, and the Bible* (Nashville: Abingdon, 1977); Plaskow, "Feminist Anti-Judaism and the Christian God."

109. See, for example, Rudolf Bultmann, "Prophecy and Fulfillment," trans. James C. G. Greig, in *Essays on Old Testament Hermeneutics*, ed. Claus Westermann, (Richmond: John Knox, 1963), 52, where he claims that the Old Testament is a "miscarriage," and states that "To talk of this kind of prophecy and fulfillment has become impossible in an age in which the Old Testament is conceived of as an historical document and interpreted according to the method of historical science." See also Bultmann's "The Significance of the Old Testament for the Christian Faith," in *The Old Testament and the Christian Faith*, ed. B. W. Anderson (New York: Harper and Row, 1963), 31 where he states that "to the Christian faith, the Old Testament is no longer revelation as it has been, and still is, for the Jews." See also Francis Watson, *Text and Truth: Redefining Biblical Theology* (Edinburgh: T & T Clark, 1997), 153ff.

110. Martin Luther "How Christians Should Regard Moses (1525)" is *Word and Sacrament*, ed. E. Theodore Brachman and Helmut T. Lehman (Philadelphia: Fortress, 1955), 166.

111. Ibid., notes 9, 11, 16.

112. "To talk of this kind of prophecy and fulfillment has become impossible in an age in which the Old Testament is conceived of as an historical document and interpreted according to the method of historical science." Bultmann, "Prophecy and Fulfillment," 52.

113. Of course, this is a huge topic which this project cannot address fully. It would be interesting, however, to study the kind of biblical interpretation which supported and nurtured the piety influencing, for example, the York Uprising or the Inquisition as compared to that of the Third Reich.

CHAPTER THREE

1. "The aesthetic model—among whose numbers are Mary Daly, Helga Sorge, Carol Christ, Christa Mulack and Starhawk—is on the whole post-Christian, matriarchal, goddess-based, with mystical, gnostic and romantic tendencies. Sin is seen as what disrupts and prevents the harmony and beauty of the cosmos and the divine presence and immanence in creation. The ethical

direction is exemplified by Carter Heyward, Rosemary Ruether, Dorothee Soelle and many others" (Mary Grey, "Have the Wellsprings Run Dry? Re-Sourcing Tradition in Feminist Theology," *Feminist Theology 3* [1993]: 49–50). See also Lucia Scherzburg, *Grundkurs in Feministische Theologie*, Mainz: Grünewald, 1995.

2. Elisabeth Schüssler Fiorenza, et al. eds., *Searching the Scriptures*, vol. 2, *A Feminist Commentary* (New York: Crossroad, 1995), 10.

3. Daphne Hampson, ed., *Swallowing a Fishbone? Feminist Theologians Debate Christianity* (London: SPCK, 1996).

4. Valerie Saiving, "The Human Situation: A Feminine View," *Journal of Religion* 40 (1960): 100–12. The author now uses the name Saiving.

5. Saiving, "The Human Situation," 108.

6. Judith Plaskow, *Sex, Sin and Grace: Women's Experience and the Theologies of Reinhold Niebuhr and Paul Tillich* (Washington, D.C.: University Press of America, 1980), vii.

7. Ibid., 3.

8. Ibid.

9. Ibid., 2–3.

10. Ibid., 11.

11. Susan Brooks Thistlethwaite, *Sex, Race, and God: Christian Feminism in Black and White* (New York: Crossroad, 1989), 77–79.

12. For a treatment which acknowledges that sin was not always defined throughout the tradition as pride alone, see Wanda Berry, "Images of Sin and Salvation in Feminist Theology," *Anglican Theological Review* 60 (1978): 25–54.

13. This has been but a brief review of the debate. For further reading, see Mary Daly, *Beyond God the Father: Toward a Philosophy of Women's Liberation* (Boston: Beacon, 1973); Mary Grey, "Falling into Freedom: Searching for New Interpretations of Sin in a Secular Society," *Scottish Journal of Theology* 47 (1994): 223–43; Mary McClintock Fulkerson, "Sexism as Original Sin: Developing a Theacentric Discourse," *Journal of the American Academy of Religion* 59 (1991): 653–75; Christine Smith, "Sin and Evil in Feminist Thought," *Theology Today* 50 (1993): 208–19; Delores Williams, "Sin, Nature and Black Women's Bodies," in *Ecofeminism and the Sacred*, ed. Carol J. Adams (New York: Continuum, 1993), 24; Delores Williams, "A Womanist Perspective on Sin," in *A Troubling in My Soul* (Maryknoll, N.Y.: Orbis, 1993), 130–49.

14. Daly, *Beyond God the Father*

15. Mary Potter Engel, "Evil, Sin, and Violation of the Vulnerable," in *Lift Every Voice: Constructing Christian Theologies from the Underside*, ed. Susan Brooks Thistlethwaite and Mary Potter Engel (San Francisco: Harper & Row, 1990), 155.

16. Fulkerson, "Sexism as Original Sin", Daly, *Beyond God the Father*.

17. Anne Carr, *Transforming Grace: Christian Tradition and Women's Experience* (San Francisco: Harper & Row, 1988); Sue Dunfee, "The Sin of Hiding: A Feminist Critique of Reinhold Niebuhr's Account of the Sin of Pride," *Soundings* 65 (1982): 316–27; Louie Adeline Andrews, "Sin with a Feminine Flair: Failing to Self-Actualize" (Ph.D. diss., Florida State University, 1985); Carter Heyward, "Is a Self-Respecting Christian Woman an Oxymoron?" in *Christian Perspectives on Sexuality and Gender*, ed. Elizabeth Stuart and Adrian Thatcher (Grand Rapids: Eerdmans, 1996), 68–83; Catherine Keller, *From a Broken Web: Separation, Sexism and Self* (Boston: Beacon, 1986); Sally Ann McReynolds and Ann O'Hara Graff, "Sin: When Women Are the Context," in *In the Embrace of God: Feminist Approaches to Theological Anthropology* (Maryknoll, N.Y.: Orbis, 1995), 161–72; Letty Russell, *Human Liberation in a Feminist Perspective: A Theology* (Philadelphia: Westminster, 1974); Williams, "A Womanist Perspective on Sin."

18. "Feminist theology had diagnosed women's problem not, as the old teaching would have it, in the temptation to prideful self-assertion, but rather to a deep lack of self-worth. Yet ironically the remedy it proposed became in its turn the problem. It made pride of self into a

goal, and the inevitable concomitant was guilt. The threat of chronic guilt and self-dissatisfaction generates in the individual the need to project these distressing emotions on to one who can take them away from the self, i.e., the scapegoat" (Angela West, *Deadly Innocence: Feminist Theology and the Mythology of Sin* [London: Cassell, 1996], 82).

19. For example, Dunfee, "The Sin of Hiding"; Williams, "A Womanist Perspective on Sin."

20. Serene Jones, *Cartographies of Grace: Feminist Theory and Theology* (Minneapolis: Fortress, forthcoming), 256.

21. Ibid., 256–57.

22. Ibid., n. 67, p. 275.

23. Ibid., 260.

24. Ibid., 267–68.

25. This is not necessarily the case with biblical feminism, as pointed out in chapter 2. See also Elaine Storkey, *What's Right with Feminism?* (Grand Rapids: Eerdmans, 1986); June Steffensen Hagen, ed., *Gender Matters: Women's Studies for the Christian Community* (Grand Rapids: Academie Books, Zondervan, 1990); Aída Besançon Spencer, *Beyond the Curse: Women Called to Ministry* (Nashville: Thomas Nelson, Publishers, 1985); Aída Besançon Spencer, ed., *The Goddess Revival* (Grand Rapids: Baker Book House, 1995); Mary Stewart Van Leeuwen, ed., *After Eden: Facing the Challenge of Gender Reconciliation* (Grand Rapids: Eerdmans, 1993).

26. "Essentialism is most commonly understood as a belief in the real, true essence of things, the invariable and fixed properties which define the 'whatness' of a given entity. . . . Constructionism (the position that differences are constructed, not innate) really operates as a more sophisticated form of essentialism" Diana Fuss, *Essentially Speaking: Feminism, Nature and Difference* [New York: Routledge, 1989], xi–xii.

27. Denise Riley, *Am I That Name? Feminism and the Category of "Women" in History* (Minneapolis: University of Minnesota Press, 1988).

28. For critiques and refinements of the notion of "experience" as theological norm, see Tiina Allik, "Human Finitude and the Concept of Women's Experience," *Modern Theology* 9 (1993): 67–85; Sheila Greeve Davaney, "The Limits of the Appeal to Women's Experience," in *Shaping New Vision: Gender and Values in American Culture*, ed. Constance H. Buchanan Clarissa W. Atkinson, and Margaret R. Miles (Ann Arbor, Mich.: UMI Research Press, 1987), 31–49; Sheila Davaney, "Problems with Feminist Theory: Historicity and the Search for Sure Foundations," in *Embodied Love: Sensuality and Relationship as Feminist Values*, ed. Sharon A. Farmer, Paula M. Cooey, and Mary Ellen Ross (San Francisco: Harper & Row, 1987), 79–95; George Schner, "The Appeal to Experience," *Theological Studies* 53 (1992): 40–59.

29. Kathryn Tanner, "Respect for Other Religions: A Christian Antidote to Colonialist Discourse," *Modern Theology* 9 (1993): 2.

30. West, *Deadly Innocence*, 146.

31. Grey, "Falling Into Freedom," 240–41 (italics hers).

32. Sarah Coakley, "Kenosis and Subversion: On the Repression of 'Vulnerability' in Christian Feminist Writing," in *Swallowing a Fishbone? Feminist Theologians Debate Christianity*, ed. Daphne Hampson (London: SPCK, 1996), 83–84.

33. Karl Barth, *Church Dogmatics* 4.2 (Edinburgh: T. & T. Clark, 1958): 381; hereafter CD.

34. CD 4.2: 399.

35. So E. P. Sanders has observed regarding Pauline theology in *Paul and Palestinian Judaism* (Philadelphia: Fortress, 1983).

36. CD 4.2:401.

37. CD 4.2:400.

38. See CD 4.2: 404–5, 412, 432, 452, 468, 482–83, 494.

39. CD 4.2:538.

40. CD 4.2:539.

41. See Gerhard Gloege, "Zur Versöhnungslehre Karl Barths," *Theologische Literaturzeitung* 3 (1960): 162–86; Herbert Hartwell, *The Theology of Karl Barth: An Introduction* (Philadelphia: Westminster, 1964), 19. Notice that for Barth there is no discrete treatment of the doctrine of sin; rather, hamartiology falls under the larger rubric of reconciliation.

42. CD 4.2:403.

43. See *The Book of Common Prayer*, Church Hymnal Corporation and the Seabury Press, 1979.

44. CD 4.2: 404.

45. CD 4.2: 405.

46. CD 4.2: 407.

47. CD 4.2: 408.

48. CD 4.2: 390–91.

49. CD 4.2: 390.

50. CD 4.2: 457.

51. CD 4.2: 600–613.

52. CD 4.2: 430.

53. Still, it must also be said that Barth is no misogynist. Even in his infamous discussion of 1 Corinthians 11 and the "ordering" of man and woman, he says: "The exploitation of this order by man, in consequence of which he exalts himself over woman, making himself her lord and master and humiliating and offending her so that she inevitably finds herself oppressed and injured, has nothing to do whatever with divine order. It is understandable that woman should protest and rebel against this exploitation, although she ought to realise at once that here as elsewhere protesting and rebelling are one thing and the way from disorder to order quite another" (CD 3.4; 170).

54. CD 4.2:464.

55. CD 4.2:586.

56. Elisabeth Schüssler Fiorenza, *Feminist Interpretation of the Bible*, 130.

57. Angela West makes a similar point in her *Deadly Innocence*.

CHAPTER FOUR

1. Portions of this chapter are excerpted from addresses given at the American Academy of Religion, November 1995, and the Charleston Scholarly Engagement with Anglican Doctrine Conference, January 1997, published in *The Rule of Faith*, 27–35.

2. Mary Daly, "The Qualitative Leap beyond Patriarchal Religion," *Quest* 1 (1974), 32–43; Mary Daly, *Beyond God the Father: Toward a Philosophy of Women's Liberation* (Boston: Beacon, 1973), 75–77.

3. "A serious Christian response to (feminist) criticism of the core symbolism of Christianity either will have to show that the core symbolism of Father and Son do not have the effect of reinforcing and legitimating male power and female submission, or it will have to transform Christian imagery at its very core. This challenge has been met in numerous ways: the search for a 'usable' tradition (or set of traditions) that has always stood over against patriarchal domination; the retrieval and reconstruction of marginalized, suppressed and distorted strands of Christian thought and practice that have afforded a measure of equality for women; the broadening of the notion of 'tradition' beyonds strands customarily deemed orthodox; and the subordination of tradition as a source and norm to the primacy of women's experience" (see Ellen K. Wondra, *Humanity Has Been a Holy Thing: Toward a Contemporary Feminist Christology* (Lanham, Md.: University Press of America, 1994), 113.

4. Daly, *Beyond God the Father*, *19*; Rosemary Radford Ruether, *Sexism and God-Talk: Toward a Feminist Theology* (Boston: Beacon, 1983), 116.

5. E.g., "The history of controversy that marks the ancient theological path to the formu-

lation of Chalcedon never directly touches on the question of women; nor does the record after Chalcedon, when the meaning of its central affirmation—the unity of Christ's two natures, human and divine, joined without confusion, change, division, or separation in one person and one hypostasis—was the subject of continued debate. The classical doctrine of the Incarnation speaks of the divinity and humanity of Christ, not his maleness. The focus is on the fully human as a soteriological issue—God's redemption accomplished in a fully human history" (Anne Carr, *Transforming Grace: Christian Tradition and Women's Experience* [San Francisco: Harper & Row, 1988], 161).

6. "A feminist theologian must question whether the historical man Jesus of Nazareth can be a role model for contemporary women, since feminist psychological liberation means exactly the struggle of women to free themselves from all male internalized norms and models" (Elisabeth Schüssler Fiorenza, "Toward a Feminist Biblical Hermeneutics: Biblical Interpretation and Liberation Theology," in *The Challenge of Liberation Theology: A First World Response*, ed. Brian Mahan and L. Dale Richesis [Maryknoll, N.Y.: Orbis, 1981], 107).

7. Elizabeth A. Johnson, *She Who Is: The Mystery of God in Feminist Theological Discourse* (New York: Crossroad, 1992), 151.

8. Johnson, *She Who Is*, 153.

9. "If the model for sharing in the image of Christ be one of exact duplication, similar to the making of a xerox copy, and if Christ be reduced to the historical individual Jesus of Nazareth, and if the salient feature about Jesus as the Christ be his male sex, then women are obviously excluded from sharing that image in full" (Ibid, 73).

10. Ibid.

11. Ibid.

12. Ibid., 55.

13. Ibid., 167.

14. Joanna Carlson and Carole R. Bohn Brown, eds., *Christianity, Patriarchy and Abuse: A Feminist Critique* (New York: Pilgrim, 1989).

15. Rita Nakashima Brock, *Journeys by Heart: A Christology of Erotic Power* (New York: Crossroad, 1989), 56.

16. "Finally, to many people the model [of the atonement sacrifice] is abhorrent because it relies on victory through violent death. It seems to highlight Christianity's concentration on the death of Jesus as the content of redemption. . . . I suggest that it is not the cross as such, but our inadequate interpretation of it, and fixation on death and violence which is the problem. Feminist spirituality offers alternative metaphors, with concentration on life-giving symbols, aware that it is often through the death of a *woman* [italics hers] that patriarchy derives its symbols and illustrates its values. . . . So a Christian feminist interpretation looks not simply to the cross of Jesus but to the values this represents" (Mary Grey, *Redeeming the Dream: Feminism, Redemption and the Christian Tradition* [London: SCM Press, 1989], 124–25).

17. Carlson and Brown, *Christianity, Patriarchy and Abuse*.

18. Dolores S. Williams, "Black Women's Surrogate Experience and the Christian Notion of Redemption," in *After Patriarchy: Feminist Transformations of the World Religions*, ed. William R. Eakin, Jay B. McDaniel, and Paula M. Cooey (Maryknoll, N.Y.: Orbis, 1991), 12.

19. Williams, "Black Women's Surrogate Experience, 12–13.

20. Richard Mouw, address at the annual meeting of the American Academy of Religion, 1995.

21. George Hunsinger, "The Politics of the Nonviolent God: Reflections on René Girard and Karl Barth," *Scottish Journal of Theology* 51 (1998): 72.

22. Brock, *Journeys by Heart*, 49.

23. "Christology has become important to me for two primary reasons: (1) First, I am hooked on Jesus. I could no more pretend that the Jesus-figure, indeed the Jesus Christ of the

kerygma, is unimportant to me than I could deny the significance of my parents and my past in the shaping of my future. As a 'cradle-Christian' . . . I have no sane or creative choice but to take very seriously this Jesus Christ who is written indelibly in my own history. (2) The second reason christology is important to me is that there is no more fundamental and problematic an issue for feminists than the person of Jesus. The centrality—the Lordship—of this male god, has been employed—doctrinally, politically, psychologically, structurally—in the service of a fellowship of brothers and fathers—the Church—whose female members have been auxiliary or, in special cases, perceived to be enough 'like men' . . . to be relatively welcome in the fellowship of men" (Carter Heyward, The Redemption of God: A Theology of Mutual Relation (Lanham, Md.: University Press of America, 1982), 196.

24. Carter Heyward, "Must Jesus Be a Holy Terror?" in Our Passion for Justice (New York: Pilgrim, 1984), 217.

25. Ellen Leonard has proposed five approaches to Christology in feminist theology: "1. envisioning Christ's humanity in female terms; 2. envisioning Christ as the incarnation of female divinity; 3. beginning from the Jesus of history as prototype; 4. beginning from the Jesus of history as iconoclastic prophet; 5. relocating Christology in the community" (Ellen Leonard, "Women and Christ: Toward Inclusive Christologies," Toronto Journal of Theology 6 [1990]: 273). While her typology is a material explanation, mine attempts a formal explanation.

26. Rosemary Radford Ruether, To Change the World: Christology and Cultural Criticism (New York: Crossroads, 1981), 56; Carr, Transforming Grace,

27. Martin Kähler, The So-Called Historical Jesus and the Historic Biblical Christ, introd. Carl E. Braaten (Philadelphia: Fortress, 1998).

28. Brock, Journeys by Heart.

29. Johnson, She Who Is; Elisabeth Schüssler Fiorenza, Jesus: Miriam's Child, Sophia's Prophet: Critical Issues in Feminist Christology (New York: Continuum, 1994).

30. Biblical feminists may fit here. However, since our concern is particularly with reconstructions of Christian doctrine, we will limit our discussion to mainline feminist theologians.

31. Carr, Transforming Grace, 163.

32. Carr refers her reader to Thomas's discussion at Summa Theologia I, q. 92, a. 1–2; III, supplement q. 39. a. 1; III, q. 1–59; and especially III q. 31, art. 4 (Carr, Transforming Grace, 164).

33. Ruether, Sexism and God-Talk, 116.

34. Ibid., 119.

35. Ibid., 122.

36. Ibid., 123.

37. Ibid., 136.

38. Paula Cooey, William R. Eaken, and J. B. McDaniel, After Patriarchy: Feminist Transformations of the World Religions (Maryknoll, N.Y.: Orbis, 1990), 107.

39. Cooey, in Cooey, Eaken, and McDaniel, After Patriarchy. 121.

40. Of course, it is ironic that the "postpatriarchal" story would need to include this moment of hesitation before a male savior, for if the situation is truly postpatriarchal, the risk of bending the knee before the man Jesus may not be great at all.

41. Cooey, in Cooey, Eaken, and McDaniel, After Patriarchy, 122.

42. "For the earliest followers of Jesus his resurrection meant that the finality of death was overcome. [here a footnote says, "For the very best critical discussion of resurrection, the difficulties it poses for contemporary consciousness, and the difficulties its rejection poses to Christian faith, see R. R. Niebuhr 1957" (Resurrection and Historical Reason).] Because the resurrection presupposed the crucifixion, it meant that one might live in hope for the future while in the midst of suffering, centered by life in spite of death. It did not mean that one could avoid suffering and death. The earliest followers of Jesus expressed this apprehension of the resurrection as an individual bodily resurrection. . . . Whatever Paul may have meant by the

resurrection of the dead when he writes in [1 Cor.] 16:53 of putting on an imperishable, immortal nature, he seems to be rejecting here not only the continuation of one's physical corporeality, but possibly the continuation of what we call personality as well" (Cooey, in Cooey, Eaken, and McDaniel, *After Patriarchy*, 124). For a very different view of what Paul meant by the Resurrection of the dead, see e.g. N. T. Wright, *Jesus and the Victory of God: Christian Origins and the Question of God*, vol. 2 (Minneapolis: Fortress, 1997).

43. Cooey, Eaken, and McDaniel, *After Patriarchy*, 124–25.

44. Sallie McFague, *The Body of God: An Ecological Theology* (Minneapolis: Fortress, 1993), 160.

45. Ibid., 162.

46. Ibid.

47. Carter Heyward, *Touching Our Strength : The Erotic as Power and the Love of God* (San Francisco: Harper & Row, 1989), 114.

48. Ibid., 116.

49. Ibid.

50. "I believe that the feminist theological agenda pushes us into discontinuity with orthodox Christology, beyond even the most adventuresome theological spokespersons of the past and present Christian male collegium. I do not think that historical christological teachings that are rooted in trinitarian philosophy can be accommodated to the critical analysis of feminist Christians. . . . Christian faith and practice is necessarily destructive to most people in the world insofar as it is cemented in the insistence that Jesus Christ is Lord and Savior of all" Heyward, "Must Jesus Be a Holy Terror?" 117, cf. 212, 214).

51. Ibid., 220–21.

52. Brock, *Journeys by Heart*, 51.

53. Ibid.

54. She uses the terms "erotic" and "heart" in a idiosyncratic fashion: "Heart—the self in original grace—is our guide into the territories of erotic power. Feminism and Christianity can converge in love and justice if Christ can come to reveal erotic power. This feminist Christology, in being guided by heart, develops another way to understand Christ that will lead us away from the territories of patriarchy and into a world in which incarnation will refer to the whole of human life" (Brock, *Journeys by Heart*, 52). Cf. the following: "The Christa/Community of erotic power is the connectedness among the members of the community who live with heart. Christa/Community evidences heart, which is the conduit in human existence of erotic power" (Brock, *Journeys by Heart*, 70).

55. Ibid., 69

56. Ibid., 98, 100, 103.

CHAPTER FIVE

1. Carol P. Christ, "Why Women Need the Goddess: Phenomenological, Psychological, and Political Reflections," in *Womanspirit Rising*, ed. Carol Christ and Judith Plaskow (San Francisco: Harper & Row, 1979), 277.

2. Gerhard von Rad, *Old Testament Theology*, 2 vol. (New York: Harper & Row, 1962–1965), 1:418.

3. For an evangelical (biblical) feminist response to this kind of feminism, see Aïda Besançon Spencer, et al., *The Goddess Revival* (Grand Rapids: Baker Books, 1995).

4. *She Who Is* won the 1993 Louisville Grawemeyer Award in Religion and has been widely acclaimed as one of the most important works of feminist theology to date. We treat this work in detail in chapter 6.

5. "The three sections of this commentary work extend the call of divine Wisdom. They invite readers to read these ancient works in light of Sophia's manifold revelations; they trace

some of the submerged struggles and subjugated knowledges of inclusive Wisdom communities which still come to the fore in the diverse correspondence preserved in the canon; and finally they tell the life stories and recount the sayings of the prophets of Sophia who are her embodied presence. Like the envoys of divine Sophia/Wisdom, the contributors to this feminist commentary invite readers: 'Come eat of Her bread and drink of Her wine' (Prov. 9:1–6). By transgressing canonical boundaries and engaging in the adventurous process of reading against the kyriarchal grain, our interpretive journey can become the home/habitat of divine Wisdom and her sister-outsiders" (Elisabeth Schüssler Fiorenza, et al., eds., *Searching the Scriptures*, vol. 2, *A Feminist Commentary* (New York: Crossroad, 1995), 10.

6. Merlin Stone, *When God Was a Woman* (New York: Dial, 1976), xii–xiii.

7. Mara Lynn Keller, "Gimbutas's Theory of Early European Origins and the Contemporary Transformation of Western Civilization," *Journal of Feminist Studies in Religion* 12 (1996): 74.

8. Raphael Patai, *The Hebrew Goddess*, 3d ed. (Detroit: Wayne State University Press, [1967] 1990), 26–27.

9. Elaine Pagels, *The Gnostic Gospels* (New York: Random House, 1979), 66.

10. Daniel L. Hoffman, *The Status of Women and Gnosticism in Irenaeus and Tertullian* (Lewiston: Edwin Mellen Press, 1995).

11. Pagels, *The Gnostic Gospels*, 113.

12. Hoffman, *The Status of Women and Gnosticism*; Susanne Heine, *Women and Early Christianity: A Reappraisal*, trans. John Bowden (Minneapolis: Augsburg, 1987); Karen King, ed., *Images of the Feminine in Gnosticism* (Philadelphia: Fortress, 1988).

13. Hoffman refers to Stead's "Valentinian Myth of Sophia," which notes that the Valentinian dyad itself was ambiguous: "Valentinians held that the male sex is superior to the female, and that 'Father' is God's proper designation. Thus by his 'dyad,' if authentic, Valentinus may have intended something little different from the conception of a God attended by a female consort" (Hoffman, *The Status of Women and Gnosticism*, 27, 55); G. Christopher Stead, "The Valentinian Myth of Sophia," *Journal of Theological Studies* 20 (1969): 88.

14. Louis A. Brighton, "The Ordination of Women: A Twentieth-Century Gnostic Heresy?" *Concordia Journal* 8 (1982): 13–15.

15. Joan Chamberlain Engelsman, *The Feminine Dimension of the Divine* (Wilmette, Ill.: Chiron, [1979] 1994).

16. Of course, there are plenty of other ways of explaining the "repression" of Sophialogy. Elizabeth Johnson credits the demise of Sophia to the growth of patriarchal ecclesial structure and sexism within the Christian communities (*She Who Is: The Mystery of God in Feminist Theological Discourse* [New York: Crossroad, 1992], 98–99).

17. Engelsman, *The Feminine Dimension of the Divine*.

18. For example, while Rosemary Radford Ruether does, Elisabeth Schüssler Fiorenza finds it politically problematic (Ruether, *Sexism and God-Talk: Toward a Feminist Theology* [Boston: Beacon, 1983], 61; Schüssler Fiorenza, *Jesus: Miriam's Child, Sophia's Prophet: Critical Issues in Feminist Christology* [New York: Continuum, 1994], 159–60).

19. Gail Patterson Corrington, *Her Image of Salvation: Female Saviors and Formative Christianity* (Louisville, Ky.: Westminster/John Knox, 1992), 104.

20. Elizabeth Johnson, "The Maleness of Christ," in *The Special Nature of Women?* ed. Anne Carr and Elisabeth Schüssler Fiorenza (Philadelphia: Trinity, 1991), 113.

21. See, for example M. Jack Suggs, *Wisdom, Christology and Law in Matthew's Gospel* (Cambridge: Harvard University Press, 1970); Felix Christ, *Jesus Sophia: Die Sophia Christologie bei Den Synoptikern* (Zurich: Zwingli-Verlag, 1970); James Robinson, "Jesus as Sophos and Sophia," in *Aspects of Wisdom in Judaism and Early Christianity*, ed. Robert L. Wilken (Notre Dame, Ind.: University of Notre Dame Press, 1975).

22. Elisabeth Schüssler Fiorenza, In Memory of Her: A Feminist Theological Reconstruction of Christian Origins (New York: Crossroad, 1983), 132.

23. Ibid., 134.

24. See, e.g., Johnson, She Who Is, 92–93.

25. Schüssler Fiorenza, In Memory of Her, 133.

26. Schüssler Fiorenza, Jesus: Miriam's Child, Sophia's Prophet, 10–11.

27. Ibid., 44.

28. Ibid., 57.

29. If her portrayal of "malestream theology," however, ends up being closer to caricature than to realistic portrayal, one wonders about the necessity of the new paradigm. Instead, one might first try to amend the caricatures.

30. Schüssler Fiorenza, Jesus: Miriam's Child, Sophia's Prophet, 62.

31. Ibid., 132.

32. Ibid., 133.

33. Ibid., 132.

34. Ibid., 139.

35. If Fiorenza were to follow Engelsman's repression theory, which she does not, it would be here in the Father-Son traditions that she could point to the "repression" of the divine feminine.

36. Schüssler Fiorenza, Jesus: Miriam's Child, Sophia's Prophet, 144.

37. Ibid., 153.

38. Ibid., 161–62.

39. Of course, this is close to Dionysian spirituality, but the difference is that, for the feminist claim, the problem in comprehending the divine is the nature of language rather than the nature of the divine itself.

40. For example, see Elizabeth Johnson: "Insofar as male-dominant language is honored as the only or the supremely fitting way of speaking about God, it absolutizes a single set of metaphors and obscures the height and depth and length and breadth of divine mystery. Thus it does damage to the very truth of God that theology is supposed to cherish" (She Who Is, 18).

41. Schüssler Fiorenza, Jesus: Miriam's Child, Sophia's Prophet, 157.

42. However, Schüssler Fiorenza reads Kähler differently from the way I understand him. She seems to think that he introduces the dichotomy between the Jesus of history and the Christ of faith, while I see him as trying to show that to make such a distinction, as did the "Lives of Jesus" so popular in the nineteenth century, was to read the Gospels against the grain; e.g., "Kähler distinguished between the historical Jesus of the modern scholar and the living Christ, i.e., the proclaimed Christ of faith." Of course, as we have noted, Schüssler Fiorenza is interested in and committed to reading the Gospels against the grain because that means subverting patriarchal readings (Jesus: Miriam's Child, Sophia's Prophet, 83).

43. Johnson, She Who Is, 165–66.

44. Ibid., 166.

45. Ibid.

46. Ibid., 33.

47. Ibid., 62.

48. Ibid., 64. Note how this view of conversion experience is like Ruether's understanding of the experience of oppression, but here the elements of hope and empowerment are more strongly emphasized. See Ruether, "Feminist Interpretation: A Method of Correlation," Feminist Interpretation of the Bible 114.

49. Johnson, She Who Is, 75.

50. Ibid., 99.

51. Ibid., 39. See also: "The trivialization introduced into the doctrine of the incarnation by

androcentric stress on the maleness of Jesus' humanity fully warrants the charge of heresy and even blasphemy currently being leveled against it. Theology will have come of age when the particularity that is highlighted is not Jesus' historical sex but the scandal of his option for the poor and marginalized in the Spirit of his compassionate, liberating Sophia-God. That is the scandal of particularity that really matters" (ibid., 167).

52. Schüssler Fiorenza, In Memory of Her, 135.

53. Johnson, She Who Is, 158.

54. Ibid., 160.

55. Angela West, Deadly Innocence: Feminist Theology and the Mythology of Sin (London: Cassell, 1996).

56. "Through her revolt against the supreme God, and her covetousness, [Sophia] is the cause of the Fall; through her share in the light she is part of the pleroma and a divine being. That is all too reminiscent of the ambivalence of evil lust and holy aura, of whore and saint, of Eve and Mary, which is usually attributed to woman" (Heine, Women and Early Christianity, 121).

57. West, Deadly Innocence, 194.

58. Corrington, Her Image of Salvation, 98.

59. Ruether, Sexism and God-Talk, 138.

60. This is true, for instance, in Elisabeth Schüssler Fiorenza's description of Carter Heyward's assessment of the "classical questions of christology—for example, Was Jesus divine? Was he human? and the 'Jesus of history' vs. the 'Christ of faith' debate—are dead" (Jesus: Miriam's Child, Sophia's Prophet, 50). See also Heyward's statement: "It is my thesis here that the historical doctrinal pull between Jesus of Nazareth and Jesus Christ, the human Jesus and his divine meaning, is no longer, if it ever was, a place of creative christological inquiry. Worse, it is a distraction from the daily praxis of liberation, which is the root and purpose of Christian faith." (Speaking of Christ: A Lesbian Feminist Voice, ed. Ellen C. Davis [New York: Pilgrim, 1989], 13. Her use of the term "christic" throughout the second half of the first essay of this book, however, betrays her own use of the Jesus of history–Christ of faith dichotomy, substituting for the "Christ of faith" the term "christic." See esp. p. 22: "Whatever/whoever may be christic for us will emerge in the contemporary crossroads of religious/spiritual pluralism. . . . Whatever may be christic in the 'small places' of our lives is the same spirit of liberation as She who holds the stars and watches over the planets in their courses. Our most fully christic experiences are our most fully embodied (sensual and erotic) connections in relation to one another, other creatures, and the earth."

61. Johnson, She Who Is, 151. See also her comment on p. 162: "The biblical symbol Christ, the one anointed in the Spirit, cannot be restricted to the historical person Jesus nor to certain select members of the community but signifies all those who by drinking of the Spirit participate in the community of disciples. Christ is a pneumatological reality, a creation of the Spirit who is not limited by whether one is Jew or Greek, slave or free, male or female."

62. Sallie McFague, The Body of God: An Ecological Theology (Minneapolis: Fortress, 1993), 163.

63. See Patricia Wilson-Kastner, Faith, Feminism, and the Christ (Philadelphia: Fortress, 1983), chapter 4. Here I am not suggesting any intent or even self-conscious awareness on her part of her use of the dichotomy. Rather, I am simply pointing out that the dichotomy between the Jesus of history and the Christ of faith is part of the conceptual substructure which supports her Christology.

64. Wilson-Kastner, Faith, Feminism, and the Christ, 71.

65. Ibid., 90–91.

66. Ibid., 115.

67. Ibid., 91.

68. See, for example, Carter Heyward, The Redemption of God: A Theology of Mutual Relation (Lanham, Md.: University Press of America, 1982), chap. 2.

69. Elizabeth A. Johnson, *Consider Jesus: Waves of Renewal in Christology* (New York: Crossroad, 1990), 197.

70. Elizabeth Johnson, "The Maleness of Christ," 108.

71. Ibid., 109.

72. Rosemary Radford Ruether, "Christology and Feminism: Can a Male Savior Save Women?" in *To Change the World: Christology and Cultural Criticism* (New York: Crossroad, 1981). 63–74.

73. Johnson, "The Maleness of Christ," 112; Ruether, *Sexism and God-Talk*, n. 1, 137.

74. Johnson, "The Maleness of Christ," 115.

75. Ellen K. Wondra, *Humanity Has Been a Holy Thing: Toward a Contemporary Feminist Christology* (Lanham, Md.: University Press of America, 1994), 304.

76. "The resurrection is a mystery of faith enveloped in the mystery of God. It negates a simple literalism that imagines Jesus still existing as in the days of his earthly life, only now invisible. Jesus has truly died, with all that this implies of change: he is gone from the midst of history according to the flesh. . . . His life is now hidden in the holy mystery of God, while his presence is known only through the Spirit wherever two or three gather, bread is broken, the hungry fed. But this indicates a transformation of his humanity so profound that it escapes our imagination. The humility of the apophatic approach acknowledges that language about the maleness of Christ at this point proceeds under the negating sign of analogy, more dissimilar than similar to any maleness known in history" (Johnson, "The Maleness of Christ," 112–13).

77. "In his classic study of *The Mystical Theology of the Eastern Church*, Vladimir Lossky asserts that 'all true theology is fundamentally apophatic.' He observes that 'apophaticism is, above all, an attitude of mind which refuses to form concepts about God.' He regards all such concepts as idols and contrasts them with the lived experience of contemplative ascent toward union with the unknowable God. . . . This approach may appear to be surprisingly like the attitude of some contemporary Western theologians. For example, Sallie McFague asserts in her *Metaphorical Theology* that . . . 'No finite thought, product, or creature can be identified with God,' she says, 'and this includes Jesus of Nazareth.' Her thesis is that theological language should employ metaphor instead of doctrinal conceptualization. Contemporary Western theologians sympathetic to this approach often appeal to the apophaticism of Christian mystics, for whom an over-whelming experience of the divine discloses the limitations of human language. Some might also appeal to the teachings of Eastern Christianity in support of their case for what amounts to a dissolution of dogma. However, let me suggest that any such appeal represents a funda-mental misunderstanding and misuse of the Orthodox tradition" (Verna E. F. Harrison, "The Relationship between Apophatic and Kataphatic Theology," *Pro Ecclesia* 4 (1995): 318–19.

78. "The inclusive 'all of us' ['are being transformed into that same image from one degree of glory to another' (2 Cor. 3:18)] makes clear that the whole community, women as well as men, are gifted with the transformation 'into the same image,' in Greek the same εἰλον, that is, the image/icon of Christ. . . . No distinction on the basis of sex is made, or needed. Being christomorphic is not a sex-distinctive gift. The image of Christ does not lie in sexual similarity to the human man Jesus, but in coherence with the narrative shape of his compassionate, liberating life in the world, through the power of the Spirit. Theologically, the capacity of women and men to be *sym-morphos* to the *eikon* of Christ is identical" (Johnson, "The Maleness of Christ," 114).

79. "Amid a multiplicity of differences Jesus' maleness is appreciated as intrinsically impor-tant for his own personal historical identity and the historical challenge of his ministry, but not theologically determinative of his identity as the Christ nor normative for the identity of the Christian community. . . . Ideally, if the equal human dignity of women is ever recognized in ecclesial theory and praxis, this discussion about the maleness of Christ will fade away. In a more just church it would never have become such an issue" (Johnson, "The Maleness of Christ," 115).

80. Teresa Berger, "A Female Christ Child in the Manger and a Woman on the Cross, Or: The Historicity of the Jesus Event and the Inculturation of the Gospel," trans. Mary Deasey Collins, *Feminist Theology* 11 (1996): 33.

81. Ibid.

82. This is all the more apparent in light of Berger's repeated attempts at self-clarification; e.g., "To accuse me of a sex-change of Jesus is absurd. Again, to say it plainly: I have no difficulties with the second person of the Holy Trinity becoming human and being born of a woman in male form . . . all interpretations of my inquiry which focus on the historicity of the Jesus event miss my very clearly formulated concern. It is not about the (historic) 'gender' of the God who became (hu)man two thousand years ago but rather about the inculturation of the Gospel in contemporary cultures" (Berger, "A Female Christ Child in the Manger," 35, 37).

83. Karl Rahner, *Schriften zur Theologie* 16 (Zürich: Benziger, 1984), 330–31, quoted in Berger, "A Female Christ Child in the Manger," 38.

84. Berger, "A Female Christ Child in the Manger," 37.

85. E.g., compare the following: "If in a patriarchal culture a woman had preached compassionate love and enacted a style of authority that serves, she would most certainly have been greeted with a colossal shrug. Is this not what women are supposed to do by nature?" (Johnson, *She Who Is*, 160).

86. Susanne Heine, *Christianity and the Goddesses: Systematic Criticism of a Feminist Theology* (London: SCM, 1987), 141.

87. E.g., the argument by E. L. Mascall: "the priesthood of Christ is, in no merely biological sense but in some profound and mysterious sense which lies behind and provides the ground of the biological differentiation, a male function, and can we doubt that this is the basis of our Lord's choice of men alone to be his Apostles and of the Church's instinctive sense that the personal exercise of the communicated and participated priestly office of Christ must be restricted to men?" In *Why Not? Priesthood and the Ministry of Women: A Theological Study*, ed. Michael Bruce and G. E. Duffield (Abingdon, Berkshire: Marcham Manor Press, 1976), 112.

88. Wayne A. Meeks, "The Image of the Androgyne," *History of Religion* 13 (1973): 168 n. 9.

89. R. R. Reno, "Feminist Theology as a Modern Project," *Pro Ecclesia* 5 (1996): 405–26.

90. The 1976 Vatican "Declaration on the Question of the Admission of Women to the Ministerial Priesthood" makes this mistake when it argues that "when Christ's role in the eucharist is to be expressed sacramentally, there would not be this 'natural resemblance' which must exist between Christ and his minister if the role of Christ were not taken by a man: in such a case it would be difficult to see in the minister the image of Christ. For Christ himself was and remains a man" ("Declaration on the Question of the Admission of Women to the Ministerial Priesthood," *Origins* 6 [1977]: 522). My point, with all due respect to the magisterium, is that this is a fundamental misunderstanding not only of the sacrament and of the priest's role in the sacrament (certainly a matter debated between Protestants and Catholics) but also of classical Christian eschatology as well. The logic of the argument could likewise demand that all Roman Catholic priests be Jews.

CHAPTER SIX

1. Elizabeth A. Johnson, *She Who Is: The Mystery of God in Feminist Theological Discourse* (New York: Crossroad, 1992), 227. See also, as examples of this trend in feminist Trinitarian theology, Catherine Mowry LaCugna, *God for Us: The Trinity and Christian Life* (San Francisco: HarperSanFrancisco, 1991); Susan Brooks Thistlethwaite, "On the Trinity," *Interpretation* 45 (1991): 159–71; Rebecca Oxford-Carpenter, "Gender and the Trinity," *Theology Today* 41 (1984): 23ff.; Gail Ramshaw Schmidt, "Naming the Trinity: Orthodoxy and Inclusivity," *Worship* 60 (1986): 491–98.

2. "Rather, the universe, both matter and spirit, is encompassed by the matrix of the living

God in an encircling which generates uniqueness, futurity, and self-transcendence in the context of the interconnected whole. Holy Wisdom transcendingly embraces all of finite existence in an inclusive relation that sets it free and calls it to communal, personal, and cosmic shalom" (Johnson, *She Who Is*, 232).

3. Ibid., 235.

4. Ibid., 211.

5. Ibid., 139.

6. Ibid., 242.

7. Ibid., 243.

8. Ibid., 43.

9. Ibid., 15–16.

10. Ibid., 45.

11. Ibid., 47.

12. Ibid.

13. Ibid., 56.

14. "Only if the full reality of women as well as men enters into the symbolization of God along with symbols from the natural world, can the idolatrous fixation on one image be broken and the truth of the mystery of God, in tandem with the liberation of all human beings and the whole earth, emerge for our time" (ibid.).

15. Ibid., 57. Could she have meant here "religiously deficient" rather than "deficiently religious"?

16. Ibid., 77.

17. Ibid.

18. Ibid., 56.

19. Ibid., 7.

20. Verna E. F. Harrison, "The Relationship between Apophatic and Kataphatic Theology," *Pro Ecclesia* 4 (1995): 318–32; Verna Harrison, "Word as Icon in Greek Patristic Theology," *Sobornost* 10 (1988): 38–49.

21. Johnson, *She Who Is*, 225. It must be pointed out that, even with the implicit essentialism running just under the surface, Johnson is aware of the possible pitfalls this can present and tries to account for the differences and distinctions in her discussion of women's experience such as is offered in the refinements of Thistlethwaite, et al.: "women's interpreted experience is as diverse as concrete women themselves so that 'the' perspective of women is not a unity nor immediately to hand" (Johnson, *She Who Is*, 10).

22. Ibid., 231.

23. Some of the important documents from the patristic period that deal with the issues at stake have been collected for convenient reference, with a helpful introduction in William Rusch, trans. and ed., *The Trinitarian Controversy* (Philadelphia: Fortress, 1980). On baptism, see Aidan Kavanagh, *The Shape of Christian Baptism: The Rite of Christian Initiation* (New York: Pueblo, 1978); and Laurence Hull Stookey, *Baptism: Christ's Act in the Church* (Nashville: Abingdon, 1982). On addressing God as Father, see W. Marchel, *Abba, Père ! La Prière du Christ et Des Chrétiens* (Rome: Pontifical Biblical Institute, 1971); Peter Widdicombe, *The Fatherhood of God from Origen to Athanasius* (Oxford: Clarendon, 1994); Jane Schaberg, *The Father, the Son, and the Holy Spirit: The Triadic Phrase in Matthew 28: 19b* (Chico, Calif.: Scholars Press, 1982). See also my fuller consideration of this topic in "What's in a Name? On the Ecumenical Baptismal Formula," *Pro Ecclesia* 6 (1997): 1–20.

24. For example, Gregory Nazianzen struggled with a similarly literalistic understanding in the theology of the Eunomians who baptized not "in the Name of the Father, Son and Holy Spirit" but "in the Name of the Creator and unto the death of Christ." He pokes fun at their literalism, suggesting that their error lies in their considering "our God male because he is called God and Father" (*Fifth Theological Oration* 31, On the Holy Spirit, 7). Those who accept as true

Mary Daly's motto, "If God is male, then male is God," share the same basic logic of the Eunomnians (Mary Daly, *Beyond God the Father* [Boston: Beacon Press, 1973], 19). Athanasius himself tried to point out that "the title Father has its significance and its bearing only from the Son" and that we who call upon God as Father do not intend to imply that God is male but that our God is the Father of the Son, not a vague creator-deity. Thus we call God not according to what God has done or made but according to who God is: "When they call Him Unoriginate, they name Him only from His works, and know not the Son any more than the Greeks; but he who calls God Father, names Him from the Word" (Athanasius, *Fifth Theological Oration*, 31).

25. Cf. LaCugna's statement that to refuse to call God Father is to concede that God the Father is male as according to patriarchy ("Baptism, Feminism and Trinitarian Theology," *Ecumenical Trends* 17 (1988): 65–68). Also, see Elisabeth Schüssler Fiorenza, *In Memory of Her: A Feminist Theological Reconstruction of Christian Origins* (New York: Crossroad, 1983), 150: "The 'father' God is invoked here [Luke 11:2–4, 12:30; Mark 11:25], however, not to justify patriarchal structures and relationships in the community of disciples but precisely to reject all such claims, powers, and structures."

26. Even if it does seem to stretch the point too far to say that the Trinitarian formula is the only name of God for Christian worship and theology, it is clear that "Father, Son, and Holy Spirit" is a scripturally derived name for God and features in the dominical command to baptize in Mt 28:19. See Alvin F. Kimel, "The God Who Likes His Name: Holy Trinity, Feminism and the Language of Faith," in *Speaking the Christian God: The Holy Trinity and the Challenge of Feminism* (Grand Rapids: Eerdmans, 1992), 188–208. In Scripture, names are generally transliterated and sometimes translated (usually when an etiological explanation of some sort follows), and titles are usually translated and only occasionally transliterated. Some take this observation to indicate that "Father, Son, and Holy Spirit" is a title and not a name: Ted Peters, "The Battle over Trinitarian Language," *Dialog* 30 (1991): 44–49; David S. Cunningham, "On Translating the Divine Name," *Theological Studies* 56 (1995): 415–40. However, the divine name (YHWH), which is usually pointed in the Massoretic text with the vowels of the title "Adonai," is pointed to read "Elohim" (god) when the text bears "Adonai YHWH" (Lord LORD), e.g. Deuteronomy 3:24; 9: 26. I owe thanks to Brevard Childs for this observation. In other words, the pointing of the generic title (Adonai) under the tetragrammaton (YHWH), which holds the space for the divine name itself, is replaced by the pointing of a generic noun (Elohim) when repetition of the title would occur in the reading of the text. So, we have a name (YHWH) which is read as a generic title (Adonai), but when it appears in conjunction with this generic title, it is read as a generic noun (Elohim). In some instances, the proper name (YHWH), the generic title (Adonai), and the generic noun (Elohim) are transliterated and *not* translated in non-Hebrew versions, while at other times, the proper name is translated as a generic title and sometimes as a generic noun. This is simply to point out that the distinction between titles and names for God in the Bible is more complex than either Kimel, Peters, or Cunningham would suggest. However, the biblical depiction remains: Jesus commands his followers to make disciples, which, he explains, consists of teaching the practice of his commandments and baptizing by the authority of or in reference to the One God named by the phrase "Father, Son, and Holy Spirit."

27. For example, see Deborah Malacky Belonick, "Revelation and Metaphors: The Significance of the Trinitarian Names Father, Son and Holy Spirit," *Union Seminary Quarterly Review* 40 (1985): 31: "It is a dogma of the Orthodox Christian Church that efforts to describe the divine nature of God are ultimately inadequate, since God is ineffable and essentially unknowable. Even on the Feast of Epiphany when Orthodox Christians celebrate the revelation of God as Trinity, they are reminded of this in the hymnography of the Church: 'Great art Thou, O Lord, and marvelous are Thy works: no words suffice to sing the praise of Thy wonders.'" Malacky Belonick fails to distinguish, however, between the prayer's assertion that all words are insufficient to the task of *singing praise* and her own inference that all words are insufficient to the

task of *naming* God. The plural form of the word "Name" in her title is significant. In classical Christian confession, the Trinitarian name has no plural and takes no plural pronouns. See the incisive critique of this type of feminist argument in Verna E. F. Harrison, "The Relationship between Apophatic and Kataphatic Theology."

28. For a recent interesting attempt to warrant the claim that God speaks in Scripture, see Nicholas Wolterstorff, *Divine Discourse: Philosophical Reflections on the Claim That God Speaks* (Cambridge: Cambridge University Press, 1995).

29. Ruth C. Duck, *Gender and the Name of God: The Trinitarian Baptismal Formula* (New York: Pilgrim, 1991), 153.

30. Philip Ellis Wheelwright, *Metaphor and Reality* (Bloomington: Indiana University Press, 1962); Max Black, *Models and Metphors* (Ithaca: Cornell University Press, 1962); Paul Ricoeur, *Interpretation Theory: Discourse and the Surplus of Meaning* (Fort Worth: Texas Christian University Press, 1976).

31. Duck, *Gender and the Name of God*, 14.

32. E.g., "Calling God the 'Father Almighty' who demands the death of his child as a sacrifice for human sin may unintentionally and unconsciously encourage fathers to use their power over children in harmful ways, and may encourage children to accept this lot" (Ibid., 54–55).

33. Ibid., 111; Sallie McFague, *Models of God: Theology for an Ecological, Nuclear Age* (Philadelphia: Fortress, 1987), 55–60.

34. Cf. the distinction between thin and thick description in Clifford Geertz, *The Interpretation of Cultures: Selected Essays* (New York: Basic Books, 1973).

35. E.g., "The liturgy of baptism, and particularly the pivotal words spoken during the administration of water, must express the hope of new life in Jesus Christ and not the old ways of patriarchy" (Duck, *Gender and the Name of God*, 122).

36. As for the extent to which the doctrine of the Trinity is "biblical," this itself was, of course, no small issue of debate in the Trinitarian controversies. Both the Athanasian and Arian positions, of course, argued on the basis of Scripture. The Nicene position argues on the basis of such passages as Is. 53:8; Ps. 36:9; Prov. 8:30; Mt. 3:17; 11:27; Jn 1:1, 3, 18; 5:23; 10:30; 14:9, 28; Rom. 8:32; Gal. 1:9; Col. 1:15–17; Heb. 1:2, 3; 1 Tim. 6:3–4; 1 Jn 5:1, etc. Arius, in turn, appealed to biblical passages such as Rom. 11:36, Ps. 110:3, Jn. 16:28, and those following him appealed to Is. 1:2, Ps. 45:7, etc. Of course, the most important text for warranting the use of the name "Father, Son, and Holy Spirit" in baptism itself comes from the dominical injunction in Matthew 28:19.

37. Thus, she might reasonably look to the so-called binitarian formulae in Rom. 8:11; 2 Cor. 4:14; Gal. 1:1; Eph. 1:20; 1 Tim. 1:2; 1 Pet. 1:21; and 2 Jn. 1:13 and the "triadic formula" (not considered yet "Trinitarian" in the full-blown sense) in Mt. 28:19; 1 Cor. 6:11; 12:4ff; Gal. 3:11–14; Heb. 10:29; and 1 Pet. 1:2 (cf. 2 Cor. 13:14) for a "biblical" understanding of the "persons" of the Godhead.

38. Cf. Roberta Bondi: "If the language of 'Father' and 'Son' leads away from the gospel the Creed is to witness to, then there is even greater reason to avoid undue attention to its words while ignoring its intended content. As for that content, it was surely not meant to include sexual identity within the Trinity itself, as God relates to God's self, apart from the creation. As the Fathers found in the struggle with Arianism, that language about God be biblical is not as important as that it witness to the truth. The term 'homoousios' is not biblical, nor must the language we use be biblical if the language misleads its hearers" ("Some Issues Relevant to a Modern Interpretation of the Language of the Nicene Creed, with Special Reference to 'Sexist' Language," *Union Seminary Quarterly Review* 40 (1985): 28). The implication of Bondi's argument is that since the Nicene fathers used nonbiblical language, we should be able in our time to use nonbiblical language to proclaim the truth of the gospel. However, we must note

that the Nicene fathers never assumed an Archimedean leverage point apart from the canonical metanarrative in order to find the "truth of the gospel."

39. E.g.: "I believe . . . that scripture is a prototype for metaphors that reveal God's nature, inviting rather than excluding new metaphors for Christian witness. We may take our lead from the very diversity of scriptural metaphors for God. Forbidding graven images, scripture uses a plurality of names to speak about God. Those who pick out just a few names for God from scripture and call them uniquely revelatory reject scripture's own method and substitute idols of their own" (Duck, *Gender and the Name of God*, 24).

40. For example, Duck can use the non-canonical *Gospel of Thomas* to her advantage over against the canonical scriptures when it supports her position, and where it does not she can disavow it. Thus, she argues that the *Gospel of Thomas* and the *Gospel of the Hebrews* "indicate" that Jesus called God Mother, but she later states that "The Gospel of Thomas is not in my view an adequate witness to God's self-revelation in Jesus Christ; the author even says that women must make themselves men to enter the reign of heaven" (Ibid., 68).

41. Baptism in the name of Jesus will be treated more thoroughly later. Duck refers, of course, to Acts 2:38; 10:48; 8:16; 19:5; Romans 6:3; and 1 Corinthians 6:11b and also cites Hans Conzelmann, *An Outline of the Theology of the New Testament* (London: SCM, 1969), 49. Schaberg, *The Father, the Son, and the Holy Spirit*, 10–11. Duck does not point to Conzelmann's statement on the same page from which she draws her evidence, which would detract from her argument: "There is remarkably little interest in liturgical regulation in the New Testament." If Conzelmann is right here, Duck is looking for such regulation (focusing on the name of Jesus to the exclusion of that of the Father, Son, and Holy Spirit in the baptismal formula) in the wrong place.

42. Duck, *Gender and the Name of God*, 129.

43. Ibid., 7.

44. See, for example, Rosemary Radford Ruether, *Women-Church: Theology and Practice in Feminist Liturgical Communities* (San Francisco: Harper & Row, 1985), 130. The following words are to be repeated three times, once at each administration of water by either sprinkling or immersion: "Through the power of the Source, the Liberating Spirit and the forerunners of our hope, be freed from the power of evil. May the forces of violence, of militarism, of sexism, of racism, of injustice, and of all that diminishes human life lose their power over your life. May all the influences of these powers be washed away in these purifying waters. May you enter the promised land of milk and honey and grow in virtue, strength and truthfulness of mind. And may the oil of gladness always anoint your head."

45. This alternative is similar to what Athanasius disputes in his *First Discourse against the Arians* 9:34, where he insists that baptism is "not into the name of the Unoriginate and Originate, nor into the name of Creator and creature, but into the Name of the Father, Son and Holy Ghost."

46. For example: " 'Creator, Redeemer, Sustainer' is a contemporary reincarnation of modalism which naively equates one function each to one person each, an idea wholly denied by classical theology" (Gail Ramshaw, "Naming the Trinity: Orthodoxy and Inclusivity," *Worship* 60 [1986]: 492). See also Catherine LaCugna, "Baptism, Feminism and Trinitarian Theology," 68.

47. David S. Cunningham suggests the Trinitarian phrase "Source, Wellspring and Living Water" but does not propose it for use in liturgy or for sole replacement for the classical formula. ("Developing Alternative Trinitarian Formulas," *Anglican Theological Review* 80 [1998]: 8–29). See also his *These Three Are One: The Practice of Trinitarian Theology* (Oxford: Blackwell, 1998).

48. Duck, *Gender and the Name of God*, 189.

49. Ramshaw, "Naming the Trinity: Orthodoxy and Inclusivity"; Gail Ramshaw, *A Metaphorical God: An Abecedary of Images for God* (Chicago: Liturgy Training Press, 1994); Gail Ramshaw, *Words around the Font* (Chicago: Liturgy Training Press, 1994).

50. Athanasius: *Discourses against the Arians* 1. 9. 33–34.

51. John 14:16, 26; 15:26; 16:7; 1 John 2:1.

52. Gail Ramshaw, *God beyond Gender: Feminist Christian God-Language* (Minneapolis: Fortress, 1995), 77, n. 7.

53. Ramshaw Schmidt, "Naming the Trinity: Orthodoxy and Inclusivity," 493.

54. Ibid., 497.

55. E.g., "If our current descriptions of the orthodox Trinity do not convey our assemblies of prayer into God's life, surely other biblical language than Father-Son-Spirit can assist us, that we may be propelled into that God praised by the New Testament writers, the Cappadocians, and contemporary Americans alike. Inclusive language may be a new idea, but inclusivity is the deepest truth of the triune God. Let us work together toward this goal, that we find the words to dance around that God of both Nicaea and New York City, of both orthodoxy and inclusivity" (Ibid., 498).

56. Ramshaw, *God Beyond Gender*, 91.

57. Augustine, *On Christian Doctrine* 1.5.

58. Brian Wren, *What Language Shall I Borrow? God-Talk in Worship: A Male Response to Feminist Theology* (New York: Crossroad, 1989), 143; McFague, *Models of God*, 91–92.

59. See, for example, Wren, *What Language Shall I Borrow?* 251–52, n. 1.

60. James F. Kay, "In Whose Name? Feminism and the Trinitarian Baptismal Formula," *Theology Today* 49 (1993): 531; Duck, *Gender and the Name of God*, 163.

61. "The sacrament [of Christian baptism] is not conferred validly in any other names. . . . Thus Gregory wrote to Bishop Quiricus, 'Those heretics who are not baptized in the name of the Trinity [Father, Son and Holy Spirit] such as the Bonosians and the Cataphrygians . . . because the former do not believe that Christ is God,' since they consider him a mere man, 'and the latter are so perverse in their belief that they hold the Holy Spirit to be a mere man,' viz. Montanus, 'all these are baptized when they convert to the Church because the baptism they received in their state of error was no baptism at all since it was not received in the name of the Holy Trinity [Father, Son and Holy Ghost]' . . . Note the words of the Decretal of Alexander III: 'In the case of a doubt about a person's baptism, he is to be baptized with these words added: 'If you have been baptized, I do not rebaptize you; but, if you have not been baptized, I baptize you, etc' " (Thomas Aquinas, *Summa Theologiae*, 3a.66, arts. 5 and 9). The recent rebaptisms at the Paulist Center in Boston were based on such an understanding of baptism.

CONCLUSION

1. Rachel Wahlberg, " 'The Woman's Creed,' " in *Growing Together in Unity: Discussion Documents for the Faith and Order Commission* (Bangalore, 1978), 16–30; Susanne Heine, *Christianity and the Goddesses: Systematic Criticism of a Feminist Theology* (London: SCM, 1987), 28.

2. Michael Root, "The Narrative Structure of Soteriology," *Modern Theology* 2 (1986): 150–51.

3. Root, "The Narrative Structure of Soteriology," 151–52.

4. "This places the interpretation of Scripture at the center of the crisis because communal authority, in the Christian sphere, depends on consonance with the Bible. There is agreement on this among all the major traditions despite their differences on the interrelations of Bible, tradition, and magisterium. The primacy of Scripture is fundamental for the patristic tradition the Orthodox follow, the *sola scriptura* for the Reformers, and, on the Roman Catholic side, the servant role of the magisterium in reference to Scripture was clearly asserted in *Verbum dei* at Vatican II (as was also, though less explicitly, the interpretive rather than independent authority of tradition)." [In a footnote Lindbeck adds: "I here follow the general view that although Vatican II did not explicitly reject a two-source interpretation of Trent's statements on Scripture and tradition, it nevertheless favors a one-source construal."] George Lindbeck, "Scripture, Con-

sensus, and Community," in *Biblical Interpretation in Crisis*, ed. Richard John Neuhaus (Grand Rapids: Eerdmans, 1989), 91.

5. See also Mary Stewart Van Leeuwen, ed., *After Eden: Facing the Challenge of Gender Reconciliation* (Grand Rapids: Eerdmans, 1993) and those considered under biblical feminism.

6. Letty M. Russell, "Practicing Hospitality in a Time of Backlash," *Theology Today* 52 (1995): 477.

7. Susan T. Foh, *Women and the Word of God: A Response to Biblical Feminism* (Grand Rapids: Baker, 1980); Manfred Hauke, *God or Goddess? Feminist Theology: Where Does It Lead?* trans. David Kipp (San Francisco: Ignatius, 1995).

8. Heine, *Christianity and the Goddesses*.

9. Daphne Hampson, *Theology and Feminism* (Oxford: Basil Blackwell, 1990); Daphne Hampson, *After Christianity* (London: SCM, 1996); Mary Daly, *Beyond God the Father: Toward a Philosophy of Women's Liberation* (Boston:Beacon, 1973); Mary Daly, *Gyn/Ecology: The Metaethics of Radical Feminism* (Boston: Beacon, 1978).

10. Rosemary Radford Ruether, "Christology and Feminism: Can a Male Savior Save Women?" in *To Change the World: Christology and Cultural Criticism* (New York: Crossroad, 1981), 63–74.

11. See also Mary M. Solberg, *Compelling Knowledge: A Feminist Epistemology of the Cross* (Albany: State University of New York, Press, 1997). This work does not fall under any of the doctrines we have considered here, but is an important feminist engagement with a classical theme, Luther's theology of the cross. I would argue that it is of the narrative pattern.

12. *De haeresibus, Patorologia Latina* 42: 19. He also said that those are "not heretics who are taught heresy but who seek truth," which, of course, puts more responsibility on the teachers than the students. See Augustine, *Epistle* 43.1; *Corpus Scriptorum Ecclesiasticorum Latinorum* 34, no. 2: 85.

13. Daphne Hampson and Rosemary Radford Ruether, "Is There a Place for Feminists in a Christian Church," *New Blackfriars* 68 (1987): 7–24. See also Anne Carr, "Is a Christian Feminist Theology Possible?" *Theological Studies* 43 (1982): 279–97.

14. An example from the previous generation might be Charlotte von Kirschbaum, *The Question of Woman: The Collected Writings of Charlotte von Kirschbaum*, ed. Eleanor Jackson (Grand Rapids: Eerdmans, 1996).

SCRIPTURE INDEX

Genesis, 21–22
  1:31, 110
  3, 34
  3:16, 110
  3:18, 22
  4:10, 23
  9, 24
  15, 24
  22, 23
  24:22, 23
  27:27, 144n.78
  28:12, 25
  32, 45
  48:16, 25

Exodus, 3:14, 112

Psalms, 115
  36:9, 164n.36
  45:7, 164n.36
  110:3, 164n.36

Proverbs, 8:22–31, 91
  9:13–18, 100
  8:30, 164n.36

Isaiah, 115, 124
  1:2, 164n.36
  53:8, 164n.36

Jeremiah, 45–46, 51–52, 88
  7:16–20 46
  44:15–25, 46

Matthew, 89, 92
  3:17, 164n.36
  4:1–11, 74
  10, 44
  11:25–27, 164
  26:72
  28, 44
  28:19, 121, 164nn.36–37

Mark, 13:46, 124

Luke, 15:4–10, 115

John, 89, 95
  1:1, 3, 18, 164n.36
  5:23, 164n.36
  10:30, 164n.36

John (continued)
  14:9, 28, 164n.36
  15:1–11
  16:28, 164n.36

Romans, 7, 60
  8:11, 164n.37
  11:36, 164n.36

1 Corinthians, 1:27, 48
  4:14, 164n.37
  6:11, 164n.37
  8:36, 125
  11, 153n.53
  12:4 ff., 164n.37
  12:12–17

2 Corinthians, 5:17, 110

Galatians, 1:9, 164n.36
  3:11–14, 164n.37
  3:27–29, 109

Ephesians, 1:20, 164n.37

Colossians, 1:15–17, 122, 164n.36

1 Timothy 1:2, 164n.37
  6:3–4, 164n.36

1 Peter, 1:2, 164nn.36–37

Hebrews, 1:2–3, 164n.36
  10:29, 164n.37
  12:2, 70

1 John, 1:13, 164n.37
  5:1, 164n.37

GENERAL INDEX

A-T/R, 17–21, 130–131, see also T/R-A
Abigail, 67
Abram, 24
abuse, 74–76
Ackerman, Susan, 45–47, 51, 88, 100
Adam/Christ typology, 57
Ambrose, 25, 48, 144n.78
Anabaptists, 24
Anselm, 14–15
anthropology, 32–33, 62, 78–80
anti-judaism, 51–52
apocalyptic literature, 95–96
apologetics, 108
    ad hoc, 15
    vs. dogmatics, 14–15, 17–18, 26, 132–133
    see also logic
Allik, Tiina, 148n.71
Aquinas, 79, 166n.61
Arians, 5, 89–90, 120, 123, 164n.36
Athanasius, 5, 71, 120, 123, 134, 162n.24,
    164n.36, 165n.45
atonement, 99
Auerbach, Erich, 9
Augustine, 25, 48–52, 55, 62, 124–125, 135,
    167n.12

authority, 43
    biblical, 44, 48
    women's experience, 43, 48, 57, 61, 74, 97–
    98, 112–115, 162n.21
    see also canon

backlash, 131
Badran, Margo, 138n.19
Ball, Mieke, 41
baptism, 117–127, 164n.35, 165n.41, 165n.44
Barth, Karl, 10–12, 14, 63–68, 107–108,
    141n.30, 152n.41, 153n.53
Bathsheba, 67
de Beauvoir, Simone, 32
Belonick, Deboray Melacky, 163n.27
Berger, Theresa, 107–108, 161n.82
Bondi, Roberta, 164n.38
Brock, Rita Nakashima, 74, 84–85, 133–134,
    156n.54
Bultmann, Rudolph 14, 29–31, 53, 108,
    133

Cady Stanton, Elizabeth, 32, 52
Calvin, John, 10, 21–26, 62, 144n.78
Cannon, Katie, 59

canon, biblical, 26, 42, 63, 85, 96
  authority of, 42–43, 56, 62
  feminist, 55–56, 42
Carr, Anne, 78–79, 134, 153n.5
Chalcedon, 70, 79
Cheney, Emily, 44, 49
Chicago School, 10, 138n.17, 139n.3
Childs, Brevard, 138n.17, 139n.3, 163n.26
Christa, 78, 83–84, 105
Christa-community, 84–85
Christ of faith, 13–14, 96–97, 104, 141n.26
  Christ figure, 13–14, 24, 73, 77–78
  Jesus of history, 13, 141n.30
  Jesus of history vs. Christ of faith, 78, 101–
    109, 159n.60, 159n.63
  see also Jesus of history
Christian, William, 7, 16–20, 28–29, 43, 48–
    50, 55, 117, 142n.56, 142n.57,
    142n.63, 142n.64
Christology, 70–110
claims, alien, 17–19, 50, 55, 142n.49, 143n.59
  authentic, 17, 19, 55, 130, 143n.63
  truth, 27
  see also doctrine
Clement, 89
Coakley, Sarah, 63, 131, 134
consciousness, feminist, 31–33, 42
consensus fidelium, 19, 143n.64
constructionism, 32–33
Conzelmann, Hans, 165n.41
Cooey, Paula, 81–82, 155n.42
Corrington, Gail Patterson, 91–92, 100
cross, 73–74, 99
Cunningham, David S., 163n.26, 165n.47

Daly, Mary, 29–30, 37, 59, 70, 81, 119, 131,
    134, 162n.24
Dame Folly, 100
David, 67
Deism, 116
demythologization, 30–31
doctrines, authentic, 16–17, 19–20, 55, 130,
    143n.63
  core doctrine, 141n.42
  extra-narratival, 50, 55, 59, 62, 130, 133
  governing doctrines, 16, 19, 27–29, 43–44,
    48, 53, 55, 59, 62, 68, 130
  primary doctrines, 6, 16, 18–19, 26, 28,
    59, 69
  see also apologetics; claims

dogmatics vs. apologetics, 14–15, 17–18, 30,
    141nn.32–33,
Duck, Ruth 119–121, 164n.32, 165n.40,
    165n.41

Engelsman, Joan, 37, 87–92, 96, 114, 158n.35
Ephraim, 25
essentialism, 32–33, 112, 116, 146n.24,
    152n.26
ethnocentrism, 33
experience, 14–15, 42–44, 57, 59, 62
  of conversion, 97–98, 158n.48
  prethematic, 113–114
  women's, 43–44, 57, 61, 74, 97–98, 112–
    115, 162n.21
extra-narratival, 14, 50, 53, 55, 61–63, 108,
    130, 132, 148n.71, see also extra-textual
extra-textual, 12, see also extra-narratival; intra-
    textual

Faludi, Susan, 131
Feuerbach, Ludwig, 29–31, 41, 50, 91, 96
Fiorenza, Elisabeth Schuussler, 34, 37, 39, 41,
    55, 87, 91–92, 94–96, 111, 115, 134,
    147n.40, 148n.53, 148n.66, 154n.6,
    156n.6, 157n.18, 158n.29, 158n.35,
    158n.42, 159n.60
Foh, Susan, 37, 131
Ford, David, 139n.3
Frei, Hans, 5–6, 8–14, 16–17, 20, 26, 30,
    102, 130, 132, 135, 138n.17, 139n.3,
    140nn.6, 9, 141n.26, 141n.25,
    141n.30, 141n.32–33, 141n.42,
    141n.63–64
Freud, Sigmund, 35
Friedan, Betty, 32, 57

Gimbutas, Marija, 87–88
Goddess, 52, 86–89, 93
Goddess-killers, 52
Goldenberg, Naomi, 134
Goldstein, Valerie Saiving, 32, 57–58, 62, 64–
    65, 98, see also Saiving, Valerie
Gospel of Hebrews, 165n.40
Gospel of Thomas, 90, 165n.40
Green, Garrett, 30, 139n.3, 145n.4
Grey, Mary, 63, 74, 131, 134, 150n.1, 154n.16

Hampson, Daphne, 62, 77, 99, 119, 132, 134
Harrison, Verna, 107, 160n.77, 164n.27

Hauerwas, Stanley, 139n.3
Hauke, Manfred, 131
Heine, Susanne, 159n.56
Henry, Carl, 140n.6
hermeneutics
    allegorical, 11, 13, 22–23, 25–26, 44–45,
        48–49, 83–86, 144n.72, 144n.78, 103
    biblical feminist, 27, 36, 38–41, 48, 132,
        137n.2, 156n.3
    canonical, 10, 12, 13
    classical, 14–15, 53, 68, 83, see also
        Lindbeck
    general, 11–12
    illustrative vs. storied, 20
    mainline feminist, 27, 38–40, 51, 129–133
    narrative vs. non-narrative, 17, 20, 26, 61–
        62, 72–78, 93, 100, 109–110, 112–
        113, 116, 127–133, see also reading,
        narrative
    phenomenological, 10–13
    special, 11–12
    of survival, 40
    of suspicion, 36–37, 39–31, 42, 47, 50
    of trust, 39, 41
    typological, 10, 12–13, 21–23, 25–26,
        144n.72
    see also interpretation; Lindeck; reading;
        sense; understanding
Heyward, Carter, 59, 77, 83–84, 105,
    134, 154n.23, 156n.50, 159n.60,
    159n.60
Hoffman, Daniel, 90, 157n.13
Holmer, Paul, 139n.3
homoousios, 5
Hunsinger, George, 139n.3
Hurston, Zora Neale, 59
Hippolytus, 123
history-like, 10, see also Frei, Hans;
    interpretation

Image of Christ, 71–73, 109
interpretation, feminist
    biblical, 27–28, 36–41, 48, 58, 68, 132,
        152n.25, 147n.49
    mainline, 27–28, 38–40, 44, 48–49, 51, 53,
        58, 68, 129–133
    see also hermeneutics; reading; sense;
        understanding
intra-textual, 12–13, see also extra-textual
Irenaeus, 17, 19, 142n.46

Jacob, 25–26
Jesus of History, 13, 141n.30
    Christ of faith 13–14, 96–97, 141n.26
    Christ figure, 13–14, 77–78
    Jesus of History vs. Christ of Faith, 96–
        109, 159n.60, 159n.63
    see also Christ of faith
Jesus Seminar, 101, 103
Job, 91
John the Baptist, 100
Johnson, Elizabeth, 70–72, 92, 96–98, 103–
    108, 112–122, 134, 157n.16, 158n.40,
    159n.61, 160n.72, 160nn.79–80,
    161n.85, 162n.14, 162n.21
Jones, Serene, 60–62
Julian of Norwich, 63, 126

Kähler, Martin, 96, 102, 108
Kant, Immanuel, 29–31, 50, 158n.42
Kay, James F., 126
Kelsey, David, 138n.17, 139n.3
Kimel, Alvin, 4–6, 163n.26
von Kirschbaum, Charlotte, 147n.47
Kroeger, Catherine Clark, 137n.4
kyriocentrism, 94–95

La Cugna, Catherine, 4–7, 163n.25
van Leeuven, Mary Stewart, 37
Leonard, Ellen, 155n.25
Lerner, Gerda, 34–36, 147n.37
Lessing, Gotthold, 101
Lévi-Strauss, Claude, 45
Lindbeck, George, 4–7, 10, 16, 20, 28, 134,
    138n.17, 139n.3, 141n.42, 143n.64,
    166n.4
    classical hermeneutic, 3, 10, 12, 14–15, 53,
        137n.2, see also hermeneutics;
        interpretation; sense; understanding
    posthermeneutical context, 12, 141n.24
    postliberal theology, 10, 141n.24
logic of belief vs. logic of coming to belief,
    14–15, 17–18, 130, 132, 141n.35, see
    also apologetics vs. dogmatics
Logos, 95
Lowe, Walter, 139 n. 3
Luther, Martin, 30, 52–53, 61

Manasseh, 25
Marcion, 101, 122
Mariology, 91

Marshall, Bruce, 139n.3
Martin, Francis 3
Martyr, Justin, 89
Mascall, E. L., 161n.87
McFague, Sallie, 4, 82–83, 103, 119
Meeks, Wayne, 139n.3
Morse, Christopher, 126

Nabal, 67
Nag Hammadi, 90
name, divine, 112–117, 163n.26–27
narrative, biblical, 3, 8–10, 12, 26, 48, 50,
    53, 57, 62–63, 103
  identification, 5–6, 15, 20, 22
  passion, 99
  realistic, 9–10
  relation to orthodoxy, 6, 17, 20, 75–76
  see also hermeneutics
Nazianzen, Gregory, 162n.24
New Criticism, 11
Nicene creed, 73, 106, 122, 164n.37
Niebuhr, H. Richard, 139n.3
Niebuhr, Reinhold, 57–58
Nietzsche, 91
Nygren, Anders, 57

Olmsted, Richard H., 141n.35
Origen, 89
Osiek, Carolyn, 37
Ostriker, Alice, 51

Pagels, Elaine, 87, 89–90, 99
panentheism, 116–117
Patai, Raphael, 87–88
patriarchy, 6, 29–31, 33–34, 40, 42, 48, 51–
    54, 59, 67, 77, 80, 89, 92, 94–95,
    100, 104
  kenosis of, 63, 106
Peters, Ted, 163n.26
Placher, William, 139n.3
Plaskow, Judith, 52, 58, 61, 134
protoevangelium, 22

Q source, 92, 99
Queen of Heaven, 45–47, 51, 88
Qumran, 95

Rahner, Karl, 107–108, 111, 143n.58
  anonymous christians, 143n.58
Ramshaw, Gail, 123–126, 165n.46, 166n.55

reading, narrative, 8–9, 11, 14, 17, 20, 55,
    62, 93, 129–133, 139n.1, see also
    hermeneutics; interpretation;
    understanding
  cultural-linguistic approach, 12
  extra-textual theology, 12, 14, 105–108,
    131, 133, 135
  illustrative vs. storied, 20
  intra-textual theology, 10, 12
  narrative identification of God, 3, 5–8,
    116, 139n.3
  penumbral narrativist, 134
  realistic narrative, 9–11, 13–14, 140n.9, see
    also Frei, Hans
    geschichtlich, 140n.9, 141n.30
    historisch, 140n.9, 141n.30
    history-like, 13, 102
ReImagining, 87
Reimarus, H. S., 101–102
revelation, 41–42, 50, 53, 115
Ricoeur, Paul, 10–11, 138n.17
  second naiveté, 11–12, 141n.25
Righter trial, 141n.42
Riley, Denise, 33, 135, 146nn.26–28
Root, Michael, 20, 140n.4
Ruether, Rosemary Radford, 37, 40–42,
    55, 78–79, 106, 132, 157n.18,
    158n.48, 158n.51, 165n.44
rule of faith, 17, 19, 48–49
rule of love, 48–49
Russell, Letty, vi, 132, 147n.45

Sackenfeld, Katharine Dods, 149n.73
Saiving, Valerie, 32, 57–58, 62, 64–65, 98, see
    also Goldstein, Valerie, Saiving
Sandys, Edwina, 83–84
Schleiermacher, Friedrich, 29–31, 43, 97, 132–
    133, 141n.31
Schner, George P., 139n.3
Schwartzentruber, Paul, 139n.3
Schweitzer, Albert, 102, 109
second naiveté, 12
sense
  literal, 12–13, 26, 144n.78
  plain, 12
  simple, 24, 144n.77
  see also hermeneutics; interpretation;
    reading; understanding
sin, 65
  original, 56

pride, 65–68
sloth, 64–66
women's, 57–60
Solberg, Mary, 167n.11
Sophia, 78, 86–101, 111–117, 133, 158n.51
Christology, 93–100
sophialogy, 95–99
Spelman, Elizabeth, 146nn.24–25
spirituality, apophatic, 91, 106, 115–116,
163n.27
Starhawk, 62, 134
Steussy, Marty, 36
Stone, Merlin, 87
Storkey, Elaine, 39, 134
Swidler, Leonard, 37

T/R-A, 17–21, 130–132, see also A-T/R
Tanner, Kathryn, 139n.3
theism, classical, 116
Thistlethwaite, Susan, 58–59, 61, 162n.21
Thomas the Contender, Book of, 90
Tillich, Paul, 14, 58, 114, 133
Torjesen, Karen Jo
Tracy, David, 10, 138n.17
Trible, Phyllis, 37, 41
Trinity, 4, 7, 76, 91, 98–99, 111–120,
163nn.26–
27, 164n.36
Abba, Servant, Paraclete, 123
Creator, Redeemer, Sustainer, 122–123
Father, Son and Holy Spirit, 67, 118, 121–
122, 127
Father, Son, Holy Spirit, One God, Mother
of us all, 126
Fountain, Offspring, Wellspring, 123
God, Redeemer, Holy Spirit, 128

God the Creator, Christ the Redeemer,
and the Holy Spirit, our Constant
Companion, 126
Mother, Lover, Friend, 125–126
Riverside formula, 126
Spirit-Sophia, Jesus-Sophia, Mother-Sophia,
112, 122
typology, 10, 12–13, 22–23, 25–26, see also
hermeneutics
turn to the subject, 29–30

understanding, disfigurational, 129, see also
hermeneutics; interpretation; reading;
sense

Valentinianism, 90
Vanhoozer, Kevin, 138n.17
Vincent of Lerins, 143n.64

Walker, Alice, 59, 148n.55
Wallace, Mark I., 144n.69
Webster, John, 139n.3
Werpehowski, William, 139n.3, 141n.33
West, Angela, 62, 99–100, 131
Wicca, 134
Williams, Dolores, 40, 74–77
Wilson-Kastner, Patricia, 104–105, 159n.63
Wire, Antoinette Clark, 41
Wisdom, 87, 91–92, 94–98, 106, 112, 117
womanism, 43, 148n.55
women-church, 148n.66
Wondra, Ellen, 106, 153n.3
Wrede, William, 101–102
Wren, Brian, 125–126

Yale School, 5, 8, 16, 138n.17, 139n.3